ArtScroll Series®

Rabbi Nosson Scherman / Rabbi Meir Zlotowitz

General Editors

RABBI
CHAIM PINCHAS
SCHEINBERG

Lectures to Women

Published by

Mesorah Publications, ltd

HEART to HEART TALKS

Compiled and edited by
Rabbi Moshe Finkelstein

assisted by
A. Rappaport

FIRST EDITION
First Impression … May 2000

Published and Distributed by
MESORAH PUBLICATIONS, LTD.
4401 Second Avenue / Brooklyn, N.Y 11232

Distributed in Europe by
J. LEHMANN HEBREW BOOKSELLERS
20 Cambridge Terrace
Gateshead, Tyne and Wear
England NE8 1RP

Distributed in Israel by
SIFRIATI / A. GITLER
10 Hashomer Street
Bnei Brak 51361

Distributed in Australia and New Zealand by
GOLDS BOOK & GIFT SHOP
36 William Street
Balaclava 3183, Vic., Australia

Distributed in South Africa by
KOLLEL BOOKSHOP
Shop 8A Norwood Hypermarket
Norwood 2196, Johannesburg, South Africa

ARTSCROLL SERIES®
HEART TO HEART TALKS
© *Copyright 2000, by* MESORAH PUBLICATIONS, Ltd.
4401 Second Avenue / Brooklyn, N.Y. 11232 / (718) 921-9000 / www.artscroll.com

Cover Photo: Courtesy of Tzvi Goelman

ISBN:
1-57819-502-0 (hard cover)
1-57819-503-9 (paperback)

Typography by CompuScribe at ArtScroll Studios, Ltd.

Printed in the United States of America by Noble Book Press Corp.
Bound by Sefercraft, Quality Bookbinders, Ltd., Brooklyn N.Y. 11232

We are honored and privileged
to dedicate this book to

Rebbitzen Basha Scheinberg תליט"א,

our esteemed Rebbetzin, who has with selfless
devotion always been a mother and a pillar of
strength to the *kollel* wives and to the *yeshivah*.

For decades, she has been the partner of the
Rosh Yeshivah שליט"א in all his endeavors.

May she be granted a *refuah shelemah*
and the strength to continue her noble work
for many more years together with the
Rosh Yeshivah and may they
be *zocheh* along with all of us
לקבל פני משיח צדקנו בקרוב.

מכתב ברכה

Rabbi CHAIM P. SCHEINBERG
Rosh Hayeshiva "TORAH ORE"
and Morah Hora'ah of Kiryat Mattersdorf

הרב חיים פינחס שיינברג
ראש ישיבת "תורה אור"
ומורה הוראה דקרית מטרסדורף

Rosh Chodesh Nissan, 5760

It is a source of great joy to me that this *sefer* has been published.

While I have been unable to review the entire manuscript, I know that I can rely on Rabbi Moshe Finkelstein, a very devoted *talmid*, who has invested countless hours in its preparation.

May he and all the individuals who have helped him be granted much *hatzlachah* in all their endeavors.

רחוב פנים מאירות 2, ירושלים, ת.ר. 6979, טל. 537-1513 (02), ישראל
2 Panim Meirot St., Jerusalem, P.O.B. 6979, Tel. (02) 537-1513, Israel

TABLE OF CONTENTS

INTRODUCTION

It is with gratitude to *Hashem Yisbarach* that we present this book of talks by our *Rosh Yeshivah Moreinu v'Rabbeinu shlita*.

Over 35 years ago *Moreinu v'Rabbeinu HaGaon HaRav* Chaim Pinchas Scheinberg *shlita* transferred Yeshivah Torah Ore from the U.S. to the newly-founded neighborhood of Kiryat Mattersdorf in Jerusalem, where he eventually became the communal *moreh horaah* and a source of guidance and inspiration.

He brought with him a group of about 25 students and a handful of young *kollel* families who formed the nucleus of Torah Ore in Eretz Yisrael.

Over the years Yeshivah Torah Ore has grown into an institution of 650 students (including a large *kollel*) who have been drawn to the *Rosh Yeshivah shlita*. In addition, the *Rosh Yeshivah* has gained recognition as one of the world's leading *marbitzei Torah* and *poskim*. Despite his advanced years (may he live to 120) the *Rosh Yeshivah* continues to give *shiurim* throughout the day and sets aside time to answer questions in halachah and offer personal advice for the general public.

The talks compiled here started many years ago through the initiative of Rabbi Menashe Feiger and Rabbi Tzvi Zobin. Through the constant efforts of the Zobins these talks continued for 25 years.

In addition to the information and inspiration that the women gained from these talks, they were given an opportunity to ask questions. Some of these questions and answers are included in this book. While some of these questions and answers are general guidelines, others are responses to a particular situation and may not necessarily apply in exactly the same manner to everyone. Therefore, in cases of doubt, a proper halachic authority should be consulted.

With all the extreme care that was taken to precisely transmit the words of the *Rosh Yeshivah shlita,* some errors may have entered into the editing, transcription, or typing. Any such error is the result of our human failings and not a reflection on the *Rosh Yeshivah* and his talks. May Hashem bless our efforts and may this be a helpful tool for the public.

ACKNOWLEDGMENTS

Thanks to the *Rosh Yeshivah's* son-in-law *HaGaon HaRav* Chaim Dov Altusky *shlita* for reviewing parts of this *book.*

Special thanks to the *Rosh Yeshivah's* son Rav Simchah Scheinberg *shlita* for his constant encouragement.

Very special thanks to Rabbi Tzvi Zobin for reviewing this work and making stimulating suggestions. His concern and friendship are gratefully acknowledged.

A special thanks to my colleagues in Yeshivah Shaare Chaim, Rabbis Dovid Krohn, Moshe Lewis and Eliezer Parkoff. Rabbi Parkoff helped with his halachic consultations which were most appreciated, and in many other aspects of the book.

My thanks as well to: Rabbi Herschel Pincus for his halachic advice and warm concern; Reb Shlomo Zalman Rappaport for his continuous assistance; Reb Shlomo Furst was extremely helpful in organizing the question and answer section, which had accumulated over many years, and also reviewed the manuscript; Reb Nosson Fabian for his arranging and technical assistance; Reb Yitzchok Mickler for reviewing the original manuscript; Reb Shmuel Landon for his hours of assistance in many areas of this book; Reb Ben Zion Davis for diligently checking the sources and making many valuable corrections.

Many other Rabbanim were helpful in the preparation. I can only mention a few: Rabbi Avrohom Pincus *shlita,* Rabbi Yosef Stern *shlita,* Rabbi Mendel Weinbach *shlita,* Rabbi Efraim Winkler *shlita,* Rabbi Yisroel Apelbaum, Rabbi Yisroel Berl, Rabbi Shimon Boxer, Rabbi Yisroel Goelman, Rabbi Noach Orloweck, Rabbi Elchanan Peretz, Rabbi Chaim Septimus, Rabbi Tzvi Sharlin, Reb Yosef Ahron Meir Gottleib. My talmidim in Yeshivah Shaare Chaim were very helpful in many details of this book, especially Sion Houllou.

My thanks to Mr. Shmuel Blitz and Rabbi Avrohom Biderman and the Artscroll staff for their encouragement and professionalism in bringing out this book.

Rabbi Yosef Stern of Congregation Agudas Achim of Midwood was gracious enough to take time out from his heavy schedule to review the final manuscript. We are deeply indebted to him for his expertise.

We want to thank the many women who did the painstaking work of transcribing the talks from the tapes.

Our thanks to: Mrs. Esther van Handel for her initial work on the transcripts and her continual advice;

Mrs. Aviva Rappaport for exercising her extraordinary talent for capturing the spoken style of the *Rosh Yeshivah* and rendering it into book form.

Our heartfelt thanks to Rebbitzen Ruchoma Shain for her help in suggesting a title; to Mrs. D. Friedman for her hard work; to Mrs. Bracha Parkoff for giving encouraging suggestions and for always being there when she was needed; to Rebbetzin Tzippora Heller for making important comments; and to Mrs. S. Makover for arranging the hundreds of transcriptions on the computer disk which greatly facilitated the organization of the book.

I want to thank my parents Mr. and Mrs. Samuel Leon and Pauline Finkelstein שיחיו. May they be blessed with health and happiness for many years to come and have *nachas* from their children and grandchildren.

In truth, my wife, Matil תחי׳ה, deserves most of the credit for this book. From the very beginning, she was most instrumental in insuring the transcription of the material, and she has been involved in every phase of this book, giving crucial and positive guidance throughout. We are very grateful to Hashem for granting us the *zechus* of publishing this book. May we continue to have much *nachas* from our entire family.

Moshe Finkelstein

Jerusalem
Rosh Chodesh Nissan, 5760

THE ADVANTAGE OF BEING JEWISH

1

The secular world often wonders what advantage there is to being Jewish. After all, they say, to be a happy, healthy, charitable, and law-abiding citizen one certainly does not have to be Jewish — nor religious at all, for that matter. What is it then, they wonder, that makes the Jewish religion great?

The question is a pertinent one. Judaism embodies the principles of charity, humanity, maintaining sound physical and mental health, etc. But these are all matters of common sense. Common sense dictates that we should be charitable and sympathetic. Feelings of pity within us motivate us to act in certain ways. Even animals possess them: A cat has pity on her kittens, and a cow nurses her offspring. There are certainly qualities that are innate.

What, then, is the connection to religion? It doesn't seem that these principles have much to do with religion at all. They are merely things that a person inherently understands — and Jewishness does not in any way seem to be more notable in these areas than does any other religion.

But there is one point that this view overlooks: If charity and compassion are so logical, why were Bilaam or Hitler, may their names be blotted out, such cruel people, even worse than animals? Didn't Hitler realize he was cruel and murderous? Why don't terrorists today have these feelings of mercy and compassion? Where are *their* "innate" feelings of pity? What of all the renowned people who didn't act in accordance with these basic traits that some claim do not require religion at all?

The answer is simple: If we, as Jews, didn't have the Torah's laws governing human nature to bind us, then, as Rav Yisrael Salanter said so beautifully, "A person gets lost in his fantasies" (*Iggeres HaMussar*).

Many times, we do things irrationally. If a father hits his child when he is furious, he is taking leave of his senses at that time. He could have educated or disciplined his child in a nice, positive, and instructive way. As our Sages say, "A person would never sin unless a *meshugas*, an irrationality, entered his mind." In other words, our emotions overwhelm our logic and our faculty of understanding.

But the G-d-fearing Jew has *yiras Shamayim*, fear of Heaven. Rav Yisrael Salanter gives a beautiful parable to explain this: If a crazy person were to tell you that the glass of water in front of you contained poison, would you brush him off by saying, "Who has to listen to him. He's a *meshugeneh*, crazy!"? Would a rational person listen to a *meshugeneh* in this case? Yes, because he might be right! A sensible person would not touch the glass of water until even the slightest possibility of danger was ruled out. Although a *meshugeneh* might be out of touch with reality, he still knows the danger of drinking poison, and his warning would make any normal person hesitate before drinking the water, because he wouldn't want to take a chance.

Our Sages over the centuries have told us about the final reckoning we will eventually have to give for all our deeds when, after 120 years, we reach the World to Come. They have warned us that at that time our transgressions will point accusing fingers and our good deeds will come to our defense. If a person would heed even a lunatic's warning about poison, why wouldn't any sane person heed the words of our Sages regarding reward and punishment?

A person who fears Heaven doesn't want to take any chances. He doesn't want to risk poisoning his soul. When I visited the Chofetz Chaim in his home, he was hard of hearing. He had a yeshivah student at his side who would shout into his ear and tell him what his visitors said. Once the Chofetz Chaim was asked, "Rebbe, why don't you have an operation?" — which could have improved his hearing a great deal. To this he replied, "Good tidings they will yell into my ear; *lashon hara* they surely won't. If I have my hearing, I may hear *lashon hara.*"

It was said that for the Chofetz Chaim hearing *lashon hara* would have been like eating pork. Knowing the prohibitions that *lashon hara* entails, the Chofetz Chaim stayed away from it as if it were pork or poison. This is what Torah can do: It can show us what a sin means. It isn't just a logical approach. Everyone knows it isn't nice to slander, yet people keep on speaking *lashon hara*. If one would know the stringency of the sin — that it's like an electric shock to the soul — he would stay away from it. And that is the purpose of our religion: to show the stringency of the matter.

It is a simple thing, perhaps, for the individual whose simplicity keeps him from violating these rules. But for all others, there must be something more: fear of G-d.

During *Sefiras HaOmer* we mourn the deaths of Rabbi Akiva's students. The Gemara says Rabbi Akiva had 12,000 pairs of students — that is, 24,000 students — and they all died between Pesach and Shavuos because they didn't treat each other with enough respect (*Yevamos* 62b). The world then remained desolate until Rabbi Akiva came to the great masters in the South and taught them Torah. His disciples were Rav Meir, Rav Yehudah, Rav Yossi, Rav Shimon, and Rav Elazar ben Shamua, and they brought Torah back to *Klal Yisrael*.

Our Sages ask a very pertinent question about this: Rabbi Akiva's students didn't treat each other with enough respect, but was that sin great enough to cause the deaths of 24,000 students and have the world remain desolate of Torah? Even if they themselves had to be punished, why did the Jewish people have to suffer a loss that we still mourn today?

The answer is that treating each other with respect was a matter of *bein adam lachaveiro*. For people on their lofty level, lack of this quality was enough to bring devastation to the world of Torah. If their conduct was such that they didn't understand how to treat other people, then their Torah was not what it should be. In fact, it went against the very basic principles of Torah.

Remarkably, the students died only between Pesach and Shavuos. Why? Because during this time the Jewish nation prepares itself to receive the Torah, and Torah without knowing how to treat other people is not our Torah. The tenets of *bein adam lachaveiro* are the very foundation of Torah. A student who does not respect other people and does not understand the importance of another person cannot remain loyal to Torah. Hashem had to take these students away to show the world what the Torah really means to us; then, other students, who would have the correct understanding of what *bein adam lachaveiro* means, needed to be produced.

The secular world won't accept this as an answer, but we know how important the tenets of *bein adam lachaveiro* are and how relevant they are to keeping the mitzvos. "*V'ahavta l'rei'acha kamocha,* You shall love your fellowman as you love yourself" (*Vayikra* 19:18) is the foundation of the Torah, and without that, there can be no proper understanding of Torah at all. Thus, the students received the appropriate punishment.

There is another dimension as well. Their lack of respect for each other wasn't just a failing between man and his fellow, between Reuven and Shimon. Our respect for each other is also connected to the *tzelem Elokim,* because each individual is created in Hashem's image and contains an aspect of Him (*Bereishis Rabbah* 24:27). So it isn't just a matter of Reuven and Shimon — spirituality itself is at stake.

When we respect each other, we are showing that we respect Hashem. The pain of each individual is the pain of Hashem. And the lack of awareness of other people is a lack of awareness of Hashem Himself. It's all one.

Of the Ten Commandments, five govern interactions between man and his fellowman. We can't separate them from the other five, which govern interactions between man and his Creator, because they are one unit. Each complements the other, and we can't have one without the other. And this is the very foundation of Torah.

Most people don't understand this. They seem to think that we can have *bein adam lachaveiro* without Torah. This is false, because without the understanding of *bein adam lachaveiro,* a person will never perform these mitzvos to the fullest extent, because he regards Yaakov as Yaakov. And if Yaakov insults him, he has no respect for him.

But we are to take a lesson from Hashem Himself, whose *chesed,* lovingkindness, to Adam HaRishon began, say the Sages, *after* the sin, not before. When Hashem made Adam and Chavah garments and clothed them, that is the beginning of *chesed* in the Torah.

The *mussar* giants ask, though, why the first *chesed* isn't considered to be the placing of Adam in *Gan Eden*. As we say in the blessing under the *chuppah*, "Gladden the beloved companions as You gladdened Your creatures in *Gan Eden* of old." The most enjoyable time Adam and Chavah had was in *Gan Eden*. The Sages tell us that the angels used to roast meat for them, that they made the best dishes for Adam HaRishon. Our wish to every bride and groom is that Hashem make their joy as great as that of Adam HaRishon in *Gan Eden*. There is no greater happiness in the world. And all of us wish, after our 120 years of life, to go to *Gan Eden*, for the greatest pleasure one can have is *Gan Eden*. So wasn't placing Adam and Chavah in *Gan Eden* the first *chesed*? Why isn't that considered the beginning of *chesed* in the Torah?

The answer simply is that it was a *chesed* that is logical. Everyone can understand that the great Adam HaRishon deserved *chesed*. If we were to see the Chofetz Chaim, we would run to do *chesed* for him. But when we see a bad person, we stay away. After the sin Adam HaRishon should be considered a rascal. After all, he brought destruction to the world. Is it possible to do *chesed* for him? Yet, Hashem Himself made garments for Adam HaRishon. And that is the beginning of the Torah type of *chesed*.

Torah *chesed* isn't logical *chesed*. Logic takes things at face value. If this fellow is a rascal, if he did something terrible, he deserves punishment. But we understand that there is something higher. We understand that this individual possesses *tzelem Elokim*, the Divine image, that he has a soul, that there exists a G-dliness within him that might motivate him and direct him to become a *baal teshuvah* and do wonderful things. That is exactly what happened with Adam HaRishon. Therefore, the first blessing we make under the *chuppah* is *yotzer ha'adam*, about the creation of Adam HaRishon. Even after the sin, he repented and did *teshuvah*, and today we are all children of Adam HaRishon.

So even an ordinary person has a chance, with the help of Hashem, to make a wonderful comeback, as we often see with *baalei teshuvah*. It is remarkable. Today some of them have learned through the entire *Shas*, and they teach Torah and influence others as well. These very individuals, who were at one time irreligious, repented fully because of that reservoir of spirituality within us that will — somehow, sometime — remind the individual of who he really is and motivate him to do *teshuvah* and become a great person. That is the Torah's concept of *tzelem Elokim*.

But the world doesn't understand this. It takes things at face value — Reuven is Reuven and Shimon is Shimon. But Reuven is not Reuven. Reuven is a child of Hashem. And Hashem's concept of *bein adam lachaveiro* does not follow the rules of logic. Human beings, who act according to logic, would not do any *chesed* for Adam after the sin.

Adam gave Chavah her name, *Em Kol Chai*, after the sin (*Bereishis* 3:20). Why did he wait so long, until after the sin, to give her a name?

The answer is that before the sin she didn't need a name to say that she was a great person, for her greatness was evident. It was for this reason that Adam had no name, just *Adam*, which means "made from the earth." A name always signifies the virtues and capabilities of the individual. If you give a name to something, it somehow defines the essence of the thing. Adam and Chavah didn't require names before the sin because their greatness was obvious; they spoke for themselves without names.

But after the sin, when Chavah brought destruction to the world, why would we give her the name *Em Kol Chai*, the Mother of All Living Beings? We should call her the Mother of Death because she brought death to the world!

But this is the greatness of our holy Torah. Even after she sinned, she still is Chavah, and all living beings must be thankful and indebted to Chavah, the *Em Kol Chai*, because she had greatness within her, despite her sin.

If a person does something foolish, that does not invalidate his inherent greatness. That is the Torah concept of *bein adam lachaveiro*. It is a higher dimension of understanding what *chaveiro* means. It's not just Reuven or Shimon, or Rochel or Leah — it is the soul, the *tzelem Elokim*, of an individual that signifies his greatness. And therefore his obligations are much higher. The world does not understand this. To give Adam honor, to work for him, to do *chesed* for him — even after his sin — that is the Torah concept of *chesed*. We understand the greatness of Adam because we know he has the *tzelem Elokim* that somehow may bring him back to his original greatness.

The dimensions of Jewishness are entirely different from the logical concept of respect for an individual. Being a Jew means that we have emotions that are higher than animalistic feelings. It isn't the doing of *chesed* that is important, it's the love of *chesed*.

Many people do *chesed*, but do they love to do *chesed*? The Sages say in *Avos d'Rabbi Nassan*: Iyov asked, "Why am I worse than Avraham Avinu?" Iyov also did *chesed*. But Iyov waited for people to come to his door and then he did *chesed* for them, while Avraham sought the poor and needy to do *chesed* for them, as in the case with the angels. There is a difference. *Ahavas chesed* means you love to do *chesed*. You feel that something is missing in your life and you want to satiate yourself, so you have to do the *chesed*. The nations of the world will do *chesed*, but only when the poor and needy come around. They can't stand seeing the poverty and they are touched. They do have feelings of pity, but only because of what they see. If they don't see it, though, it does not bother them at all.

The Jewish people merited to reach the level of Avraham, where the Torah is a *Toras chayim*, a living Torah, which means that it rules and oversees every phase of our lives. Part of this is loving *chesed*.

We see in the song *Eishes Chayil* that the virtue of the *eishes chayil* is "*Toras chesed al leshonah*" (*Mishlei* 31:26). What is the meaning of *Toras chesed* being "on her tongue"? Is it enough just to talk about *chesed*?

The answer is that when something is an innate part of you, you automatically talk about it. You don't have to make any effort to do so because it is part of you. We speak our language because it comes automatically. The *eishes chayil* possesses *chesed* automatically; it is a part of her. And the love of *chesed* is so ingrained in the Jewish people that the *eishes chayil* does it graciously, without anyone even asking her. She seeks the needy to do *chesed* with them and she feels she's missing something when she doesn't do *chesed*.

The 24,000 students of Rabbi Akiva lacked recognition of what *bein adam lachaveiro* meant. And this meant a lack of recognition of Torah, not just *bein adam lachaveiro*. I will respect my fellowman because this person was created in the image of Hashem, and respecting him is respecting Hashem. If we don't respect him, we don't respect Hashem either. And then there is no Torah. So Rabbi Akiva's students were taken from this world to show the world that Torah without respect for our fellowman is not Torah. Torah is one, with the *tzelem Elokim* embracing both *bein adam lachaveiro* and *bein adam laMakom* together, as one unit.

The students died, the Sages say, of croup (*Yevamos* 62b), probably because they said something negative about their fellowman, so their punishment was centered in the throat. They died between Pesach and Shavuos, a time when we prepare for Torah. The world doesn't understand this concept of Torah because it has divorced one from the other. People think that a person can be a G-d-serving Jew, observing *bein adam laMakom* without *bein adam lachaveiro*, making them two separate ideas. But it isn't so. It is all one: *bein adam laMakom*. If a person has the realization that he is a child of Hashem, and that Hashem and the Jewish people are one, he is elevated from his natural inclinations to the level of serving Hashem. Even after he sins, a person is still Hashem's child, so respect him.

In the home, we must set an example for our children. Never be vicious or lose control. On the contrary, show graciousness, goodness, and lovingkindness to a child and you will see how influenced he will be. He will love you much more. He will understand the greatness of being a Jew, and what Torah means to us. That in itself is something wonderful. It rubs off on a child when he sees your actions and conduct, that you don't lose control and spank him when you are angry but that you act in a respectable, pleasant, and instructive way, with lovingkindness.

Toras chesed — the graciousness, familiarity, and respect, the beautiful and emotional feelings of lovingkindness of Torah — belongs to the woman. The holy Torah is higher than the common sense approach to life of the non-religious. When you merit the pleasure felt in appreciating the greatness of doing a *chesed*, you will benefit more than the individual receiving the *chesed*. And that is what it means to be Jewish and to live a life of Torah.

QUESTIONS & ANSWERS

Q

What is *yiras Shamayim*? What mitzvos should one encourage in one's household to increase *yiras Shamayim*?

A

Yiras Shamayim is fearing *Hashem Yisbarach* and being afraid to transgress any of His mitzvos. When you fear someone, you won't do anything that goes against his wishes. Increase *kavod haTorah* and you will increase *yiras Shamayim*. If you increase Torah study and the respect and honor given to Torah, you automatically increase *yiras Shamayim*. Torah, more than anything else, brings a person closer to Hashem.

Q

What happened to the Torah and *yiras Shamayim* that there was in previous generations? How did we lose it?

A

The Reform Movement began in Germany because of German culture. The *Meshech Chochmah*, Reb Meir Simchah of Dvinsk, prophesied 40 years before the rise of Hitler, may his name be blotted out, that this embrace of German culture is what would bring the Holocaust. German culture entered the Jewish home, causing the Reform Movement. It traveled into Galicia, but *baruch Hashem* there the *gedolim* stopped it; it never reached Poland at all. But some places were hit hard.

Q **If someone is selfish and self-centered, how can he work on becoming a *baal chesed*?**

A The Rambam says that this trait is cultivated by doing many acts of *chesed*. The more times you do an act of *chesed*, the more it impresses you and the more the *middah*, trait, then becomes ingrained in you.

Q **Will doing acts of *chesed* without necessarily having good intentions eventually bring a person to do *chesed* with proper intentions?**

A Definitely. Habituate yourself to doing acts of *chesed* and the good intentions will follow.

Q **What happens if one feels that he cannot do unlimited *chesed*?**

A We have to remember that we always have *siyatta diShemaya*; *Hashem Yisbarach* always helps. There are many ventures that a person undertakes and at first he thinks he will not be successful. As we know, over the course of a lifetime, there are many major steps one takes. But remember, with *bitachon* we have everything, and one must make the attempt.

Physically, our strength is limited, yet we get bouyed, filled with *ruach*, spirit, inspired to do many things. So although physically we are limited, *Hashem Yisbarach* gives us the ability to see things through. Think, for example, of the airplane that carries so much weight with such a small engine. It's the *ruach*, wind, that carries it; so too, the body might be frail and weak but the *ruach* supports it. People explain this phenomenon by saying that there is a reservoir of energy a person taps into to do a great feat, but we believe that there is spiritual help from Hashem. You will be able to accomplish what you aim to if you strongly want it and are willing to fight for it; then it will be done. The *ruach* gives us the courage and inspiration to go on, and Hashem gives the success.

2 THE PURPOSE OF THE CREATION OF WOMAN

We are all familiar with the blessing under the *chuppah*, "*yotzer ha'adam*, Who fashioned the man," and "*asher yatzar es ha'adam b'tzalmo*, Who fashioned man in His image." I often wondered why the Sages instituted these blessings thanking Hashem for creating Adam, to be said under the *chuppah*. What connection do these blesssings have with the *chasan* and *kallah*? Many years have elapsed since they were born!

To understand this we must examine carefully the purpose of the creation of Adam as well as the purpose of the creation of Chavah. Referring to the blessings under the *chuppah,* some of our commentators explain that the first expression, "*yotzer ha'adam*, Who fashioned the man," is a general reference to the creation of Adam, and the second, "*asher yatzar es ha'adam b'tzalmo*, Who fashioned man in His image," refers to the creation of Chavah as well as the creation of Adam (see *Rashi* on *Kesubos* 8a).

There is a very basic idea here. As we know, Hashem caused Adam to be unconscious and took one of his "*tzela*" to create Chavah. Although the usual translation is "rib," it really means "side." The Midrash asks why Hashem took one of Adam's *sides* for the creation of Chavah. We might think that Hashem should have taken a section of the head, a part of the body that is more important than a rib. But Chavah was to be formed only from the part that is hidden and inconspicuous, the side of the body, for a person's sides are usually covered by his arms, even when he is undressed. Therefore, Hashem created Chavah only from the rib, from the side of the body.

When each limb was formed, Hashem said to Chavah, "Be a *tzenuah*." Chavah was formed in such a manner so that she should possess the attribute of *tzenius*. This word doesn't mean only modesty, but also humility. Chavah was born with the spirituality that prepared her for the future: to become the wife of Adam HaRishon. As the Sforno points out, "Hashem formed Chavah from the *tzela* so that she should have the same *tzurah*, form, as a man, along with his qualities and characteristics." *Tzurah* usually refers to spiritual form, not the physical body. Physically, the reproductive organs are the only differences between a male and a female. Other than that, Chavah had everything in common with Adam (*Bereishis* 2:22).

So, from the very beginning of Chavah's creation, she wasn't formed only for the perpetuation of the species. There was a component in the very structure and composition of Chavah that gave her the preparation, in the spiritual sense, to become Adam's wife.

We all know that Chavah was born as an *ezer k'negdo*, a helpmate "in opposition to" Adam (*Bereishis* 2:18), which seems contradictory. Our Sages say, "When the husband merits it, when there is a life of happiness and peace, then she is a helpmate, *ezer*, to him; but if not, *chas v'chalilah*, she becomes an opponent, *k'negdo*" (*Yevamos* 63a).

But there is another explanation in the commentaries, one that you have probably heard: The *ezer* consists of *k'negdo*; the opposition is part of the helpmate. Just imagine if Chavah had been born with all the same qualities, all the virtues as well as all the bad attributes, as Adam. Of what would the union be comprised? Together they would just intensify the qualities each already had: the good qualities would become greater, but the bad ones would become worse. They wouldn't complement each other. It is only the opposition that does this. Electricity is produced in the same way. Two elements meet and the friction creates electricity. So it is the *k'negdo* that is in essence the *ezer*.

The Sages tell us something very interesting concerning this. You probably know of the great *Amora'im*, Rav Yochanan and Reish Lakish. The Gemara tells the story of this partnership (*Bava Metzia* 84a). Reish Lakish had gone astray and become the head of a group of gangsters. One day, Rav Yochanan was bathing in the Jordan River when Reish Lakish saw him and jumped into the Jordan. It seems that this was an outstanding jump, for Rav Yochanan said to him, "Your strength should be used for Torah. You have the power to become a great man."

Reish Lakish answered Rav Yochanan, "Your beauty" — Rav Yochanan had a beautiful face — "belongs to women."

Rav Yochanan said to Reish Lakish, "If you will return to Torah and become a *ben Torah*, I will give you my sister, who is more beautiful than I, for a wife."

Reish Lakish accepted the deal. The Sages tell us that Reish Lakish became the study partner of Rav Yochanan, and the two became wonderful friends. After a while, Reish Lakish died and the Gemara says that Rav Yochanan suffered immensely from the loss. The rabbis suggested to Rav Yochanan, "Let's look for another study partner for you." They thought of Rav Elazer ben Pedas, who was also a great *Amora*, with a very sharp, deep mind. They thought he would be a good challenge for Rav Yochanan as a study partner. The two sat together and began learning. For every *chiddush* Rav Yochanan said, Rav Elazar said to him, "I'll prove that you're right," and he brought proofs to show that everything Rav Yochanan said was right.

We would be very happy to have a study partner like this, but Rav Yochanan was dissatisfied. He said to Rav Elazar, "Are you as wise as Reish Lakish? You don't compare as a study partner to Reish Lakish! When I would say something to Reish Lakish, he would ask me 24 questions to contradict what I said and I would answer him with 24 answers. In this way, we elaborated on the halachah much more. But you just prove that I'm right! I know that I'm right. I want to hear something *against* what I'm saying, so that I can elaborate on the halachah more."

Rav Yochanan was so dissatisfied with his study partner that he tore his clothes.

This is a remarkable story. It shows what the right study partner means to a person. Rav Yochanan needed opposition to prove his point, for only through opposition did he become the great Rav Yochanan. So we see that the *k'negdo* is a kind of opposition that brings out the greatness of a person.

We find the same idea in many halachos. For instance, an *eishes chaver*, the wife of a Torah scholar, is considered like a Torah scholar. And the commentators say that one must stand up for an *eishes chaver* the same way we stand up for a Torah scholar. The reason for this is not just that she is the wife of a scholar but that she made her husband into a scholar. How did she do it? Not by always agreeing with everything he did. As it says about the mother of King Solomon: She made her son great. She was the one for whom *Eishes Chayil* was written (*Mishlei* 31:1). King Solomon considered his mother an *eishes chayil* because she reprimanded him after he married Pharaoh's daughter. It was she who put him back on the right track. So it is the opposition, not just agreement, that brings out the greatness of an individual.

And this is why the Torah says *ezer k'negdo*, for Chavah's role was not to always agree with Adam. The *ezer* could also be in the form of *k'negdo*; if she saw him doing something wrong, she would tell him. This should only be done respectfully, of course, and not critically. Chavah was created — and all women after her — with the ideal spiritual qualities to bring out the best in her husband.

The Gemara asks a question that is apparently not easy to understand: "With what do women gain merit?" (*Berachos* 17a). The Chofetz Chaim asked, "Why does the Gemara ask this question? Women have mitzvos of their own, and they are obligated in negative commandments just like men, so of course they have merits!" (*Chovas HaShemirah*, Ch. 13).

The explanation seems to be that indeed, they have merits, but to merit *techiyas hameisim*, revival of the dead, they need Torah. As the Gemara says, the "dew" of Torah will give one the merit of *techiyas hameisim* (*Kesubos* 111b). Only Torah has the quality of giving life to a person. So the Gemara asks what merits women have, because although women are obligated in other mitzvos, those mitzvos do not have the life-giving quality that Torah has. With what, then, will they merit *techiyas hameisim*?

The Gemara in *Berachos* answers that their merit is bringing their children to *cheder*, enabling their husbands to study Torah, waiting for their husbands to return, and giving their husbands permission to learn in other cities. In other words, enabling someone else to learn Torah gives the person herself the merit of Torah.

Constantly women nowadays seem to deplore their situation. When they say the morning blessing, "for having made me according to His Will," they don't say it happily. This is wrong. Women play a major role in spiritual life. They were not born just to be servants or housemaids. Of course, a woman should be a good homemaker, but that is not the true purpose for which she was created.

Chavah was created to be a helpmate in the spiritual sense. She was formed from the *tzela*, which symbolizes *tzenius*, humility and modesty. These are spiritual virtues, which made her great spiritually, so that she could be a helper to Adam as he climbed the ladder of spirituality to become the great Adam HaRishon. Waiting for one's husband to come home from yeshivah, or taking the children to *cheder* gives a woman spiritual merits. Of course, homemaking is in and of itself a big *chesed*, and a woman's physical activities at home are mitzvos, but this was not the sole purpose of the creation of Chavah. She was built to become the spiritual helpmate of Adam. You could say she was built from the side so that she would always be at Adam's side to help him along.

Therefore, we say the blessing *yotzer ha'adam* under the *chuppah* many years after the person was born, even though it would seem to be more appropriate to say it at the time a child is born. The prefix "*ha*" means that we are not referring to the general creation of mankind but to the specific creation of Adam HaRishon. He is that special individual who was created for a certain purpose in life, and this spiritual aspect continues to be found within each person.

The next blessing also talks about the creation of that man who was to become the complete man. The Zohar says that before marriage a man is considered a half-person. The spiritual completion of the body takes place under the *chuppah*, when he gets his helpmate in the spiritual aspect of life. Then he becomes a whole man. Thus, the next blessing, "Who fashioned the man in His image, in the image of His likeness and prepared for him — from himself — a building for eternity," means that he and his wife together form one whole body. We say these blessings under the *chuppah* to indicate that with this union they will become the complete body in the spiritual sense. We cannot say the blessing at birth because at that point the person is not complete; he will only become complete after marriage. In fact, the Gemara even says that a person only merits perfection in Torah after marriage (*Yevamos* 62b).

So we see that Chavah made Adam into the great man he became. She was the *Em Kol Chai*, the Mother of All Living Beings. Every woman should be happy when she says, "for having made me according to His will," for her role is like that of Chavah, to form with her husband one complete unit to attain their mutual spiritual goals.

QUESTIONS & ANSWERS

Q How should a woman act when speaking to men?

A The conversation should be as brief as possible.

Q If a woman is sitting on a bus and a man sits on the seat next to her, should she get up?

A Preferably, she should try to find a way to leave that seat without embarrassing the other party. A person must be very careful in these situations not to insult someone. It's a very big sin to embarrass someone. If this is impossible, she must be careful to avoid any contact with him.

Q How thick do a woman's stockings have to be?

A If the stockings are so sheer that you can see the leg through them then it is not acceptable.

Q The *Rosh Yeshivah* mentioned that the man is able to attain greatness through the woman. If the husband is not successful in his learning is it because of the wife?

A You can't make a blanket statement like that. It would all depend upon the individuals and on the setup of their married life. There are many factors involved here. But *sometimes* she is at fault. As the

Chofetz Chaim says, she might be too demanding. She may want to purchase new clothes frequently and they can't afford it, so he has to look for a job. But if she is modest and doesn't seek too much, then he is able to learn. You can't make a blanket statement about this, but a good wife, dedicated to Torah, should spur her husband on. Don't worry about making a living, but give your husband a little more faith and encouragement. Remember — the burden of making a living weighs heavily on the husband's mind. Sometimes he becomes depressed and feels like a failure. It is the duty of the wife at those critical moments to spare him and save him.

Many times, out of despair, the husband will leave the yeshivah. The wise woman will say, "Don't worry, my dear husband, Hashem will help us!" That is being the true *ezer*, helpmate, during those critical moments. But do not become the *posek*; ask the opinion of *gedolim*. People always run to ask a rav if a *milchig* spoon falls into a *fleishig* pot. And what is a spoon worth? Why don't they ask a rav when it concerns whether or not to leave the yeshivah, which is the person's whole spirituality? Unfortunately, they don't come to ask this question. A wise woman should encourage her husband at these critical moments — because she can make him or break him at such times.

What if someone is unhappy learning?

It is essential that he search for ways to find success, because experience teaches us that if one leaves the yeshivah out of failure he will be the unhappiest individual in life. He will constantly think that he didn't make it and his children will think that they, too, will be unhappy learning Torah. It's the person who learns Torah who will be a happy person. Maybe his goals and expectations of himself were unrealistic. A reorientation may change his attitude toward himself. Lack of money is a momentary pressure that sometimes causes people to leave. Running away, though, is not the answer.

Q Do you need to be brilliant to achieve success in Torah?

A No one needs brilliance. There are many brilliant people in this world who accomplish nothing. It is a person's *mesiras nefesh*, self-sacrifice, that counts and that enables him or her to achieve things in life.

Q You mentioned before that a woman merits *Gan Eden* when she encourages her husband to learn and brings her children to yeshivah. But what about a single woman?

A Supporting Torah, a Yissachar-and-Zevulun partnership, is just as good. Zevulun was the one who supported Yissachar, who studied Torah. By supporting Torah you get the same reward as one who studies Torah. If you have a husband, your support of Torah is helping your husband to learn. If he is not a *ben Torah*, or if a woman is not married, then supporting Torah is just as good.

Q Is there also reward for sending girls to Bais Yaakov?

A Yes, this is a definite connection to Torah. The Chofetz Chaim explains that it is an important mitzvah to see that girls have a strong Torah education.

Q Why do we need Bais Yaakov today if in the olden days there weren't any?

A Our *bubbies* didn't have a Bais Yaakov because in their times their lives were full of the *kedushah*, sanctity, of Torah. Their homes were filled with Judaism, so there was no need for the Bais Yaakov to teach them this. Today, unfortunately, the streets are not what they should be. Imagine what would happen to the children without a Bais Yaakov! A Bais Yaakov had to be founded; it became the shelter that gave the inspiration needed. In Europe, before World War I, they didn't need a Bais Yaakov, for Torah was stronger. Shabbos observance was on a high level. The homes were *batei mikdash*. But many homes today are somewhat deficient of the spirit of Torah, and therefore the Bais Yaakov becomes necessary to supplement the traditional home in its highest sense.

Q **Why was it necessary for those who learned Torah during the time of the Gemara to leave their home-towns?**

A At that time, there weren't local yeshivos as there are nowadays. The outstanding yeshivos were in Sura and Pumbedisa, so they had to travel, just as in Europe people traveled to the Mir Yeshivah and the Volozhin Yeshivah, among others. Small towns had elementary yeshivos, but for *yeshivah gedolah* students had to travel. Some, like Rabbi Akiva, left for many years. In that case, the wife had to give her husband permission, because otherwise he wasn't allowed to go. The permission a wife gives her husband to go learn Torah is a merit for her.

Q **What does the Gemara mean when it talks about a woman gaining merit by "waiting for her husband" to return home?**

A Sometimes her husband will come home late at night from yeshivah. This means she has to wait for him to serve him supper. This is very hard for her, especially for a mother with children, who would like to go to sleep early. But she waits for her husband, and this goes toward the making of a great man.

Q What about other families, where the father is not studying full time in a *kollel*? How do they earn merit?

A Scheduling set times for Torah study also brings merit. Also, people earn merit for supporting the study of Torah, since it is as if they are learning Torah themselves.

Q Should a woman push her husband to do more than what he thinks he is supposed to do in learning?

A This is a very difficult question. Men do not like to be pushed. But you might say tactfully, "My dear husband, maybe you should devote more time to learning."

Q If a woman sends her husband to the yeshivah half-heartedly, does she still gain merit?

A Of course she does. But even if she sends him off half-heartedly, she should try to do it with a smile. This will make him happier in his learning — for which his wife shares in the merit.

Q If a husband is sitting and learning, should one encourage him to go out and do *chesed,* or is it better for him to sit and learn?

A He should sit and learn. There are halachos that guide us concerning when a person should stop learning to do a *chesed*, such as doing so only when there is no one else who can do that *chesed*. Remember: Torah study outweighs everything.

Q Should the husband go to yeshivah for third *seder* in the evening or should he stay home with the children while the wife goes out for a little while?

A I always feel that a wife should go out sometimes during the week to have a change of scenery. This helps maintain *shalom bayis*, marital harmony. It's so important after a hard day and she deserves it. But each case should be considered individually. If a woman goes swimming or out to a lecture, it is a good break for her, and her husband will have a better wife, thus helping him learn better. If she's feeling low, it will affect his learning and *shalom bayis*. Of course, a woman should not go out at the expense of the home, for the home comes first. But if her husband is wise, he will be understanding and give her the opportunity to go. The best solution is to find a reliable babysitter if possible.

Q **There's one question that's bothering me: Our husbands' goal in this world is to reach the greatest height in learning and my husband feels that he can get the best learning during the *kollel* years, before he goes out and gets a job. Then what happens? If he gets a job, let's say, teaching second grade, how can he achieve and go higher?**

A Even the *shiur* given to a second-grade class can bring tremendous spiritual satisfaction. There are influential people today, leaders of American Jewry, who are the former *talmidim* of *marbitzei Torah*. Can you imagine the satisfaction a rebbe has when he says, to himself, "Ah, that's a *talmid* of mine! Forty years ago, I toiled and did everything in my power to impart to him the *ruach* of Torah, and now he's one of the leading Jews in the United States." Nothing can equal that pleasure. After leaving *kollel*, a man assumes the role of becoming a *marbitz Torah*. Teaching any grade is a great task filled with *chesed*. There is a certain satisfaction in being a *marbitz Torah*, in teaching and giving of yourself to a *talmid*, in conveying to someone else what you have acquired in yeshivah. In imparting Torah knowledge, a man enjoys the fruits of his labors.

When a person says a good *shiur* and sees that those listening are deriving satisfaction from it, it gives him the impetus to keep up his work. It has nothing to do with money, it's spiritual. When a *rosh yeshivah* comes into the yeshivah and sees it full of *talmidim* learning, it gives him the courage and inspiration to continue the work. It is this sense of spiritual elevation that carries the teacher of Torah on.

Q

My husband teaches, but we are finding it hard to make ends meet. Should I encourage him to leave teaching?

A

Financial consideration should not be the only guideline about *parnasah*. A person must have *bitachon* in Hashem. Becoming a *marbitz Torah* is totally an act of *chesed*, and remember: One who has the pleasure of *chesed* will enjoy life. *Chazal* tell us that jealousy, desire, and pursuit of honor remove a man from this world. Someone who runs after these desires will never enjoy life because he feels that the world and everyone in it owes him. His soul is never full, as *Chazal* say, "A man does not die with half of his desires fulfilled." It is only the *baal chesed* who enjoys the true essence of life. There is a certain satisfaction in being a *marbitz Torah*. There is a certain satisfaction in teaching and giving of yourself to a *talmid*, in conveying to someone else what you acquired in the yeshivah. The fruits of this work give the teacher a spiritual elevation. Again, it's the *ruach* that carries him on. It's all in a life of Torah ideals. The real *melamed* and *rosh yeshivah* is not the one who punches a clock. Such a person never has success. This rebbe works hard with his *talmidim*, giving them all individual attention. It is the *middah* of *chesed* that makes one into a successful *rosh yeshivah*. The *talmid* sees that the rebbe is devoted and he thereby imparts to his *talmid* a love for Torah.

Q **How interconnected is the wife's spiritual level with her husband's? Do they get the same share in the World to Come or is each credited separately?**

A You can rest assured that you get a great deal of credit. Hashem will take care of it.

TRUE BEAUTY

When students tell me they must have exactly such-and-such in order to function as good *talmidim*, that they want a perfect set-up for themselves — wonderful *chavrusahs* to study with, excellent *shiurim*, and everything exceptional and ideal — I call them "incubator *talmidim*."

These are the students who have complaints, if anything is lacking, if something is missing, if their rooms in the dorm aren't the best, if the beds are a little hard. They say that without having what they are missing, they cannot function properly.

Of course it helps to have all these things. Having the right *chavrusah* is wonderful. But the outstanding student, the exceptional *talmid*, will always function as a good *talmid* no matter what the circumstances because, "Such is the way of Torah: Bread in salt shall you eat, water in measure shall you drink, and on the earth you shall sleep." A good student functions regardless of the situation, just as a good businessman will function as a good businessman even if he has deficits and even if business is not going well that particular day.

When we look at the life story of Queen Esther, for example, we see that she was unlike most girls, who have the reassurance and backing of their parents when it comes to a *shidduch* or anything else important in life.

Every child wants parental approval, especially that of the mother. It's human nature. A girl will never begin any venture of major importance without consulting her parents, and she is very right to act this way. Yet, although Esther was an orphan, nevertheless, under Mordechai's guidance, she grew up to become Queen Esther, all because she was not an "incubator *talmid.*"

What did Esther possess that made her the great Queen Esther? We are told that she "found favor in the eyes of all who saw her" (*Esther* 2:15). In other words, she captivated everyone who saw her. Not only that, but "the king loved Esther more than all the women, and she found more favor and kindness before him than all the other maidens" (*Esther* 2:17). Esther had some special quality that captivated people — even King Achashverosh — something more basic than beauty: her *chein.*

Queen Esther's *chein* captivated all who saw her, including the king. Achashverosh saw perhaps thousands of woman, but Esther struck a chord in his innermost nature. Her lovely personality was her greatness, and it was for this virtue that she was chosen to redeem the Jewish people.

What exactly is *chein*? We say a certain person has *chein*, a certain charm. Is it something physical? No, it's not that at all. A girl may have charm even if she is not beautiful. *Chein* is a spiritual value, not a physiological one. It is a spiritual attribute and the woman who has it captivates people with her graceful attitude and poise and by her conduct, for which people love her. We find a source for this in the Torah: "*Ya'er Hashem panav eleicha vi'chuneka*, Hashem should make His Face shine upon you" — this is the light of Torah — "and give you *chein*" (*Bamidbar* 6:25).

Chein is a spiritual quality that appeals to others, a spiritual virtue that captivates and draws other people, something magnetic. When the personality is full of *chein*, people love the individual, not because of external beauty, but because of spiritual virtue. For example, the Torah tells us that when Yosef was in Egypt, "his master perceived that Hashem was with him and whatever he did Hashem made succeed ... and Yosef found favor in his eyes" (*Bereishis* 39:4). Here again we find *chein* as appeal, as a magnetism by which Yosef's master became attached to him.

Yosef was a great individual, a magnetic personality, full of smiles, full of goodness, full of sweetness — full of *chein*, the spiritual quality you can see on a person's face.

What was the beginning of Yosef's greatness, the starting point that led to the redemption from the Egyptian exile? Yosef was imprisoned in Egypt, as were Pharaoh's baker and cupbearer. One morning Yosef noticed that they were somewhat distressed. "Why do you look so sad?" he asked — and there is the turning point (*Bereishis* 40:7). Many people wouldn't have noticed the change in their faces. So what if they were sad? The egotist wouldn't have paid any attention. It is only the *baal chesed*, the person who is interested in the other person's welfare, who will notice a change in expression.

Yosef asked why they looked sad, and from this followed his interpretation of their dreams, which began his redemption. If Yosef hadn't noticed their faces, they wouldn't have asked him to interpret their dreams, and when Pharaoh dreamed, they wouldn't have given Yosef's name as the interpreter of dreams. None of it would have happened.

People who notice a change in the other person are those people who possess the quality of *chesed v'rachamim*, caring about others. They notice every change in the other person, whether he is happy or sad, while a person who is interested only in himself will never notice anything.

Our Sages tell us that when *Klal Yisrael* accepted the Torah at Sinai they did not want to accept the Oral Law. However, "*kafa aleihem har k'gigis*" — they were forced to accept it, for if not, they would have died (*Shabbos* 88a). This situation was changed at the time of Mordechai and Esther, when *Klal Yisrael* willingly confirmed their acceptance of the Oral Law, thus indicating their acceptance of the complete Torah.

Our Sages compare the acceptance of the Torah at Sinai, and the acceptance of the Torah in the time of Achashverosh in the verse, "The Jews had light, *orah*, and gladness and joy and honor" (*Esther* 8:16). Our Sages tell us that *orah* is Torah.

When the Jewish people received the Torah at Sinai we are told, "and Israel rested, *vayichan*, there, opposite the mountain" (*Shemos* 19:2). The Hebrew word for *rested* is in the singular here, yet it should be in the plural, as it is two words earlier in the phrase, "they rested, *vayachanu*, in the wilderness." Rashi and other commentators note that the singular usage tells us that the Jewish people were not separate individuals when they received the Torah but were united into one. This was the basic requirement for receiving the Torah.

We have 613 mitzvos equal to the limbs and sinews of a person's body, with each limb having its own mitzvah. But can each of us fulfill all 613 mitzvos? Of course not. Someone who is not a Kohen cannot perform the mitzvos that a Kohen is commanded to do, while only a king can perform the mitzvos of a king. With so many mitzvos that we cannot fulfill, how can we have 613 mitzvos equaling our 613 limbs and sinews?

The answer is that "*Torah tzivah lanu Moshe morashah kehillas Yaakov.*" Moshe has given us Torah, but we can only fulfill it when we are *kehillas Yaakov*, when Yaakov, the Jewish people, is one *kehillah*, community (*Devarim* 33:4). When we are one, then you get partial credit for the mitzvos I do and I get partial credit for the mitzvos that you do. This way — when we are one unit acting as one — all of us together can fulfill all 613 commandments. But if there is no peace and love between us, there can be no complete fulfillment of the 613 mitzvos.

During Mordechai and Esther's time there was a similar confirmation of acceptance of the Torah. Then, too, all *Klal Yisrael* had to be as one. This explains why we send *mishloach manos*, gifts of food, and give *matanos l'evyonim*, presents to the poor. These were not commanded on any other Yom Tov, not Pesach, Shavuos, or Succos. Why do we give such gifts only on Purim? There are many reasons, but one is very basic: If *matanos l'evyonim*, caring for the needy, and *mishloach manos*, brotherhood between each and every individual, prevail, then we can have acceptance of the Torah.

That was the greatness of Queen Esther. Toward the end of the *Megillah* we read that dispatchers were sent to all the Jews "*lekayem es iggeres ... shalom v'emes*, with words of peace and truth to establish these days of Purim" (*Esther* 9:29). Then it says, "For Mordechai the Jew was viceroy to King Achashverosh; he was a great man among the Jews and found favor with the multitude of his brethren; he sought the good of his people and spoke for the welfare of all his seed" (*Esther* 10:3). A united *Klal Yisrael*, Jews combining into one and caring for each other, was the essence of the Purim miracle. That's why Esther was selected, for she possessed *chein v'chesed*.

She was crowned not because of her physical beauty but because of her *mesiras nefesh*, self-sacrifice. When Mordechai said, "If you don't take action, Hashem will bring the salvation in another way," Esther fasted for three days. Uppermost in her mind was her *mesiras nefesh* for *Klal Yisrael*, the ultimate virtue of *chein v'chesed*.

It does not matter if a woman is not learned, not part of what we used to call "the sophisticated intelligentsia." It is the *Yiddishe tochter*, the Jewish daughter, who possesses that *chein v'chesed,* that virtue of caring for others, who earns our admiration. The woman who has in mind, "Did I do a deed of *chesed* today? Did I do anything good for my neighbor?" is beloved by all. It is she who has that magnetic personality, that special touch of giving that endears her to others. She is the *baalas rachamim*, the *baalas chesed*, and this can be recognized immediately in her wonderful personality. People trust her because they know she is a person who cares about them.

In some neighborhoods, people pass each other without even a greeting. I don't think this is intentional, but the virtue of the *Yiddishe tochter* does not allow this. There is the basic feeling of caring for others. When you meet a friend or neighbor, you don't have to spend half-an-hour talking about what she's preparing for supper that day. You may be a busy woman, but stop and say hello. It only takes a minute or two. This may sound like a little thing but it is not little. It is the personality one cultivates, the interest one takes in other people, that takes only a minute or two but makes such a big difference.

Torah is all *chesed* from beginning to end. A person who is self-absorbed and feels no connection to *Klal Yisrael* cannot fulfill the Torah because he cannot fulfill all 613 mitzvos on his own. Only if I share in the merit of your mitzvah and you share in the merit of mine can we individually and together reach the full 613.

So show a little appreciation for other women, show them love and that you care about them. Help each other and work toward developing a total devotion to each other. Consolidate all ties into one group, in the spirit of "I care for you, you care for me; I care for your children, you care for mine."

This is the true beauty of the Jewish woman.

QUESTIONS & ANSWERS

Q   **How much should a woman sacrifice her family and her own needs to do** *chesed*?

A   A woman's *chesed* should be unlimited, as long as it does not come into conflict with the home, husband, and children. This is her only limitation, because her first obligation is to her husband and family.

Halachah should be her only limitation. Halachically, a woman should not do *chesed* at the expense of her husband and children. When her family's needs are not fulfilled, she shouldn't leave to do *chesed* for other people. She owes her time and energy to her family first. She has to curb her desire to do *chesed* for others in order to be fair to the home, and dare not neglect her home by doing *chesed* for other people. Yet she must remember: Charity *begins* at home, but it shouldn't end at home.

If a woman has free time, she can do *chesed* for everyone, and it should be unlimited. Remember, *chesed* should always be as unlimited as her schedule allows. A person who does *chesed* will always be happy and content, knowing that she is fulfilling the virtue of *chesed* for which she was created.

A wife often feels how much she sacrifices and wonders how much she can take. A *kollel* wife whose husband is always learning gives up some companionship, and it's a struggle. She may feel stressed, but if she would appreciate and realize how much *chesed* she is doing, building her own home, giving emotional support to her husband and children — the future — she would be proud. She should feel wonderful and happy.

You'll appreciate *chesed* and you'll feel wonderful when you do *chesed* only when you recognize the greatness of *chesed*, whether it is in the home or for those outside the home.

Q **Can you do the mitzvah of *bikur cholim*, visiting the sick, by telephone?**

A Yes, in a way. Ask the person what you can do for him. The mitzvah of *bikur cholim* is not just to ask him how he feels but what you can do for him. Visiting is very important but it's not everything. If you can't ask about the patient's needs in person, you can do it by phone.

Q **Can you fulfill the mitzvah of *nichum aveilim*, comforting the mourner, by phone?**

A *Bish'as hadchak*, if there's no other way, you can, by phone or letter. However, it is better to go to the person's home.

Q **How can we comfort a person who is ill with a serious disease?**

A Tell him that Hashem is the *Borei refuos*, Creator of all remedies. Tell him not to give up hope. Researchers might come up with some medication that will cure his disease. Many illnesses that formerly were fatal are today easily curable. *Borei* is in the present tense; Hashem is always creating new cures.

In *Mishlei*, the Vilna Gaon says *simchah*, happiness, cures diseases. The psyche has an effect on the body. A happy person will not suffer the same as one who is sad. Two people might have the same disease but the one who is happy will be cured sooner.

Q **Should you continue *davening* for someone who had an illness such as mononucleosis or hepatitis even after they have survived the dangerous part?**

A Yes, *daven* for them until they are completely recovered. You do not know the extent of the damage that might have occurred. It takes a long time to recover from such illnesses.

Q **When one calls from a public phone and our token or coin does not go down but we get a line anyway, do we owe the phone company for the call?**

A Yes, you do.

Q **Is it permissible to copy tape cassettes?**

A All commercial tapes produced by any company should not be reproduced without permission. Likewise, things should not be photocopied. If everyone would do so, the rightful owner would go out of business. If the tape is no longer being sold, you may copy it on condition that it is not injurious to the copyright holder.

Q **If I copied a copyrighted tape and then found that this is forbidden, am I still allowed to listen to it?**

A No, do not listen to it. Do not use anything that has been taped from a copyrighted tape.

Q **Is it right to ask a person for a debt from years before?**

A One can remind someone that a debt is still outstanding, but one should be careful not to ask someone to repay a loan if he knows that the person is unable to repay it at that time. On the other hand, if a person owes money and is unable to repay it at that time, he himself should go to the lender and say that he is very sorry but he is unable to repay him at the moment. He should also say that he realizes that he still owes him money and will repay him as soon as possible.

Q **Is a shopkeeper allowed to withhold stock from customers until the prices go up?**

A Why not? That is business. If he would have faith, though, he would realize that Hashem could give him money from other sources as well.

Q **Many women nowadays are fed up with the drudgery of never-ending household chores, even though we know these are great mitzvos of *chesed*. And although we know kids will be kids, it's hard to keep calm when they get on our nerves. How is a woman supposed to cope?**

A She can learn from Queen Esther to succeed in overcoming all the tribulations she encounters with the aid of prayer, *bitachon,* and patience.

Prayer: The power of *Tehillim* can change one's life. David HaMelech, the author of *Tehillim*, was constantly fleeing for his life, but his spirit never faltered. The *Tehillim* he wrote sustained him through his terrible trials, and these same *Tehillim* continue to sustain the Jewish people today. One draws hope from saying even a single psalm, especially if she believes in what she is saying.

Bitachon: She must not despair. If she succumbs to her natural feelings, she will give up. Her task is to overcome these feelings and develop the inner strength that will keep her going. It is a difficult task, but if she has *bitachon*, Hashem will help her. She must think: "Today may not have been so bright, but tomorrow, with Hashem's help, will be sunnier." Such thoughts will help her succeed.

Patience: She must bear in mind that personal growth is a slow and gradual process. She must think: "Thank G-d, I am a little gentler today, I'm more good-natured, I did more *chesed* today." In this way she will gradually change her nature, which is the greatest accomplishment in life.

All women can become outstanding personalities in their own homes. If you work on your personality gradually, with prayer, *bitachon*, and patience, I assure you that you will always achieve your goals.

4

When the Jewish people saw that Moshe was delayed in coming down from Har Sinai, they gathered around Aharon and demanded that he make them a new "god" to replace Moshe. Aharon then instructed them to take the jewelry from their wives and children to use for the Golden Calf. But, our Sages tell us, the women would not give in so easily and refused to contribute their jewels. And so, the Torah tells us, "the people removed the gold rings from their ears"— *the people*, meaning only the men (*Targum Yonasan ben Uzziel* on *Shemos* 32:3).

Because of their loyalty, women were given the days of *Rosh Chodesh* to observe as minor festivals, as days to be freed from major household chores. Until the Golden Calf, both men and women celebrated the sanctity of *Rosh Chodesh*, but after the sin, only the women continued with this privilege, their reward for maintaining their faith in Hashem and Moshe Rabbeinu (*Shulchan Aruch* 417).

Why did the women refuse to contribute their jewelry? What was the source of their loyalty?

It came from their special approach to life, as shown in this story from the time of the holy Alshich.

A wagon driver once heard from the Alshich that there exists in Judaism a concept of *bitachon*, absolute blind faith. The wagon driver thought to himself, "Why should I waste my time in worthless toil and labor? I will put my faith in Hashem and He will provide." And so he made himself comfortable by the fire and began to recite *Tehillim*. When his family came to complain, telling him that he should be out with his wagon earning a living so that they would have food, he explained his new-found philosophy: "Why should we work if Hashem will reward us for our faith?"

So as not to starve, his family sold the wagon and donkey to a local farmer. Soon after, the farmer went to seek his fortune in a forest. Finding a buried treasure, he proceeded to load the donkey with as much gold as the animal could carry. Suddenly a large boulder fell from the mountainside and killed the man, at the same time frightening the donkey so that it ran back to its former master. When the donkey arrived at the house of the wagon driver, the family discovered the sacks of gold it was carrying and realized that their *bitachon* had been richly rewarded.

Upon hearing of this amazing incident, the students of the holy Alshich demanded an explanation from their rebbe. After all, why should the power of *bitachon* be so much greater in the wagon driver than in them?

The Alshich explained with a parable: "If one puts a rod into the hard earth, it will hold its own. But the same rod driven into soft earth will be shaky and ultimately fall.

"The wagon driver does not question. To him the idea of *bitachon* is very simple: One must trust in Hashem. But your minds, trained to probe and analyze all aspects of a question, automatically do the same to a concept such as *bitachon*. The result is that questions that remain without answers may arise in your minds. And although this would not, *chas v'shalom*, destroy your faith in Hashem, you would nevertheless trust less strongly than the simple wagon driver" (*Madregas HaAdam*, Ch. 5).

Women have a natural ability to see to the heart of things. Their ability to do so is a special gift from Hashem. A woman will not try to analyze and rationalize everything she encounters. At Sinai when Hashem gave the Torah, all of Israel cried out, "*Naaseh v'nishma*, We will do what Hashem commands us and only then question and analyze." What happened in the short time that elapsed between this total acceptance and the making of the Golden Calf?

The Ramban explains that the Jewish people wanted the calf, not as a god, but as a leader to replace Moshe Rabbeinu (*Shemos* 32:1). They were frightened when Moshe went up to the mountain and did not return, and they wanted a new symbol of leadership. But why weren't they more patient? They had only miscalculated by a few hours. Couldn't they have waited a little longer?

The Sages tell us that the Satan came and confused the world, making the people think that Moshe had died (ibid., *Rashi*). However, only the men were affected in this way. Their analytical, rational minds told them that something must have happened to Moshe. But the women, with their direct, trusting approach to life, understood only that Moshe had said he would return and so return he would; the Jewish people had merely to wait.

We can now understand how a woman's nature is different from a man's, and as a result, how her role in life also differs. A woman's nature, her practical approach to life, enables her to run a home and care for children as only she can. An analytical approach to homemaking would lead to utter chaos; nothing would get done. It is not difficult to conjure up in one's mind a picture of what things would be like if each time a woman prepared a meal, she analyzed philosophic points of view on each course.

In addition, a woman appreciates the tremendous *zechus*, merit, in caring for children. When a woman takes care of her children, she is performing *chesed shel emes*, true kindness for her children. They will never be able to repay her for all that she does for them: nursing and feeding them at all hours, washing them, seeing to all their needs. Such is truly the *chesed shel emes* to which our Sages refer, and it is only a woman who can do this. A man's mind can't work this way. A man looks at household chores as mundane tasks that only serve to interrupt his *avodas Hashem*. His analytical mind will not permit him to see the relative importance of such things as preparing meals and caring for children. So while he analyzes and probes, the woman must be relied upon to guard the home with her unshakable, simple faith in Hashem.

Just as each woman was able to see beyond the confusion at Sinai, only the woman, with her direct approach to life, can deal with the daily problems of bringing up a family. And only the woman can have such strong, unwavering faith and trust no matter how difficult her situation may become.

QUESTIONS & ANSWERS

Q **Can a woman wash clothes and do other** *melachos* **on** *Rosh Chodesh*?

A The *minhag* is for women not to wash clothing and sew on *Rosh Chodesh*, but if you need the item, you may. Some also have a *minhag* not to iron. If you have a different *minhag*, you should follow your *minhag*. Other *melachos,* such as washing floors, etc., are permitted.

Q **How do I know if I have a high level of** *bitachon*?

A Once a man came to Rav Yisrael Salanter complaining, "I bought a lottery ticket and I had *bitachon* I would win, so why didn't I win?"

Rav Yisrael said to him, "Let's say you bought a ticket for a $1,000 prize. If I had come to you before the lottery and offered you $999 for your ticket, would you have sold it to me?"

"Of course."

"Then you didn't have real *bitachon*. If you had real *bitachon,* you wouldn't have sold your ticket for a cent less than $1,000. The fact that you were willing to sell it for less, shows you didn't have true *bitachon*."

This is the truth. You can't fool yourself, saying, "I've got *bitachon*," when you really don't. Some people have *bitachon* when they have a nice savings account. Then they sit and learn the chapter on *bitachon* in *Chovos HaLevavos,* and oh, how *geshmack* it is! But when a person has nothing in his pocket, no savings at all, that is the test. With real *bitachon* there are no doubts whatsoever.

Q **A person can understand intellectually and rationally that one needs to have *bitachon*, but practically, what can a woman do for her nerves?**

A Always remember to be happy when you do your work.

My father had a dry-cleaning store, and he had a worker who ironed the clothes. It was over 120 degrees under that pressing iron — unbearable, especially with the New York humidity. But this worker sang while he worked and the heat didn't bother him. It's all in your frame of mind. People who are happy do not feel the burdens and hardships they encounter.

Q **How can a woman stay calm if her children scream a lot?**

A She should try to project a positive attitude. It's not enough to put on a tape to distract them; you have to sing along with it. Then you'll feel wonderful and they'll sing with you.

Q **How should I react if everything goes wrong during the day and I'm upset when my husband comes home?**

A Why should you say everything went wrong? Things always go wrong — that's part of life. So feel good that you are doing what you can. Just do as much as you can. Don't be upset if you aren't up to doing the cleaning that day. Take everything calmly. Hashem gave you energies to do whatever you can and He doesn't demand the impossible from you. So feel happy. Would you feel bad if you were confined to bed and the house was a mess? You would not feel bad at all because it would be impossible for you to do it all. So always take things with a bright perspective. Just do whatever you can, and you have fulfilled your job. You don't have to be a perfectionist; only Hashem is perfect.

Q **Is it wrong at the end of the day to leave the house as it is and to skip baths for the kids and say you'll take care of it the next day?**

A If reason dictates to you that you are too tired, then don't give the kids a bath today. A *bissel shmutz* won't hurt them, and you will bathe them tomorrow. Think: Today I had a hard day. I'll go to sleep and rest my nerves and *b'ezras Hashem* tomorrow will be better.

Q **Is it okay to want to get out of the house occasionally?**

A I always advise women to get out of the house a bit, to have a good time, a change of scenery, and go swimming. Women who complain of boredom come back invigorated after going swimming.

Q **What is the meaning of the verse, "Hashem is my Shepherd, I shall not want"?**

A Hashem is likened to a shepherd, the commentaries say, for just as a shepherd cares for each individual sheep, Hashem provides for each person individually. Young and old, he gives each one according to his needs.

A person who truly believes these words has the merit of great faith; however, becoming such a person is easier said than done.

Q I am worried that I am not on the proper level of *bitachon.*

A We must realize that developing the highest levels of *bitachon* is a very slow process. We have to seek advice on how to attain that degree of *bitachon*, and not fool ourselves. We must work on *bitachon* little by little, adding more each day. We must say to ourselves, "Even though the problem child is annoying me very much, I am not as upset as I was yesterday." Gaining *bitachon* is a gradual process, and we hope to eventually merit it. It is not practical to close our eyes to everything and talk ourselves into *thinking* we have *bitachon.*

BUILDING YOUR HOME

5

The Torah begins the instructions for building of the *Mishkan*, the Tabernacle, with Hashem telling Moshe to say to the Jewish people: "*V'yikchu li terumah me'es kol ish asher yidvenu libo*, Hashem spoke to Moshe, saying: Speak to the Children of Israel and let them take for Me a portion, from every man whose heart motivates him" (*Shemos* 25:2).

Why are the people asked to *take*, *v'yikchu*, a portion when they are supposed to be *giving* contributions toward the building of the *Mishkan*? Why doesn't it say *v'yitnu*, "*they should give*"?

Delving further, we might also ask what the word *li* signifies. Rashi says it means "*lishmi*," for the sake of My (Hashem's) Name. The motivation for contributing to the building of the *Mishkan* was to be purely for Hashem's sake. And we know that this holds true for all the mitzvos that we do. Mitzvos must be performed with intent. Before doing any mitzvah, we have to remind ourselves that we are doing it because Hashem commanded us to do so.

Similarly, the Rambam explains that although non-Jews have seven mitzvos and the righteous gentiles who fulfill them merit the World to Come, this holds true only when they do these mitzvos because Moshe Rabbeinu received them at Sinai (*Hilchos Melachim* 8:11). If they perform these mitzvos because their logic dictates that they do so — out of rationalism — they will not earn the World to Come. Compensation is only given if they realize that they are doing Hashem's Will.

We act on the highest level when we do everything *l'sheim Shamayim*, solely because Hashem told us to do so. Here, too, with the building of the *Mishkan*, the word *li* indicates that all the efforts involved should be 100 percent for Hashem's sake.

This takes us back to our original question: If this is the highest form of doing Hashem's Will, wouldn't the most appropriate term have been "*v'yitnu li*, let them *give* Me"? Shouldn't the people *give* for building the *Mishkan* because Hashem has commanded them to do so?

The question is one that has brought forth many explanations from our Sages. The Malbim explains that Hashem did not say *v'yitnu* because He didn't want the Jewish people's contribution to the *Mishkan* to come from an *obligation* to give but rather from their desire to give. He wanted them to be the ones to take from themselves, to give 100 percent on their own accord.

Of course, each and every mitzvah is done because it is Hashem's Will. However, it seems to me that when it comes to mitzvos between one person and another, these mitzvos should also be done because we feel for our friend and not just because Hashem has told us to act in a certain way. A person has to care about his friend and not be cold, without any feelings at all. The only proper approach when it comes to *bein adam lachaveiro*, the mitzvos between one Jew and another, is to have feelings of sympathy for other people. This will enable us to do things graciously.

On the verse, "When you lend money to My people, to the poor man who is with you ...," Rashi explains that when it comes to lending money, the word *with you* teaches us that we should put ourselves in our friend's position as though we were the ones borrowing the money (*Shemos* 22:24). How would *we* like to pay back the loan? Wouldn't we want easy terms, with the option of either paying it out in installments, or returning as much as we can at one time? Lending money is a mitzvah, but it shouldn't be done just because we must, but because we feel our friend's plight.

So it is with all mitzvos between one person and another. Our approach must be to fulfill these mitzvos relating to interpersonal relations out of a gracious feeling toward the other person. Therefore, *v'yitnu* would not have been the proper term, because the *Mishkan* was a place where people would come and beseech Hashem and seek mercy. It was a place for prayers and supplications, a place of Divine mercy. The contributions to build this unique Sanctuary had to come from willing hands and hearts filled with a longing to help build a place of Divine mercy — not from people who gave because they were so commanded.

The concept of purity of intent being necessary for building the *Beis HaMikdash* is a theme found elsewhere as well. The Midrash tells us that there was a dispute among the 12 tribes as to where the *Beis HaMikdash* would be built. Each one wanted it to be built in his territory. Hashem answered them: None of you will merit this because you all participated in the sale of your brother, Yosef (*Bereishis Rabbah* 99:1). Even though all was done in accordance with Hashem's Will, and the brothers had their reasons and justifications for acting as they did, the bitter feeling they displayed toward their brother Yosef prevented them from having the actual building of the *Beis HaMikdash* in their portion of Eretz Yisrael. Only Binyamin, who did not participate in the sale in any way, was given the privilege of having it built in his territory.

We also learn that David HaMelech, despite his yearning to build the *Beis HaMikdash* and his pleading with Hashem to be allowed to do so, was denied this privilege for a similar reason. Our Sages ask why the prayer says, "*Mizmor shir chanukas habayis l'David*, A psalm, a song for the inauguration of the Temple by David" (*Tehillim* 30:1). After all, David HaMelech did not merit to build and dedicate the *Beis HaMikdash*. They answer that this refers to the great *mesiras nefesh* he had when he entreated Hashem to build the *Beis HaMikdash*. He said that he would not allow his eyes to slumber until he saw the *Beis HaMikdash* erected. The reward for this great *mesiras nefesh* is that the building of the *Beis HaMikdash* is accredited to him.

But why wasn't David HaMelech allowed to build the *Beis HaMikdash*? The Rambam answers: David spilled a lot of blood in the wars he fought (*Shemoneh Perakim*, Ch. 7). Although this was done only in connection with destroying idol worship, and although he was a kind and merciful ruler of his people, nonetheless, since he had shed blood Hashem did not allow him to build the *Beis HaMikdash*.

It is remarkable that David, who longed to see the *Beis HaMikdash* built and who was willing to go without sleep until it was, could have no share in its building because of wars that were Divinely commanded. Yet, since the *Beis HaMikdash* was designated a sanctuary, bloodshed could be no part of it.

Furthermore, as the Midrash explains, the *Beis HaMikdash* was to serve another purpose, that of a dwelling place for the *Shechinah*, the Divine Presence. When Hashem gave the Torah to the Jewish people, He said to them: I have sold to you My Torah as it says, *"Ki lekach tov nasati lachem,* and I have also sold Myself," so to speak. In this sense, *v'yikchu li* means that we are to *take* Hashem. This is compared to a king who had an only daughter. One day a prince came and married the girl. Time passed, and the prince wanted to return to his country. The king said to him, "This is my only daughter and I cannot part from her. I cannot tell you not to take her, though, for she is your wife. But please do me a favor. Wherever you go, make a little room for me so that I can live with you, because I cannot leave my daughter" (*Shemos Rabbah* 33:1).

Similarly, Hashem said to the Jewish people, "I am giving you the Torah but I cannot part from it. I can't take it back, though, because I gave it to you. So please, wherever you go, make one little room for me in which I can dwell."

From all this we understand that the *Beis HaMikdash* was a place of mercy designated to receive all prayers and entreaties because the *Shechinah*, the Divine Presence, was to dwell there.

The moral: The *Beis HaMikdash* could be built only through heartfelt contributions given without any pressure or coercion. Otherwise, it would not have the purity and sanctity necessary for a dwelling place of the *Shechinah*, which is itself total mercifulness and graciousness. After all, can Hashem dwell in a place where there is friction and bickering? The *Shechinah* can only be found when we do things *lishmi*, fulfilling Hashem's Will for His sake alone, with a sense of *v'yikchu*, taking, or accepting, with the commandment, the feeling and understanding that it has to be so.

This is the basis of the *Beis HaMikdash*. It is a place of

full Divine mercy and an expression of total Divine Will. Thus was the *Mishkan* built in the times of Moshe Rabbeinu, and the forthcoming *Beis HaMikdash* will be built on the same premise.

Our Sages tell us that as long as there is the unwarranted hatred of *sinas chinam*, bickering and fighting, the derogatory speech of *lashon hara*, and no *ahavas Yisrael*, there will be no *Beis HaMikdash,* but only ruin. As long as *sinas chinam* exists among the Jewish people, there will be no *Beis HaMikdash* because the *Beis HaMikdash* represents mercy, prayer, and entreaty (see *Yoma* 1:1, *Yerushalmi*). The way to repent for *sinas chinam*, as the Prophet says, is only through giving charity and through feeling for other people, which, as we said, is fundamental to the building of the *Beis HaMikdash*. Any connection to cruelty will block the *kedushah*, sanctity, from permeating it. It must be a place of 100 percent mercy.

Let us apply this to our own *Beis HaMikdash*, our home. The last *berachah* under the *chuppah* is, "*asher bara sason v'simchah, chasan v'chalah, gilah, rinah, ditzah v'chedvah, ahavah v'achvah, v'shalom v'reus*, Hashem created the *chasan* and *kallah*, and these many forms of *simchah*, and also love, brotherhood, peace, and friendship." Marriage, as we know, is the union of two disparate people. The *berachah* ends with these beautiful words, from which we learn that it is *ahavah, achvah, shalom* and *reus,* the love of kindness and mutual feeling they have for each other, that together build the *Beis HaMikdash* of married life.

As our Sages have so beautifully stated, when you look at the Hebrew words for man and woman, *ish v'ishah*, you see that the man has the *yud* and the woman has the *hei*, which together form the *yud-kei* of Hashem's Name. If the two people are worthy, the *Shechinah* will dwell with them. If, however, they are not worthy and they drive away the

Shechinah, the *yud-kei* is removed and only the *aleph* and *shin* remain; they spell *eish*, a fire that consumes them. When there is no *achvah v'shalom*, there is no dwelling place for the *Shechinah* and you cannot have a *Beis HaMikdash*.

People go to the *chuppah* to form a mutual relationship in which each one wants to benefit from the marriage. True, they want to be united — but it depends where you put the "I." If you misplace it, then "united" becomes "untied." If the "I" is not where it should be, then destruction and ruin are the outcome.

A main cause of marital troubles is what they call nowadays a "non-nurturing personality." Some people find it hard to give to other people. They lack the warmth and willingness to share themselves. On the outside, they may seem friendly enough, but at home, in their closest relationships, there is something missing.

We must remember that a non-nurturing personality does not disappear at the *chuppah*. It is carried into the new home and can affect the children, who will wind up in trouble later in life. The tragedy nowadays is that we have great geniuses whose basic understanding of marriage is distorted. We see this tragic devastation in so many marriages today. We find brilliant people who are dedicated public servants, yet don't make good husbands. This stems from earlier years when they were not given the proper love they deserved. They were not nurtured as children, and so love and affection did not become part of them. A good nature has to be cultivated. The Rambam advises us to do as many acts of *chesed* as we can in order to cultivate the trait of *chesed* within us (*Avos* 3:15).

You cannot compare a soldier who has had years of training and preparation and has earned his medals on the battlefield to a soldier who isn't prepared to go out to battle. The inexperienced soldier is more likely to be killed.

So, too, it takes years of preparation for a person to develop his feelings for other people. We must start at the very beginning of the child's life by hugging and kissing him as much as we can. In this way, we will cultivate feelings of love in the child's mind and heart. We will also gain his confidence, and he will grow up to become a good-natured individual. When we have a nation of people raised like this, then we can have a *Beis HaMikdash*.

We see, then, that we have to go to the *chuppah* with a feeling of *give* and take, not *take* and give. The attitude should be, "I am going to do for you, and eventually I will receive as well." The intent should be solely to help one's spouse in every way possible. Only then does a person get more than he gives. A person who begins his married life with the attitude, "I will take and then I will give," brings only destruction and devastation.

Many troubled couples come to me asking for advice. I always ask first why they want to break up. The usual reason given is "incompatibility" and "lack of communication." But why should this be so? They got to know each other during the meetings, they thought they were compatible. What happened? They found the companionship quite suitable — why do they want to break up after a few months of marriage? What happened to their communication?

The answer is simple. It's easy to feel wonderful being together for a few hours, but being married and living in the same house is totally different. The couple found themselves compatible only as boy and girl, not as man and wife. They went to the *chuppah* with this same feeling: I remain what I am; you remain what you are. But when they are together, united as man and wife, what happens? He pulls in one direction, she pulls in the other, and only trouble is found.

A home is a miniature *Beis HaMikdash* and must be built on the same premise: not with *v'yitnu* but with *v'yikchu.* Each partner's giving must be totally 100 percent, and of his or her own accord. This means that no one has to force you to give a smile or a word of appreciation but rather you must do it on your own. A person has to feel that his or her spouse deserves this after a hard day. They need a word of encouragement, and each partner should appreciate what the other has done instead of criticizing him or her. Mutual appreciation makes a sound basis for the home.

Remember, the more you give, the more you will get; the more you take, the less you will give — and get. If you learn this important lesson in life and do things of your own accord, following the example of *v'yikchu li,* then *b'ezras Hashem,* you will make a beautiful home that will be a true *Beis HaMikdash.*

QUESTIONS & ANSWERS

Q Are there any *tefillos* that are a *segulah* for *shalom bayis*?

A No. You can *daven* for someone that Hashem should give him the idea of making *shalom*, but that is not enough. You must solve the problem properly.

The problem today is that there is no compatibility. Couples don't see eye to eye and neither person is willing to compromise. She wants to be the winner and he also wants to be the winner. What is lacking is *vitur*, giving in. Learn to overlook things. Forgive for the sake of peace. But you will never have *shalom bayis,* and no *tefillos* will ever help, if each one is adamant. When he says, "I want what I want," and she says, "I want what I want," that's where the tragedy begins. Giving in is the wise choice that saves the home. When you make everything else trivial compared with the main goal of *shalom bayis*, then you will have *shalom*.

Q What about a husband who does not learn — is he still entitled to order his wife around?

A What difference does it make whether he's learning or not? It should not be a matter of "ordering around." A man should be strong enough to carry the burden of the family and not shift it onto his wife. A wife needs someone to lean on; she wants someone stronger to rely on. I would like to quote to you the Rambam on *shalom bayis* (*Nashim, Hilchos Ishus* 15:19-20):

And therefore, *Chazal* commanded that a man should honor his wife more than himself and love her as himself. And he should give her as much money as he can afford. He should not put fear on her and he should speak to her pleasantly and not with anger or irritability.

Likewise, a woman is commanded to show her husband great respect and honor. He should be like a king in her eyes and she should do all that he wishes and keep away from what he doesn't like.

And this is the way of the holy and pure Jewish men and woman. And in this way, their lives will be beautiful and praiseworthy.

Q **What is the husband's obligation in helping around the house and clearing the table?**

A It is said in the name of Rav Chaim Vital, the great Kabbalist and student of the Ari *z"l*, that the husband's *chesed* will be measured according to how he treats his wife. If he does no *chesed* with his wife and is lacking *chesed* at home, his acts of *chesed* with other people are insignificant. Of course he has to do *chesed*; we tell him: If a needy person were to ask for your help you would certainly help him, so why don't you also help your wife?

But the wife should not shrug off her responsibilities. It depends on the situation. If the wife is really tired, then of course the husband should lend a hand. But if she can do whatever needs to be done, then she should not waste the time that he could use to learn.

Q How careful should a wife be about asking her husband for help in the house?

A This is a very difficult question. It depends upon the nature of work in the home, upon the nature of the wife, and the nature of the husband. If you can spare your husband for learning at night, it would be wonderful. It depends on your disposition, on your attitude to work. If you remember that you get half the reward of your husband's learning, then you will feel good about your work. If you were getting $1,000 for your hour of work, you would be very happy about it. But you are getting more than that, so you can be happy about letting your husband learn another half hour or so at night. It's only the frame of mind that determines the hardship of the work you are doing. If you are in a good frame of mind, you won't feel the hardship at all.

Q If I want to give my husband more time to learn, does this mean taking in extra household help if necessary?

A Yes, if it is necessary, take in extra help. The most important thing is that your husband should have maximum time to learn. If he is a *masmid*, he is always pressed for time. There is always more for him to learn, and he needs time for reviewing as well.

Q Should a husband help on *erev Shabbos*?

A It's a mitzvah for him to help on *erev Shabbos* but he doesn't have to help all day, just as much as is necessary.

Q What if a husband offers to help with household chores?

A A good husband will of course help his wife when she really needs help.

Q If a woman sees that she needs her husband at a certain time every day, at which time she just can't manage without him, can she ask him to be there?

A Yes, definitely. There are certainly situations in which that would be the right thing to do. You are not commanded to do the impossible.

Q How much should a husband spend on a present for his wife?

A It depends on the woman's tastes and the family's financial situation. It's not how much you give but what you give. A wife appreciates that her husband cares for her. For this, any little gift will be good. But a loving husband will look for something nice. It does not have to cost a fortune, but it should look nice.

Q If a woman buys clothes so that she will look nice when her husband comes home, even though they really don't have enough money for this, is this a good thing to do or not?

A Yes, it is important to look nice for your husband. How much you spend depends upon your husband and what he considers nice. If you can buy a simple dress and it will be just as good, fine. But, without going overboard, she *should* buy something nice, and Hashem will provide for them.

Q How much should one invest in the home?

A I always tell the men that it is very important for the woman to be happy in the home. A woman who cares for her home sometimes needs a little nicer home, otherwise, she will be miserable. Some women are not bothered at all. Sometimes a man comes to ask me if he should give in when his wife wants to buy a new couch or other items for the home and the husband doesn't feel it is necessary. I say to him, "If it means that much to her, then go ahead and buy it. She'll be a much happier woman and you'll be the winner in the end. It is an investment for you to make her happy in her home." That does not mean that the woman should be lavish. But sometimes it even pays to borrow. If the home is shabby and rundown, a woman can get depressed. It depends on the woman and the individual situation.

Q **What if a wife buys a present for her husband with money she has earned, even though her husband had told her in the past not to buy gifts for him?**

A Sometimes a husband will say to his wife that he doesn't want her to buy him gifts, but he doesn't really mean it. Therefore, buying a present for your husband is not stealing and he will even thank you for it. Buying him a present will make him feel good and that can enhance your marriage and the general feeling of *shalom bayis* in the home.

Q
A **To whom should *maaser* money be given?**
Maaser, a tenth, should be given like it was to the Levi'im, to those who sit and learn. By giving to poor people who are learning Torah, it is a double mitzvah. There are yeshivah men who are in such a difficult situation that they eat all their meals in the yeshivah because they don't have enough money for food.

Q **If a wife gives a sum of money to *tzedakah* without first checking with her husband, could this be considered stealing?**

A   You can give what we call a *matanah mu'etess*, a small donation. But a *chashuvah davar*, an important donation, you cannot.

Q   **How often should a husband and wife go out alone?**

A   It depends. Sometimes a wife feels a little low in spirits. It all depends how the woman feels and how things are in the home. Sometimes you have to go out but you have to use your discretion. This should really be told to the husband, that he should care for her, and then she will care for him as well.

Q   **If a woman is upset, should she keep the fact from her husband, holding in her feelings so as not to disturb him?**

A   A person should never hold in his feelings. It can make him sick. It's always best to talk things over. She should express her feelings and get it out of her system. She should never keep things bottled up inside her. Remember, you are the ones who have to do all the housework and take care of the children; he should realize this and acknowledge your feelings.

6 A WOMAN'S WISDOM

A woman's goal in life, as we all know, is to build the home. Yet nowadays, unfortunately, this goal is not being met. There are so many divorces today. We know that divorce in pre-war Europe was quite rare, despite the misery and poor living standards of the time. A *get* was given only once in a great while. We can't imagine how poverty stricken and poor the people were then. The times were primitive and the people had nothing — not even electricity or hot water. Yet they had a peaceful and joyful life and divorce was unheard of.

Today we have endless luxuries at our disposal, but it is now, in these comfortable times, that we find marriages breaking up after only two or three months. Why is this so?

All couples start out with good intentions. Everyone wants to have a nice, spiritual, Jewish home, but some couples do not succeed. Shlomo HaMelech has given us the answer to this problem: "It is the wisdom of the woman that builds her home" (*Mishlei* 14:1). The foundation of the home lies in the insight and foresight of women who do not seek a temporary dwelling based on the physical desires of this world. Instead, they fill their lives with spiritual meaning.

The problem today is that many women seek a home that will give them pleasures and enable them to enjoy life. They want, perhaps, a combination of Torah and this world. It is remarkable to note in this connection what the Sages say about the construction of the individual. They say that a person consists of two parts: the *chomer*, the flesh-and-blood, the animal part of the human being, and the *neshamah*, the soul. Ultimately, the *neshamah* does not seek enjoyment in this world, for its pleasures are not of a permanent nature. One may enjoy a delicious, fattening meal but afterward he might suffer a stomach upset or other side effects. Eating a simpler meal would be healthier, but it is human nature to seek foolish desires. The animal part of the individual seeks things that give enjoyment to the body, and it does not care for the *neshamah's* spiritual feelings. It is these overwhelming natural feelings within us that put emphasis on the physical enjoyment of life.

We know that the result of this constant challenge between the body and the soul is that the body always wins — unless the individual understands that this friction is a part of living in this world. Most people, though, give in to these physical and emotional desires. What we must understand is that the body belongs to this world, and like anything built on physicality, it is not of a permanent nature. The body does not last forever, but rather it disintegrates over time. We all know that as people grow older they lose much of their physicality. The spirit and soul, on the other hand, belong to the next world, which is everlasting. Our Sages say that the older *tzaddikim* become, the more tranquility of mind they have. Their souls are more at ease, and they don't have all the conflicts of the mind. They are left with the spirituality rather than the physicality, and they enjoy this permanent, spiritual type of life.

This is how an individual is constructed, and this continual conflict in a person tears him apart (*Chovos HaLevavos*, Ch. 5, "*Yichud HaMaaseh*"). We often see that teenagers who have all of the pleasures in life become addicted to drugs, thinking this will bring them gratification. They are wrong, because the more they indulge in the pursuit of physical pleasure, the more cravings they will have and the guiltier they will become. They then become addicts to silence their consciences. But they are only building a temporary structure, for physical pleasure is only wonderful at the very beginning. The person doesn't always worry about the outcome because he is tempted by what is delicious and appealing to the palate.

The loftier, more spiritually inclined individual understands that only what is built from the soul is permanent. Things of the spirit last forever. The soul lives on forever, even after death; it does not disintegrate at all.

Shlomo HaMelech says that the wise woman, who understands life in its reality, will have the foresight to look ahead. We are not supposed to look for immediate gratification that gives us a certain temporary satisfaction. We are to look into the future for that which will give us everlasting satisfaction.

We read about the terrible dispute that ruined Korach and his congregation. The Gemara maintains that they will not even have a share in the World to Come (*Sanhedrin* 109b). Looking behind the scenes, we are told that Korach's wife was responsible for this devastation. Yet there was one man who was not punished: On ben Peles. He too had joined the group against Moshe Rabbeinu, for his own ulterior motives. What saved him from being punished?

We are told something very interesting here: "'Woman's wisdom builds her home ...,' this refers to the wife of On ben Peles, '... and the hands of the foolish one destroy it,' this is the wife of Korach" (*Sanhedrin* 110a). While his wife's insight saved On ben Peles, the jealousy of Korach's wife caused Korach's downfall. What was the wisdom and the foolishness of these two wives?

On's wife said, "What difference does it make to you who the leader will be? You will remain the follower whether the leader will be Moshe Rabbeinu or Korach. Why then should you fight and argue with Moshe Rabbeinu?"

Her husband answered, "What should I do? We all planned the dispute together and it is wrong for me to desert them."

His wife reasoned, "I know that the Jewish people are a holy people, especially when it comes to modesty." She gave On some wine to put him to sleep. Then she sat at the threshold of their home and uncovered her hair. Anyone coming to the door saw her and ran away, and so On was saved. This was the wisdom and insight of On's wife.

Korach's wife, on the other hand, said to her husband, "Look what Moshe did. He appointed himself king and Aharon became the Kohen Gadol. His nephews also received certain appointments but you were left out."

She goaded Korach so much that she caused him to revolt against Moshe Rabbeinu — and all because of such foolishness. What was it after all? Nothing but a little fleeting honor. By looking only at the here and now, Korach's wife ruined his life. On's wife, though, had the foresight to see that even if Korach became the leader, On's status would remain the same.

I have always wondered why these particular two women were singled out to illustrate this point. After all, as the saying goes, "Behind every great man there stands a great woman," and we have had many great women in our history who were responsible for their husband's greatness. Why were these two chosen to show that wisdom builds the home while foolishness ruins it?

I would say that this is an illustration of two extremes: On ben Peles, although a member of the *Dor HaMidbar* and consequently on a very high level, was not one of the most outstanding individuals of that generation. Korach, on the other hand, was one of those who carried the *Aron* that contained the *Sefer Torah*. This tells us that he was an outstanding Jewish leader, for the Torah would not be carried by a simple person.

We therefore have two extremes: the ordinary person, and the very great one. We can understand that the wise woman would save her home if she has a wonderful husband. They share the same views and can consult with one another and help each other. Such a woman would be instrumental in all ways in helping her husband achieve his life's goals. For instance, Sarah Imeinu, as we know, was the wife of Avraham Avinu. He converted the men, and she converted the women. They were both of the same caliber, so of course Sarah was able to help Avraham in his important work. The courage and inspiration of Avraham Avinu allowed her to play her wonderful role in life.

But what about someone who is not an outstanding individual but only average? We would think that even if his wife tried to influence him, she wouldn't be able to accomplish much. Yet, it is not so, as we see by these two extremes. We have an On ben Peles, who was an average person, and Korach, an outstanding personality who carried the *Aron*. Our Sages gave us this illustration to teach us that a woman has this great role in life even if her husband is not a tremendous Torah scholar. If she is imbued with a high level of spirituality, she can save even an average person.

At the other extreme, the man might be the greatest individual but the woman can be responsible for his downfall, as we see with Korach. It is the wisdom of the wife that can save even the lowest person, and a lack of insight that might ruin even an individual who is far beyond an On ben Peles.

Why are there so many divorces nowadays even though both sides start out with sincere intentions? It is because women don't realize how much influence they have over the direction their marriage takes. If a husband, the former *yeshivah bachur*, suddenly starts watching television or doing other things in life that cause him to go astray, his wife can use her womanly wisdom to help him get back on the right path. Sometimes, though, through carelessness or wanting to have a good time and enjoy life, a wife pulls her husband in the wrong direction. She may want his companionship and say, "How can you go away to learn and leave me alone?" But wanting to have a good time and enjoy temporary material satisfactions will not build a permanent home — for a home built on physical desires cannot be everlasting. Understanding this teaches us an important lesson: The wife plays a major role in her husband's life, whether he is an ordinary person or a great Torah scholar.

Devorah HaNeviah's husband was an *am ha'aretz*, completely unlearned, but she wanted him to have a portion among the righteous and merit the World to Come. She thought of a plan that would bring him to the *Beis HaMikdash*, where he would be able to absorb the holiness of the place, meet the leading Torah Sages of the time and so learn from them. She made beautiful thick wicks for the Menorah, and said to her husband, "Come, take these to the *Beis HaMikdash*." She put her whole heart into making these wicks thick so that they would give off more light. Hashem said, "Devorah, your intention was to give Me more light and therefore I will make your light great," and she merited to become a prophetess and to receive the light of Torah to be a Judge over *Klal Yisrael*.

Of course, all Bais Yaakov girls say that they want a *ben Torah*. But how many girls say in the same breath that they also want a nice paycheck, a nice home, etc. I would not say that they are completely wrong, but they are not entirely right either. Of course, a woman should have a nice home. If you ask me if you should buy a nice sofa, I would say that you certainly should. A woman has to have a nice home so that she doesn't face four empty walls. I always tell my students to give their wives a nice home and to do as much as they can for them.

But at the same time, the wife should not be too demanding. Hashem can help a couple have a nice home but this should not be their goal in life. They should not approach life with the attitude that they *must* have this and that. It is the spiritual view of life that forms the permanent basis of the home. When you want something in life you have to think: What does this mean to me? Some of these temporary things might harm your spirituality, your life's goal.

There are *bnei Torah* today who left education for business solely because of a wife who didn't realize that while the *kollel* type of life has its difficulties, the lasting benefits outweigh this. Even excellent *bnei Torah* can get caught up in this and spiral downward. I'm talking about people who could have made the effort to manage, but instead chose to join the race for material comforts.

This lesson is relevant to every aspect of life, including raising children. Sometimes a mother complains to me that her son is not doing well and she asks, "What can I do for him?" If I tell her that perhaps the boy needs a change of environment and that she should send him away to another school, she'll say to me, "How can I send him away to study? He has to get his degree." I tell her, "When it is a matter of life or death for the child, what does a degree mean?"

General education is played up so much today that a mother will not give up the idea of her child having a diploma even at the expense of his spiritual health. Isn't that foolishness? What is lacking is just a little understanding of the dangers to her child's spirituality and a little foresight. It means placing the child's best interests first. When this isn't done, the result is the catastrophe we see today. People lose sight of what it means to raise children. If you want to have a healthy child with a sound mind and a solid spiritual foundation, you must look ahead. This requires the woman's wisdom that builds her home.

The same applies to having a husband who is a Torah scholar. True, it means a struggle, and entails giving up much of this worldly life. But isn't it worth it? Isn't it worth giving up temporary pleasure for spiritual gain that is everlasting?

This is the essential wisdom that a wife and mother must have if she wants to build a permanent home. She must realize that there always exists friction in this world between the physical-material and the soul, and so it will be for 120 years. Our task is to give the soul the upper hand by realizing the importance of our existence, which is eternal life, not that which is of a temporary nature. The pathway of growth in Torah is always filled with struggle. However, we will enjoy life and feel that we are reaching our goal when we feel satisfaction in accomplishing our mission in life rather than causing destruction and failure. This satisfaction is only felt when we build an eternal home based on spiritual values, which are permanent.

I know from personal experience that it is a tough struggle. When my wife and I lived for five years in Mir in Europe over half a century ago, everything was very primitive. It was 20 degrees below zero in the winter, and when I took my 4-year-old daughter outside, her cheeks froze. There was minimal electricity and no central heating. Yet, *baruch Hashem*, we lived happily and gave our children the education they needed. Nothing can replace the *nachas* we have from them today. We had to struggle, but my wife had the wisdom to look ahead. She was willing to give up so many things when we married; it is only because my wife gave up the material for the spiritual that, *baruch Hashem*, all of my children are so wonderful.

With a little foresight and insight, all of you can also merit this. It should be the happiest time of your life as you go through this struggle with the noble goal and intention of building a permanent home. Although you might not realize it now, all who work for Torah merit its honor (*Nedarim* 62a). This goes without exception. My blessing to you, as I say to all my boys in the yeshivah, is, "Keep going." We all have our ups and downs, and sometimes we may get a little discouraged. But the important thing is to never give up. Keep going and you will, *b'ezras Hashem*, get there.

QUESTIONS & ANSWERS

Q I would like my husband to remain in *kollel* for many years but with the growing financial difficulties, I keep worrying about how we are going to manage. How can I overcome this worry?

A You can stop worrying only by reading about *bitachon*. You can become a *baalas bitachon*, a person who trusts in G-d. If we know that G-d will provide for us, we don't have to worry about finances. I always say, with *bitachon* we have everything; without it we have nothing. With *bitachon* you will stop worrying.

I recommend rereading the chapter on *bitachon* in *Chovos HaLevavos*. It is wonderful reading material. I know there are classes on *shemiras halashon*, but I think it would be wonderful to have a class on *bitachon* as well. A class on *bitachon* once a week would be ideal. Many women, in these difficult times, wonder how they are going to manage. But if we understand that He Who has provided for us in the past will provide for us in the future, then we don't have to worry.

Q My husband and I try to keep an open house for guests but sometimes when my husband sits down to learn and there is a knock on the door, his learning is disturbed. Is there an obligation for him to entertain our guests? Isn't it better for him to learn?

A He should close the door to the room where he is learning. If someone special comes or a great personality visits he can come out but this does not happen all the time. It all depends on who the guest is.

Q What should you do with leftover bread crumbs and pieces of bread?

A This is a big problem. You should put them into a plastic bag and leave the bag on the garbage can to let the sanitation department take it away. Some people make crumbs and give them to the birds. If the bread is edible, you are not allowed to discard it. Wrap it up and put it on the garbage can and let the garbage collectors take it away.

Q Why doesn't Hashem give us a good income without our asking for it?

A If you had a good income, you wouldn't ask Hashem for anything else! The Torah in *Parashas Vayeitzei* says that Yaakov Avinu beseeched Hashem for everything: "*lechem le'echol u'beged lilbosh*, bread to eat and clothes to wear." Hashem assured him that He would watch over him but He never promised to give him a good livelihood because had He done so, Yaakov would no longer have had to *daven* for food.

You must pray every day for livelihood. You will have it but you must pray for it because that is what Hashem wants.

Hashem gave the manna every day of the 40 years that the Jewish people wandered in the desert when

He could have given them manna for the entire year at once. This way they had to go to the field every day and pick manna. The Gemara compares this to the case of a king who had an only son. At first, the father gave his son his allowance once a year. Then he realized that this way he only saw his son once a year. The king then told his son, "From now on, you will receive your allowance day by day, for I want to see you every day."

Hashem wants to see us every day. Father's Day is not one day a year but 365 days a year. We must beseech Hashem for a good livelihood. You may have to pray for it a little more or a little less, but you must always pray for it.

THE ROLE OF WOMEN

David HaMelech taught: "It is the honor of the princess to dwell within" (*Tehillim* 45:14). A woman, the daughter of the King, is most honorable and most appreciated when she is within the walls of her home. This is the true glory of a woman.

When we read about *akeidas Yitzchak*, where Avraham was willing to sacrifice his son Yitzchak because Hashem had directed him to do so, we should stop and think: Who was responsible for the greatness of this wonderful, miraculous act? We can understand Avraham Avinu's willingness, for Hashem commanded him to do so. But Yitzchak wasn't told by Hashem to go through the *akeidah*, so why would he let himself be killed?

The answer is simple: Yitzchak knew and respected his father Avraham, and this was sufficient; he didn't need any more proof. And the way he performed the *akeidah*! It was outstanding for a young man.

Who was responsible for raising a child of this caliber, a child who had such total dedication to Hashem? You would say, "Avraham, the great patriarch, the great educator and philosopher, the most respected individual of his time." The Gemara tells us that when Avraham passed away all the leaders of the nations proclaimed: "Woe to the ship that has lost its captain!" (*Bava Basra* 91a). "Alas," they cried, "for the generation that has lost its leader."

There are two types of leaders: one who leads in peaceful times when things run smoothly, and the other who can captain the ship in stormy waters. A ship in danger of capsizing in a turbulent ocean needs a great captain, a leader with experience, to steer it to safety. Avraham Avinu, as leader of the world and recognized as such by all the rulers of the world, was not just a captain in calm waters; he was a leader in troublesome and turbulent times as well. Certainly, it was this great leader who was responsible for Yitzchak's becoming the personality and individual so totally dedicated to Hashem that nothing could stop him from doing His will.

But the credit does not go to Avraham; it goes to Sarah. The Torah tells us that after Yitzchak was born, Sarah noticed Yishmael becoming involved with idol worship, and she asked Avraham to drive him away, saying, "I don't want him to be in the presence of my dear son, Yitzchak" (*Bereishis* 21:9-10).

Avraham felt deep sorrow over this incident. Here he was, the idealist who had destroyed the idols, and now his very own son was playing with them. What a shock it was! And to think that Yitzchak might be drawn to participate! Yet Yishmael was very precious to Avraham, and Avraham was a tremendously kind person. Driving a son away from home is an act of cruelty, but he knew he had to save Yitzchak. Otherwise, it might mean the destruction of his whole hope of having a spiritual inheritor.

Who was responsible for this discovery? Sarah! It was

she who noticed Yishmael's behavior and it was thanks to her advice that Avraham sent Hagar and Yishmael away. Imagine if she hadn't discovered the truth! Yitzchak would have gone astray and we might not have a Jewish people today. It was Sarah who was responsible for Yitzchak's growth and development into the Yitzchak capable of the *akeidah* and of becoming the father of the Jewish people. It was only her total vigilance as a mother that enabled her to notice Yishmael's negative behavior, which was probably secretive, otherwise Avraham would have noticed it as well.

Many things in Jewish life require the mother's vigilance. She is the only one who can be depended upon for these things, because she is in constant contact with the child and notices things that the father will never notice. The supremacy of the woman is her life within the four walls of their home. This is the glory of the King's daughter.

In previous generations, women were not outgoing and did not seek to leave the house. They spent their days at home, which is where they found their happiness. Back then, they took pleasure, for instance, in nursing a baby. Today, many women would rather give formula than "waste" half-an-hour on breastfeeding. But the cuddling, caressing, and love the mother gives to the child are what is responsible for the healthy development of the child.

It is the job of the woman, who understands her role as a mother, to develop a well-adjusted child. We find today many mentally crippled people who have to go for treatment, all because they spent their youthful years in broken homes where they always saw fighting and bickering. The effect of conflict on a child is far-reaching and will pursue him his entire life.

An abused child doesn't deserve this abuse. It is the parents who have the problems. When a child cries, parents will often say he is a bad child, but many times, he is not at fault. Often a parent is irritable from lack of sleep. Then the child gets on his nerves and does something that isn't really as bad as the parent thinks it is. Yet although whatever the child did was really trivial, the parent lashes out verbally degrading the child, and causing him to lose his self-esteem. The effects of verbal abuse will remain with a child in his later years. Often mental illness can be traced back to a person's childhood and oftentimes the parents are responsible. Hitting a child out of anger might create fear in the child and instill in him a picture that he'll never forget.

Give the child proper care and don't abuse him. Be well rested to raise him properly. Remember that you're developing a Yitzchak Avinu — a person who will become a great man. Spiritual growth will progress, not regress, and you'll develop a well-adjusted *mentch* who will be an asset, not a deficit, to society.

The father cannot accomplish this task; it is up to the mother, with her constant vigilance and care. When a woman does her job efficiently, she should feel proud of herself for being the one responsible, just as Sarah was responsible for Yitzchak. The great Avraham didn't detect Yishmael's dabbling in idol worship; it was our mother, Sarah, who was alert and noticed. All our mothers and grandmothers were like this. The father was the breadwinner and had to go out early to work each day. He didn't know what the child was doing: whether his son was *davening*, making *berachos*, saying *Shema*, or wearing his *tzitzis*. It was the mother who was at home and aware of the child's behavior.

Thus the job of the mother isn't boring — it's holy work. Imagine if you had the Chofetz Chaim in your home and you had to cook for him, wash his floor, make his bed. Wouldn't it be an honor for you? Wouldn't it be wonderful? Just think, your son could be a Chofetz Chaim!

We often don't realize the lasting value of even the

smallest of our deeds. When the great Reb Yitzchak Elchonon Spector went to yeshivah, there were no dorms and so he boarded with one of the local residents. The poverty then was unimaginable. The allowance given by the yeshivah barely covered basic necessities and certainly did not include anything extra for new clothes. Suits were patched, and a pair of shoes had to last for many years. Reb Yitzchak Elchonon, like many others, wore his shoes down to the point where he was almost barefoot.

One day the man of the house where he had his lodgings said to him, "Let me have the *zechus* of making you a pair of shoes." But Reb Yitzchak Elchonon was a big *tzaddik* and said, "I don't need any." The man begged him until he finally agreed to accept the offer, and those shoes, which lasted 10 years or so, were the last ones he wore as a *yeshivah bachur*.

Then Reb Yitzchak Elchonon married, was received as a rav in a small town, and eventually became the great and renowed *gaon* of Kovno. One day he traveled to Vilna, capital of Lithuania, to publish a *sefer*. Upon his arrival, he received a royal welcome. The local householder at whose home he had stayed when he was a *yeshivah bachur* also came to greet him but could not make his way through the crowd of admirers. Instead, he sent him a note saying that the *baal habayis* where he had stayed wanted to give him *shalom*.

Upon reading the note, Reb Yitzchak Elchonon said, "Hurry and bring him here!" When the man came up to him, Reb Yitzchak Elchonon said to all those surrounding him, "In his shoes I became the Yitzchak Elchonon I am today."

The *gaon* remembered and was grateful for the *chesed* implicit in the gift of a pair of shoes. Imagine how much *chesed* is involved when a mother gives of herself 24 hours a day, day after day.

The mitzvah of honoring one's father and mother is one

of the Ten Commandments. Why? After all, who doesn't understand the importance of respecting one's mother and father? Why mandate it in the Ten Commandments, the cardinal tenets of the holy Torah?

The answer is simple. When a baby is tiny, the mother gives 24-hour-a-day attention and the baby does not know what's happening. Then the child stops nursing and becomes a 2- or 3-year-old. The child doesn't want to eat his cereal. What does Mama do? She runs after the child and begs him, "Do me a favor! Eat your cereal, *mein tei'era kinde*!" He's doing Mama a favor by eating. When he is older he becomes more independent and doesn't need Papa and Mama anymore. As a baby, he didn't realize what his parents were doing for him. When he grows up, he is no longer a baby but a self-reliant individual who doesn't need Papa and Mama. So the Torah says, "You'll live long years and have your own children and then you'll feel the taste of what a mother goes through in the development of a child." Children don't realize the importance of honoring parents. We don't have Father's Day and Mother's Day once or twice a year, but 365 days of the year. Every day we have the mitzvah of honoring our parents.

In the upbringing of the child, though, it is the mother who is responsible, who inspires the child, who gives him that love and care that make the child cherish and recognize what Mama and Papa means to him.

So do not in any way feel degraded. When you say, "Who makes me according to His Will," feel happy that this is your role.

Do I feel bad that I am not a Kohen? After all, a Kohen has more mitzvos than a Yisrael. No, I know that I have my own job to do. In the same way, men and women each have their own role. Carry yours out efficiently and your accomplishments will be far-reaching and limitless.

QUESTIONS & ANSWERS

Q

Was Yishmael a *rasha*, evildoer, solely because of Hagar or did Avraham have any part in this?

A

It was not only Hagar. We see that Yaakov and Eisav had the same parents, yet one was a *tzaddik* and one was a *rasha*. Terach had Avraham Avinu and the seed, as the Kuzari explains, had different impurities that had to be purified throughout the generations. Avraham had to have a Yishmael; he was not only Hagar's son but also Avraham's. He was still Avraham Avinu's child but the impurities of Terach had settled in him. Finally, Yaakov was completely pure.

Q

If the children of the *Avos* couldn't improve themselves how can we?

A

They did improve themselves, as we see with Yishmael. Yishmael did *teshuvah* at the end.

It is an astonishing fact that Torah can come from something impure. Avraham Avinu came from Terach. This shows us that a person *can* change his entire personality, both spiritually and in all ways.

Q

Is the *Rosh Yeshivah* implying that a woman should not work outside the home?

A Unfortunately, out of necessity, a woman may have to go out to work, but the home, rather than her outside job, should always be the most important thing in her life.

Q **I feel bad about not being required to learn.**

A You shouldn't feel bad because a woman is not obligated to study Torah. Your most important job is your home and giving your children their Jewish education.

You should not feel bad if you do not open a *sefer*. The Gemara says that *"ein isha ela l'banim — a woman's responsibility is to take care of her children."* You are not obligated to learn; the *chesed* you do with your children is important enough. The Abudraham says that a woman is exempt from time-related mitzvos because her time is not her own. When your children get a little older you will be able to open a *sefer,* but your immediate obligation is to the home.

Q **Does a woman get rewarded for her learning?**

A Yes, like one who is not obligated. One who is commanded to do so has a bigger *yetzer hara* urging him not to and therefore he gets greater reward for learning. But women still gain merit, as we see that they say the *Bircas HaTorah.*

Q **Why do we get rewarded for doing something we are not commanded to?**

A If I do something for you that I am not commanded to do, wouldn't you still be grateful? It's still a good thing even though it's not obligatory. In the Gemara it says that a woman can't be burdened with mitzvos when she is burdened with the home and children. But if she wants to take more upon herself, she still gets a mitzvah, because Torah raises a person's spiritual level. So if you have a spare moment, it's definitely good to learn something.

Q **Could the *Rosh Yeshivah* please give me some advice on how to improve my concentration during *davening*?**

A This takes practice. I would suggest that you treat it like a school exercise. The old-fashioned method required repetition and building on basic skills. It's hard to have *kavanah*, to concentrate during the entire *tefillah,* but I would take one *berachah* each time to concentrate on in particular. That way you get used to having your mind concentrate on the *tefillah*.

Developing concentration is a gradual process. If you concentrate on a certain matter for 10 minutes the first day, increase this the next day by another minute, and a few days later by another minute, you will gradually build up your powers of concentration and this will lead to *kavanah* as well. You can't do this for the entire *Shemoneh Esrei* at one time, but practice on one *berachah* to start with. Say to yourself, for example, "I am going to have *kavanah* on the first *berachah*." Increase your concentration solely on this particular *berachah* for the week. Next week you will add another *berachah*, and gradually over a period of several months you will develop the power of concentration and *kavanah* during *davening*.

Several months after bringing the Jewish people out of the Egyptian exile, Hashem told Moshe at Sinai, "Thus you shall say, *tomar*, to the house of Yaakov, and tell, *tagid*, the Children of Israel" (*Shemos* 19:3). Most people are familiar with the comment of our Sages that "the house of Yaakov" here means the women, and that the use of the word *tomar* instead of *tagid* indicates that they should be spoken to in a gentle voice, not harshly or firmly, because they are more sensitive.

But the truth is, a woman doesn't *need* to be told in a strict, forceful tone. Man, by his nature, needs a firm tone. But a woman is so gentle, so good, and so gracious that she understands a softer tone. That is enough to convey a message to her.

Yet if Moshe Rabbeinu's sole purpose in speaking to the women was to ask them to accept the Torah, why are they mentioned first? The answer is that these words refer not only to acceptance of the Torah but to a much deeper thought. What was conveyed to the women was their mission, their purpose in life. They are being told here that they are the ones who will convey the message to the Jewish people. They are supposed to take over, to be the teachers of the Jewish people, and this is why they are spoken to first and given prominence. It is the mother's teaching that will mean much more to the child than that of the father.

Yet a woman is not obligated to teach a child, so why is she being told to do so here?

It is because the teaching that is referred to here is the teaching that precedes all other teachings, the teaching of *chesed*. It is the mother's lovingkindness rather than the father's sternness that will give the child a beautiful, idealistic love for Torah. He will then have a natural desire to want to love Torah, because of its beauty and because of its virtue of *chesed*.

So, *tomar*, say to her. The language used is entirely different because the woman possesses that greatness, that beautiful virtue of *chesed*, of goodness. Her tone and language is of a different nature, and that is how she should be spoken to.

At the same time, we find that Shlomo HaMelech says, "Listen, my child, to the reproof of your father and do not forsake the Torah of your mother" (*Mishlei* 1:8). Here again, we are confronted with the question: What does the "Torah of your mother" involve? What is the Torah that the mother conveys to the child?

Torah without *chesed* is not Torah, and such learning can, *chas v'shalom*, make a person haughty and lacking in proper *middos*. The "Torah of the mother" is *chesed*, and this Torah must come first, before that of the father.

Our Sages tell us that there are three partners in the creation of a child: *HaKadosh Baruch Hu*, the father, and the mother. The Gemara, as explained by Rashi, says that the father provides the hard tissue, the bone; the mother supplies the soft tissue, the flesh and blood; and Hashem's share in the partnership is the *neshamah*, the soul (*Niddah* 31a).

When it comes to honoring parents, the father is mentioned first: "Honor your father and your mother" (*Shemos* 20:12). Honor, *kibbud*, is respect in a positive way — it is not fear — and a child will naturally respect his mother more than he does his father. Why? Because the mother always has a word of encouragement for him. It is she who always takes his side and defends him. When his father disciplines him, his mother gives him a kiss, so a child naturally loves his mother more than his father. The verse is saying, "I know you will give your mother respect, but I want you to respect your father too." It is emphasizing the message: Remember, your father deserves the same respect as your mother.

However, Hashem knows very well that a child will fear his father more than he does his mother, for a father is by nature the sterner, stricter parent. So when it comes to fear, the Torah puts the mother first: "A person should fear his mother and father" (*Vayikra* 19:3), meaning, "I know you will fear your father, but remember that your mother also deserves to be feared."

So we see that there are two types, the father and mother, who are two of the three partners in the life of the child. And, as we said, the father supplies the bony tissues of every child and he is the one with the stern character who gives the son a spank when he doesn't behave properly. So Shlomo HaMelech is saying, "Listen, my son, to the reproof of your father." That is the father's job, to reprimand the child, to chastise the child and lead him in the proper path. And this he does in a stern, firm way.

But "do not forget the Torah of your mother." The Torah of the mother is of a different nature from that of the father and has a special significance for the child. It is her goodness, her softness, and her gentleness that teach the child.

The child has a certain love for the mother because of her total dedication to him. A mother has a natural feeling, imbued in her by Hashem, to want to do *chesed* with her child. If not for this, a mother could not dedicate herself so completely to the child. You can get a nurse willing to work day or night shifts, you can get a 6- or 8-hour-shift nurse but you can't get a 24-hour-a-day nurse — only a mother does that. Why? Because Hashem has given her a natural love for her child.

Love is the Torah that the mother teaches the child. This is what is inculcated in the mind of the child and implanted in his heart. And that is the symbol of the mother; that is her Torah that she conveys to the child. It is unforgettable, for it is ingrained in the child from his earliest years. And when we say that each mother is a link in the chain of Judaism, we mean that it is only through her compassion and her goodness that the spiritual idea of *ahavas chesed*, which precedes Torah, is perpetuated.

Knowledge is not the essence of Torah; Torah is always accompanied by *chesed*. We say in our daily prayers, "You have given to us a living Torah" — not a Torah that is only in a book, but a living Torah, one that is implanted within us and is a deeply ingrained part of us.

But at the same time, we dare not stop there. We continue, "You have given us a living Torah and *ahavas chesed*." The living Torah is followed by love of *chesed*. What does this mean? We know that for *chesed* to take place, an action is required. You do a good deed for someone and this is an action of *chesed*. But there is a great distinction between doing *chesed* and loving *chesed*. Loving *chesed* means that you *search out* someone for whom to do *chesed*.

Avraham Avinu is the symbol of *chesed*. He was circumcised, and on the third day after the *bris*, when he was in the category of a person whose life is in danger, his suffering was so great that Hashem Himself came to visit him (*Bereishis* 18:1). Yet Avraham could not rest knowing that he was unable to do *chesed*. Our Sages tell us that Hashem let the sun shine at full strength, burning in its full fiery flame, so that no living being would be able to come and bother Avraham. But Avraham had no peace of mind. Even on the third day, when his physical suffering was at its peak, he felt such great pain at not being able to do *chesed* that he sent his servant Eliezer to look for guests (*Bava Metzia* 95b). When Hashem saw how distressed Avraham was, how saddened he was about not being able to welcome guests, He sent down angels in the guise of wayfarers, just to please him.

This is what we call *ahavas chesed*, love of *chesed*.

We presume, of course, that if there is no guest, if there is no one with whom to do *chesed*, we are exempt. But Avraham's greatness in loving *chesed* merited something extraordinary: a new creation, just so that he would be able to do *chesed*.

If the circumstance arises and you see a poor person and realize that something has to be done for him, that is called doing *chesed*. But to love *chesed* even when no one is around, to seek out the poor person, to look for the one who needs *chesed* even before he comes to you — that is a virtue. And that is what we mean when we say *ahavas chesed*, loving *chesed*. This is the height of the *middah* of *chesed*.

And this is the mother's Torah. With her motherly love, her gentleness, her graciousness, and her goodness, a mother can teach wonderful things to her children.

Women often feel miserable about having to do the housework, what some people call "the dirty work." They say to themselves, "Is that my goal in life? Is that my mission in the world?" and they sometimes feel miserable about what they call "missing the boat." They think to themselves, "With my talents and potential I could do wonderful work. Must I be stuck within the confines of the home? Must I do housework? Must I be tied down?" She feels that all this is beneath her dignity.

But the truth is, if we were to understand the significance of this so-called dirty work — which it is not, *chas u'shalom* — we would realize it is on the highest level. Doing *chesed* for one's husband and one's children is the highest ideal.

Seeing this quality of lovingkindness in his mother will teach the child the biggest and most significant lesson of his youthful years. He is too young to understand lofty philosophers and he cannot comprehend Talmudic knowledge. After all, what can a child of 4 or 5 realize and understand? But his mother's lovingkindness will last within him forever. The impression the child gets from the mother, what she conveys to the child that gives him a deep love for her, is the teaching of his mother, the Torah of his mother.

When it comes to the Torah of the mother, the verse says, "*v'al titosh*, do not forget." But when did she teach him? What teaching is there not to forget?

It is these early teachings of the mother to the child when he is not receptive to higher education, when he can only understand motherly language, the love of the mother — this is what he must not forget in his later years. The message to the child is: You will grow up and you may not need your mother anymore but don't forget, *v'al titosh*, the teachings of your mother from your youthful years, the wonderful love your mother gave you. As an adult, you won't need your mother the same way you did as a child, but remember what she did for you.

No woman should feel deprived. By fulfilling her obligations as a good wife and as a good mother, her teachings will never be forgotten by the child. And that is the role the mother plays in the life of a child. There are hardships a mother goes through in raising a child, but she will reap the harvest, *b'ezras Hashem*, in another few years, and that will compensate for all the hardships of the past.

So please, I ask of you and beg of you: Do not feel in any way deprived of your greatness. Feel happy when you do your work. Feel that you are fulfilling your share in your child's life. You are giving him the soft tissue, the kindness and the goodness. You are an equal partner with Hashem, our Sages teach us, and your share is greatness.

And may *Hashem Yisbarach* give you the strength, the time, the peace of mind, and the happiness to enjoy what you are doing.

QUESTIONS & ANSWERS

Q I've heard that if a child has fear of his parents, he will learn fear of Hashem as well.

A Fear is psychological dynamite. A fear might become an obsession. We must develop fear in a gentle manner, through respect for parents. Teach the child respect and he will have fear through love. If I love someone, I'll always be afraid that I might do him some harm, but that comes from love, not pure fear. Pure fear today is dangerous for a child.

Q If a person doesn't have a *yetzer tov* until he's bar or bas mitzvah, does that mean that any good he does until then is just because of the parent's influence or because it is ingrained in him? Can a person do good on his own?

A Of course a child possesses goodness and *Chazal* tell us that the father is *moresh livno*, that at birth the child receives the virtues of his parents. Of course the child has goodness in him, there's no doubt about it. So does a cat. A cat has pity on its kittens, doesn't it? Is this the *yetzer tov*? No, it's a natural inclination that Hashem gave to all animals and one that we share too.

Then there is something greater, that we don't understand, which we call the *yetzer tov*. It's a lofty matter, not just a natural inclination we possess at birth. So of course you'll see a child doing good things too, even though he doesn't yet have a *yetzer tov* because it's a natural capacity in human beings. But, pertaining to the *neshamah*, a *yetzer tov* is something higher that is acquired with the fulfillment of mitzvos.

Q **My 5-year-old son came home from *cheder* saying bad words. What should I do?**

A If you have other children, give them a prize for not saying the bad word. Ask the child, "Did you say a bad word today?" and give her a beautiful prize for not saying it. This is a kosher form of jealousy and will cause the child to stop saying the words. Try it and see how it works. It's miraculous. If the child who says the bad word does it again, give the other child two more prizes. The more the one child says, the more prizes the other one gets. You'll see how easily he'll stop.

Q **What can you do for a 3-year-old who is extra sensitive and cries whenever you reprimand him?**

A If a child cries too often that means he is a sensitive child who needs a little more love. Hug him, kiss him, and make him happy. Usually such a child is very delicate and just needs proper love.

Q **What should I do if my children are constantly hitting each other?**

A The main thing is not to lose control of yourself. They will grow up. I always maintain that it is normal for the child to be wild; if he is not, there could be something psychologically wrong with him. A child must have a release somehow for his feelings. That is normal. The main thing is for you not to lose control of yourself. When the child sees that you are in control of yourself, he will not take advantage of you but on the contrary, he will respect you. I say that people should have *nachas* if their children are wild and you will see that in a matter of time they will outgrow it all. In later years, he will use his intelligence in the right way. A child who has a lot of intelligence but does not release it will use it in the wrong way. So don't worry about the child.

Q

What is the best way of dealing with fighting children? Should I isolate them?

A

It depends on the child. Isolation might have a bad, long-lasting effect on a child. A sensitive child might develop a fear of being alone. Of course, you always have to stop the fighting; it's never good. A positive way of dealing with it is to employ the token system. Do not punish the naughty one but give the good child a present. If the child was bad, give the other children something. Give him a bank and deposit a coin when he does something good. He can save and then he feels proud and he can buy what he wants. Always avoid destructive methods.

Q

What happens if a child steals from his brother?

A

Envy is a natural emotion. All emotions are healthy but they have to be used in a certain way. When the *mussar* sages talk about *middos* they are referring to "measurements." Every quality must be used in proper measure. For example, we all possess within ourselves the *middah* of anger, and there are times when we must have a measure of anger. Knowing when and how much is *gadlus*. Shlomo HaMelech says, "There is a time to talk and a time to keep silent." Knowing the optimum time is what makes a person great. A child who steals is not really *stealing*; he feels a little envy so he takes the item. Let him get a little older and he will be taught, "Do not steal." I would reward such a child for those times that he does not steal by giving him something he would appreciate. This is something that will be outgrown; it just takes time.

Q **We have started giving our children stars for good deeds. Is it okay to give them money to buy things for each star, or is that likely to give them a lust for money?**

A It depends. Large sums of money would give them a lust for money. So use your discretion, and only give them money sometimes, so that they can enjoy having the money.

Q **Should you use the token system of rewards even if it causes envy between one child and another?**

A Envy might bring good results if it is used diplomatically and sensibly. For instance, if children do not behave properly at the Shabbos table, and one does behave, give that one a prize. If the others behave, they will get a prize too. Change the reward system from time to time, though, to keep it interesting.

Punishing children can teach them to be rough. The reward system accomplishes better results.

Q **If a child isn't interested in washing *netilas yadayim* for the meal, what should a parent do?**

A Each time she washes, give her something nice. Use the token system, the constructive method, particularly when it comes to fulfilling mitzvos.

Q **My daughter's teacher forbade her to go to a public library. Can't my daughter read kosher books**

A from the library for relaxation?

Yes, she can read for relaxation. Go to a *frum* library and pick out a kosher novel.

Q Could the *Rosh Yeshivah* please tell me his opinion about spacing children?

A Sometimes a woman thinks she can decide when to have her babies. But how do you know that Hashem will give you at a different time that baby who was supposed to be born now?

Many times, I explain to a woman that every Jewish baby is a great blessing. When they understand this, they are happy to bring another *eved Hashem* into the world. Of course, if there is a medical problem, one should ask his *posek* a *shei'lah*. But many times it's a matter of your mental attitude. When a woman understands the greatness of bringing children into the world and raising them to Torah and mitzvos, she will happily have children even though it's difficult. Our grandmothers had large families and lacked even the most basic conveniences. Yet they were overjoyed each time they brought a new Jewish life into the world. This understanding and joy made their hardships easier to bear. May Hashem bless all of you with this joy and may you have *naches* from all your *kinderlach*.

Q I'm often tired at the end of the day and can't always finish my work.

A Women have to learn that they can leave the kitchen with dirty dishes for the next day. This is not a crime, especially when you are worn out. Tomorrow you will be able to do it in less time and you will have more peace of mind. The house does not have to be spotless when you go to bed. Here again we get carried away by our emotions. If we would use our rational mind we would know to leave those dirty dishes. It's the mind versus the emotions. If you rest your nerves, though, your mind will be more effective.

Two children may be brought up by the same wonderful, caring parents, yet one becomes a *mentch* and the other turns out to be bad. How is this possible?

Children are born with certain tendencies. One is more irritable, one less. Some bad traits are also picked up in the street. You have Yaakov and Eisav. How? Yitzchak gave both the same *chinuch*. But Eisav was an Eisav at birth, hot-tempered and wild; Yaakov was cool and complacent, and sat in the tents of Torah. Some children have within them certain virtues.

How do you teach children to do *chesed*?

Rashi explains that it was to educate Yishmael that Avraham told him to give food to the unexpected guests. When a poor person comes to the door, let the child hand him the money. Send a child to do a *chesed* for a neighbor. Look for ways to train him to do *chesed*.

How do we teach a child to be humble?

A child does not understand what humility means. It doesn't mean regarding yourself as a dishrag. Moshe Rabbeinu knew who he was and he knew how great he was but he was the most humble of all people because he realized that all was from Hashem. He knew that what he possessed was not his but Hashem's. Humility is greatness, but both humility and its opposite, conceit, do not apply to a child.

Q I learned that the fact that Noach is called "righteous" in his presence but not "perfectly righteous" teaches us that one doesn't give full praise to a person in his presence. Does this apply to praising children?

A No. It is very important to build up the child's ego by praising him in his presence. When you praise a child you help him develop himself and create a positive self-image. Always praise children. Some children do not speak up in class because they are not given this encouragement. At their age, they will not become haughty.

Q Until what age can we praise a child without worrying that it will make him haughty?

A Certainly up to the age of 13. Many times a child is depressed because of his parents. Some parents instill too much fear in their children and the child becomes dejected. When you embarrass children in front of their friends it takes a big toll on them. A child thrives on his mother's affection, which helps a child develop mentally and physically. It is the dedication and total devotion of the mother that develops the child, and therefore you should always praise him.

Q Chazal say that a parent is obligated to teach his children fear of sin. How is a parent supposed to do this? Should we tell them there is a *Gehinnom*? Should we tell them that they might go there?

A No. Children are too young for this. It would be too frightening for them. Besides, even adults do not really know what *Gehinnom* is, so how can we explain it to a child?

Q Should we train our children to fulfill the halachah to stand up when a parent enters the room?

A Yes, definitely. The lack of Torah we see today comes from the lack of respect for it. In the olden times people used to stand up when a Torah scholar or *rosh yeshivah* passed them by, but today very few people do so. It's not that the Torah scholar wants the honor, but that there should be recognition of Torah's importance. People who have respect for a *talmid chacham*, a Torah scholar, understand what Torah means. This attitude should be cultivated in the child's mind in his younger years. When a child stands up for his mother he realizes what she means to him. A child who is not raised that way treats his mother like a dishrag, like nothing at all. Standing up is a sign of recognition of the dignity of the individual. We also stand up for an aged person. A man of about 70, some opinions say 60, has a certain amount of knowledge that is deserving of our respect. This is a wonderful practice and attitude that we must teach our children so they learn to respect other people.

A child should be taught to respect his parents. He should be made to stand up for his parents at least once a day. Today children do not stand up even for an important rabbi, because they are not taught what respect is. If a child is taught respect, he will not, G-d forbid, raise a hand to his parents or even raise his voice.

In many cases, we are the ones responsible for our children's bad behavior because we have spoiled them.

Q **How do you explain to a child who *davened* for someone who was ill that the person died?**

A This touches on the matter of *hashgachah*. There are more intrinsic problems. For example, why were six million Jews killed in the Holocaust? Why do *tzaddikim* lose children? The Chofetz Chaim gave a parable that you should always remember.

A fundraiser for a certain institution once came to a packed shul on Shabbos. To his surprise, the *gabbai* gave out the *aliyos* to people sitting on all four sides of the shul. "Why don't you give out the *aliyos* from the same row?" the visitor asked him. "It would make more sense."

"My dear *meshulach*," the *gabbai* answered, "you only came for one Shabbos and can't understand how the shul is run. This man over here was just sick and had to get an *aliyah* this week, and so with this one and that one."

So too, the Chofetz Chaim says, it is with *hashgachah*. We come to this world for 60, 70, or 80 years. We don't know the past, present, or future, and therefore we do not understand how things link together. These questions on *hashgachah* can be answered through this parable. We only see a piece of the puzzle here and there, but if we could tie it all together, it would make sense. The Gemara says that in the World to Come we will say the blessing "*hatov ve'hameitiv*, He is Good and bestows good," on the things for which we now say *dayan ha'emes*. There, we will realize that these things were really for our own good, something we cannot understand now.

One should explain, in simple language, that Hashem has His reasons, so to speak, which we can't understand, and that Hashem knows the right way to answer our *tefillos* and always does the best thing for a person.

Q **How much candy and sweets should children have?**

A Children should not be brought up on chocolate or ice cream. The way of Torah is a difficult one, not a sweet one. If children have a craving for sweets, they won't enjoy the study of Torah when they get older. It is very wrong to bribe a child with candy just to keep him quiet. This is at the expense of the child's spiritual life in later years. The child who has a craving for sweet chocolate, besides ruining his teeth and appetite, will not enjoy a yeshivah meal, nor will he enjoy the study of Torah unless he gets a chocolate bar at the same time. You can ruin your children by giving them chocolate. Give them simple, nourishing food, not even food that is too delicious. If a child is consumed by a desire for delicious chocolate, he will not develop a taste for Torah.

Q **We are having a hard time financially. Is it all right to let the children be aware of this problem and explain why they can't have things that they want, or might doing this create unhealthy fears for them?**

A No, not at all. If the child is an understanding child, matters should be made clear to him. The child should be made to feel responsibility. My mother, *a"h*, went to work when she was only 8. The sense of responsibility they had in Europe made *mentchen* out of them. Nowadays, children are pampered until they're 18 or 19. A child should be taught, "I wish I could give you such and such but it is not a necessity and it is not within our budget. Maybe Hashem will bless us with greater abundance."

The big *tzarah* in American life is that we spoon-feed children and they wind up not caring about or feeling the seriousness of life. So instead of hiding things, take the child aside and explain the situation to him in a nice way and say, "You pray to Hashem, *daven* well, and He'll give you what He knows you need."

Let your children share life with you at the age of 8 or 9, not at 18 or 19. Let them feel life in its fullness — the hardships, the responsibilities — and they'll have greater respect.

Q **Should we go through the same expense to make the same bar mitzvah party for our second son as we did for the first, even though we can now no longer afford it?**

A Yes. Borrow money and make as nice a bar mitzvah party for the second son as you did for the first. Otherwise it might cause jealousy and give the second boy an inferiority complex. He'll think that he's not as good as his brother.

For a twin bar mitzvah, give both boys the same gift, even the same book, so as not to cause jealousy.

Q **What about talking politics with our children?**

A Don't mix politics into a child's youthful years. He won't understand, it will confuse him and create conflicts and hatred, which are bad for a child.

Q **Is there something special about wrapping a 3-year-old boy in a *tallis* when taking him to *cheder* for the first time?**

A Yes. It is an old *minhag*, custom.

Q **Do you have to wait three years before first cutting a little boy's hair?**

A Many have this *minhag* but it is not obligatory. If the child has lice, you can give him a haircut. If his hair gets into his eyes, you should trim his bangs because the hair could obstruct and harm his vision and you should not let him suffer.

Is it detrimental to put pressure on a child to learn?

It might be. I find many times that parents, especially *baalei teshuvah*, expect their children to make up for what they missed as children, and often this takes a toll on the child's health. The parents forget that the child is only a child. Never make it hard for a child or expect too much from him. Let him enjoy his childhood and develop naturally. Let him play. Remember that he is only a child.

At what age can you push a child?

Each child is different because each has a different mental constitution. A child forced to go to a kindergarten against his or her will, can develop certain complexes or fears that gradually grow bigger and sometimes cannot be repaired. So go easy on a child, don't pressure. "*Chanoch lanaar al pi darko*" — the child needs his training according to his mental and emotional capacities.

Can pushing a young child of 2 to 3 into a situation where he is separated from his parents, either by entering a kindergarten or staying with a babysitter, cause internal harm if he does not want to go, even if he doesn't put up very strong protest?

This depends on the child. In some, this will create fear. There are some people getting married still "tied to their mother's apron strings" and, unfortunately, some even get divorced because of it. An unnatural attachment can harm and getting used to a stranger won't harm, but it has to be done carefully. Explain to the child; do not force. Otherwise, it might develop into a phobia. Maybe sit with the child in the new place until he becomes accustomed to it. But children *should* be taught to leave home.

Q **What if you have a child who's very friendly and goes to everyone?**

A That's very good — wonderful! You have a lovable child. But when he gets older you must curb this. Train him. It is human nature to like company, not to be isolated. The *mussar* masters say that melancholy distances people. It is a disease. But when your child gets older, you must be sure to select his friends.

Q **What can be done with a *cheder* boy who dreams during the day?**

A Well, *cheder* boys do have a tendency to dream. But make sure he sleeps well at night so he will dream at night and not during the day. He needs a good rebbe, too, of course. If he is getting enough sleep, you should check his hearing and eyesight. If necessary, check for learning disabilities. But be careful not to get angry with him, because the daydreaming is not his fault.

Q **My almost-7-year-old comes home from *cheder* at 4:20 in the afternoon. He likes to read, play, and go to friends at this time. Should we allow him this free play or should we obligate him to learn?**

A Of course you should allow him this free time.

Q **My child was *patched* in the face by his teacher. I thought one should not hit a child in the face, yet the teacher claims that in Europe this was always done.**

A I once met a very wealthy man who was turned away from Judaism because one of his teachers had been so vicious. This man was left with that picture. This is a very important point. If a child fears his teacher and every day is torture for him, you dare not sent him there. This can result in psychological and mental disorders, fears, and complexes in later years. A youngster's psychological state of mind is very important. Your husband should discuss this with a rav.

Q **How much should you encourage a child by saying, "I'll give you a toy if you sit down and learn." Or is it better that he has that hour to play outside?**

A It depends on the child. Forcing a child of even age 5 or 6 is no good. A child should be playful. The *Chovos HaLevavos* explains why an ox is born fully developed while a human being is frail at birth and must develop, not attaining its final state until years later. A child is frail and could never live with the intellect of a grown man and his pressures. Intellect and the brain must develop. Let your child enjoy life. The child also needs a sensible rebbe to give him a feeling of success and nurture the child so that he will be more receptive.

Q **Should girls memorize parts of *Chumash* by heart?**

A No.

Q **If we shouldn't force a child, does that include having a child dress himself or clean up?**

A If he is an understanding child, it would be a sign of laziness in him at a certain age not to clean up or dress himself, which is not good. Help the child if that is what he wants. Maybe he needs it. Don't push; make him understand. If he requests a candy as a reward, give it to him the first time. Next time, say, "I have no candy, but if I see you can do it today and tomorrow without one, the next day I'll give you a candy." Get him unused to the candies gradually.

Q My husband feels it is very important to learn with our twins, aged 9 years, on a regular basis, but they often give him a hard time and refuse to learn. Should we bribe them?

A The token system is excellent. You make a chart for the child. If he behaves well, if he learns, you give him a star. If he gets 10 stars, then you buy him something he wants. That works wonders. Bribe him as well as you can, in a constructive way.

Sometimes, for a father to teach a child is not too practical because a child will not receive from the parents as well as he will from someone else. This is because he is too used to them. This depends upon the nature of the child and the nature of the father. Sometimes the child is not well prepared, maybe a little irritable or maybe a little nervous. Then you should leave him alone.

Q Is it a father's responsibility to watch over his children's spiritual welfare by means of examining them on what they learn in yeshivah? Our sons are aged age 8 and 12.

A Of course. The father is obligated to look after the spiritual welfare of the child.

Q Is it a waste of Torah study time for a father to learn *aleph-beis* with his son?

A Not at all. Teaching *aleph-beis is* Torah.

Q What should a father who learns all day do when he can't spend time with his children?

A He could spend time with them on Shabbos. *Chinuch* is necessary, and on Shabbos a father can take an interest in how the child is learning. But he should be careful not to try to cram in too much all in that one day because children are frail.

Q **What if your child does not want to learn or review? What should you do? Should you just leave him alone?**

A It all depends. Sometimes a child is a little irritable or a little nervous. At those times, you should leave him alone. But if he is well rested, you should always use the prize system. Buy him something nice, a little gift from time to time. Every time he reviews, he gets a star and in the end, he gets a prize.

Q **Should a child be allowed to play with toy guns?**

A No, this is bad *chinuch*. A child should *never* be allowed to hold a gun. He should hold a *sefer*, something with *kedushah*. This has an effect on the child.

Q **Should we obligate a boy to *daven* Maariv?**

A If it will deprive him of his sleep, no. He can *daven* Minchah and then *daven* an earlier Maariv at *plag HaMinchah*. Remember, give the boy time to enjoy life. We have to care for his physical well-being as well as for his *neshamah*. If you want to have a healthy child and not one mentally deranged or frustrated, you have to see that he gets enough sleep and play in life.

Q **Should little boys *daven* three times a day?**

A Some children are frailer than others and you may have to allow him to omit some sections of the *davening*. Train him with one *tefillah* a day. At 6 or 7 years, *chinuch* begins, but moderately and sensibly. Don't force a child.

Q **What should parents do if their son doesn't want to *daven*?**

A There is something wrong somewhere in the *chinuch* of such a child. The parent should discuss this problem with the child's rebbeim to find out why he does not want to *daven*. It would be good to get him a good friend who would *shlep* him along to shul.

Q **Some people take their kids to kiddy parks, but how can this be good even if there is no problem of *pritzus*, indecency, there? Why pay money for a ride when you could take them on a hike up a mountain to see the beauty of Hashem through that?**

A Take them to a kiddy park. Children are only children and they also want to have some fun and at this age, this is what they enjoy.

Q **Must I teach my children to stand up for their older brother?**

A Yes, you should teach them to stand up for their older brother.

Q **Is it proper for a parent to tell his child how old the parent is?**

A What's wrong if you tell him your age?

Q **What do you do with boys' *tzitzis* that are old, torn, and no longer kosher?**

A You should put them in a bag and throw them away. You cannot use them as rags but you are allowed to throw them away.

Q **Should a mother treat her daughters differently from the way she treats her sons?**

A Basically, no. A mother's purpose is to give warmth, love, softness, and support to her sons as well as to her daughters. Of course, a boy must go to *cheder* and has a natural toughness, which means he can take things a little harder than the girl. So naturally you have to be a little softer with the girl than with the boy. But basically, they both should be treated similarly.

Q **In my neighborhood, there is a terrible problem of littering. How can a concerned individual do something about it?**

A Many times it's due to the children. There should be more parental supervision. Posters should be printed up and put in the shul and other places.

Q **Children today are given so many expensive toys that parents feel pressured to relax their principles so that their child will not feel that he is the oddball in the class. But if parents try to maintain a simpler lifestyle, a child may feel that his parents do not want to give him the good things in life. Is there any way to prevent a child from feeling this way?**

A Remember, as a child is trained, so he will grow. If he is accustomed to many expensive toys, he will always want more. If you buy all the toys at one time, he will get tired of them, but if you buy him a new toy every six months or so, he will appreciate them and enjoy them. If you don't get him used to expensive toys he won't feel bad at all if you don't buy them. Point out that not every child in his class has every toy.

Q **Should I put a bad-tasting substance on my 5-year-old's thumb to make him stop sucking it?**

A No, You should use a gradual process to wean the child from his thumb, because it is hard for him to break such a habit. You can use the reward system we talked about earlier.

Q **Tonight my daughter spoke *lashon hara*. Her sister said, "You will get *Gehinnom* if you say *lashon***

hara," to which the other one said, "I am not yet bas mitzvah, so I won't be punished." What should I have said to this?

A You should tell her that she is right, she is not yet bas mitzvah. But if she is not careful to refrain from speaking *lashon hara* now, it will become habitual with her. Then she may come to speak it after she is bas mitzvah as well, and then she could get *Gehinnom*.

Q Should one try to give the same amount of attention and the same size portions to two children, or should you give one of them more than the other to teach the other to be happy with what he has?

A Do not do this because you could hurt them. Also, it would only breed envy. Our Sages say that Yaakov Avinu brought about the *galus* because he favored Yosef. Do not in any way make changes that cause envy. As for a child learning to be happy with what he has, don't worry, he will learn this gradually. You can point out to him all the good things he has, for instance: heat, warm clothing in the winter, a wonderful family that loves him, food to eat, parents who care about him, etc., etc. For example, when you come into your warm house on a freezing cold or rainy day, say to your child, "Aren't we lucky to have a warm house?" He will learn to appreciate what he has and won't focus on what he doesn't have.

9 A LESSON FROM QUEEN ESTHER

The Gemara tells us that in the future all the Yamim Tovim will be nullified except for Purim (*Mishlei Rabbah* 9). The Gemara says that although the final redemption will be even more miraculous than the Exodus from Egypt (*Berachos* 12b), the miracle of Purim — which basically revolved around the personalities of Mordechai and Esther — will never be forgotten. It was the unique courage and boldness of Mordechai and Esther together that make them the stars of the beautiful story we read in the *Megillah*. Since all of us are going through hard times today and there isn't a person who isn't struggling, a little insight into the characteristics of Mordechai and Esther might be a great help to us in our times of tribulation.

The very names "Mordechai" and "Esther" are symbolic for our times. The name Mordechai in Aramaic consists of two words: *mera dachya*, a spice that diffuses fragrance only after it has been processed. As for Esther's name, we are told, "And he [Mordechai] had reared

Hadassah, she is Esther" (*Esther* 2:7). Why are two names mentioned? Was her real name Esther, with Hadassah being some kind of nickname, or vice versa?

She actually had both names, and both have deep meaning. Hadassah stems from the word *hadas*, myrtle. Esther was similar to the *hadas* in that she had a deep olive-green complexion. We also know that the leaves of this plant have a very sweet fragrance that can only be released when the leaves are bruised and crushed. As a matter of fact, some people use the crushed leaves for *besamim* during Havdalah. Just like the *hadas*, which is only fragrant when it is bruised and crushed, so too was Esther's potential brought out to its fullest by her hard life.

The name Esther is related to the word *hester*, meaning hidden. When we look deeper into the *Megillah*, we see something remarkable. For nine years, until Haman's downfall, Esther guarded the secret of her ancestry. She never told anyone that she was a Jewess. Examining her situation, we know that as the wife of Achashverosh she was constantly pressured to reveal the truth. Yet she withstood this pressure. Why?

The Midrash explains that Mordechai realized there was something unique in Esther's becoming the queen (*Esther Rabbah* 6:6). He knew that she was a righteous woman and that it had to be Divine providence that she became the wife of the non-Jewish king, Achashverosh. Mordechai realized that Hashem had something in store for the Jewish people and that Esther would be instrumental in saving them. Mordechai was aware of the impending calamity that would befall the Jews and foresaw that Esther would be the one through whom they would be saved. Had she revealed her ancestry, she would have defeated this purpose. She therefore carefully guarded her secret until the proper time. The Ibn Ezra explains that if Esther hadn't kept her secret, she would not have been able to observe her religion (*Esther* 2:10). Since Achashverosh did not know she was a Jewess, she was able to observe her religion in secrecy.

Other reasons are given, but in all cases, there was a sound reason for Esther doing this outstanding act of guarding her secret for nine years. This is due to a character trait that Queen Esther inherited from Rachel, who likewise did not reveal or give any indication to Yaakov that she was not the person he was marrying, and so he married Leah first. Esther inherited this quality of silence and discretion, which Rachel had shown under such tremendous pressure. We know Rachel's great merit in this act, for we know how much Yaakov loved her. It was an exceptionally courageous act befitting one of our *Imahos*, and this character trait was bequeathed to Queen Esther.

This incredible silence is the outstanding virtue that made Esther queen. She boldly and courageously kept her secret while under terrific pressure from a king and an entire nation. Esther did not dare reveal anything, for she knew that her silence was necessary for the salvation of the Jewish people. She knew that there would come a time when she would have to tell, and that there was a *hashgachah pratis* in store for her. Mordechai guided her, as the verse says: "... and he had reared, *imen*, Hadassah." The word *imen* is from the word *uman*, a skilled professional or expert. Mordechai was not just a tutor to Esther; he raised and reared her skillfully, so that she would understand and appreciate what *hashgachah pratis* had in store.

If we are faced with a terrible situation that is hard for us to take, we still must realize that the salvation will come and that *hashgachah* has something in store for us. We must remember that it is only a passing situation; a new time will come, a happier time, bringing a sunnier day.

Queen Esther guarded her secret for nine years, waiting for the day when she would be able to declare proudly and courageously that she was a Jewess. It was then that everyone recognized the greatness of the Jew. Had she revealed this secret beforehand, everything would have been a waste and she would not have been instrumental in bringing salvation to the Jewish people.

Esther had perfect self-control. The ability to be queen over herself is what made her queen over the world. Self-control stems from the powers of the soul, which all of us possess. The Gemara tells us that a person's greatness or inferiority is recognizable when he gets angry (*Eiruvin* 65a). The logical person does not lose control of himself. It's like a pressure cooker that has a little hole on the top to release the pressure. If you didn't have that little hole, the pot would explode. One should not bottle up his emotions, because that will cause mental anguish. However, although you have to speak, your tone of voice and how you say things make the difference.

Building a home requires self-control and knowing how and when to speak to one's husband and children. We sometimes lose control of ourselves and out of anger, say things that we later regret. Many times the regret does not rectify the damage that was done.

Raising children is a hard job, full of stress and pressure. Hashem gives a mother such a profound love for her child that she tends to him with selfless dedication, even if she goes for nights without sleep. Nevertheless, physical and mental exhaustion sometimes cause a mother to lose control and give the child a slap. Mothers should learn about the various stages of childhood, puberty, and adolescence that a child goes through. Understanding the child's development will help the mothers realize and accept that the things he does are normal for a child his age.

A child has little knowledge, and no understanding of what to do with his knowledge. He has to release his feelings, and sometimes he does so in a vicious way, perhaps by breaking or damaging things. It is normal for a child to be wild. The Gemara tells us in reference to education: "Befriend him with your right hand and repel him with your left" (Sotah 47a). Just as the right hand is stronger than the left, the befriending should be stronger than the repelling. If the child deserves punishment, give it to him. But for every slap, give him 10 kisses. And far better than slapping is withholding something that the child wants very badly. Actually, it is far better to avoid slapping entirely, because it can create a fear that might only show up later.

Of course, a parent might need to show some anger to a child who is misbehaving, but the anger should be external only; inwardly, the parent must stay calm and composed. He must not lose his self-control. If he does, he can create fears and a complex in the child that might mar him physically and emotionally for life.

In this way, we will cultivate feelings of love into our children's minds and hearts. By exercising control, we gain the child's confidence and he will grow up a nurtured individual.

Let us learn the lesson of self-control and silence from the queen whose name was Hadassah and Esther. Hadassah, the one who suffers, was Esther, the hidden one, who kept silent about her ancestry for nine years in order to redeem the Jewish people.

QUESTIONS & ANSWERS

Q Does a nursing mother have to fast on *Taanis Esther*?

A She should not fast unless fasting is usually not a strain for her. A nursing woman is obligated to fast only on Tishah B'Av and Yom Kippur, unless she fasts very well.

Q Can a pregnant woman eat or drink before Kiddush on Shabbos morning?

A She can drink a cup of coffee or tea before *davening* but should not eat solids or most other liquids.

Q Can she eat solids on Shabbos morning before Kiddush after she says *berachos*?

A The Chofetz Chaim rules that one is not allowed to eat before Shacharis. First you have to *daven* Shacharis and then you can make Kiddush. If the woman is so weak that she can't *daven*, she can use the cup of coffee for Kiddush and have a piece of cake.

Q On Shabbos, is it all right to put honey in tea or is this considered cooking?

A You can put honey in tea if the tea is not boiling hot. It should be cooled off first.

Q Can you leave laundry on the line over Shabbos?

A Yes, but not in the front of the house because it is not dignified for Shabbos.

Q On Shabbos, can you clean up a messy room and put laundry away if leaving things the way they are would disturb your Shabbos?

A Yes, you may, because doing so becomes your *oneg Shabbos*. But when putting items or laundry away, you are not allowed to pick and choose, or sort. You should dump it all into a laundry basket and sort it after Shabbos.

Q On Shabbos day is it permissible to cover the bed with a bedspread?

A If without one the bed looks ugly to you and disturbs you, it is your *oneg Shabbos* to cover it and you are allowed to do so.

Q Since talk on Shabbos should be *divrei Torah*, what do you do if a guest or a friend you met on a walk brings up *divrei chol*?

A You've touched on a delicate subject. If you're going to stifle your speech, will you enjoy your Shabbos? One could say that the only way to really keep Shabbos is to tie your hands and feet up and tie yourself to a bed. But you don't enjoy your Shabbos that way. To refrain from speaking takes many years. If you enjoy it and don't suffer from it, then refraining is a high level. But to suffer could get to be a transgression if you feel it as pressure and you don't have *oneg Shabbos*. Limit your speech, but don't stifle yourself.

BEN SORER U'MOREH

10

A man once came to me and said, "Rabbi, you can imagine my *tzaar*. When I make Kiddush, my son sits on the sofa in his dungarees. He won't even come to the table to hear Kiddush!" What we see going on today clearly portrays, to a large extent, the life of the *ben sorer u'moreh,* a child who is stubborn and rebellious. He rebels against society and Torah life especially. What has caused this terrible phenomenon?

The Gemara tells us that the *ben sorer u'moreh* was a glutton and drunkard. He lusted for the best meat and the finest wine (*Sanhedrin* 70a). The parents of the *ben sorer u'moreh* were to bring him to the *beis din* and say, "This son of ours ... doesn't listen to us ..." (*Devarim* 21:20). And although he has been punished, he persists in his rebellious ways and will not yield an inch. One determined to be a *ben sorer u'moreh* was sentenced to be stoned to death. Our Sages say that the *ben sorer u'moreh* was judged according to his ultimate destiny. They explain that there will come a time when stealing from his parents will not suffice. Just as nowadays drug addicts will steal and do anything — even kill — to get the drugs they crave, likewise the lust of the *ben sorer u'moreh* will lead him to robbery and worse. The Sages say, let him die relatively innocent now, before he kills, and not when he is guilty.

Yet this raises a question: Our Sages have told us that a person is judged and sentenced according to his current status, not according to what the future will bring forth. Yishmael is an example. After Avraham followed Hashem's command to drive out Hagar and her son Yishmael, Yishmael was near death from thirst. Hagar despaired but an angel called out to her, "Fear not, for G-d has heeded the cry of the youth in his present state" (*Bereishis* 21:17). According to the Midrash, the angels pleaded with G-d not to perform a miracle for Yishmael, because his offspring were destined to persecute and murder Jews. However, as Rashi explains, G-d responded that He would judge Yishmael only according to his present deeds and not according to what would happen in the future. Why, then, is the *ben sorer u'moreh* judged on the basis of his ultimate destiny?

The answer is simple and at the same time remarkable: The *ben sorer u'moreh* has reached the stage at which his behavior has become an innate part of his personality. Habit and practice can change a person, until even the worst acts become like second nature to him. A terrorist is trained to enjoy killing; he has developed a lust to kill. A person can radically change his inner life to the extent that habit turns into a part of his inner makeup.

The *ben sorer u'moreh* will not change. As much as his parents have reprimanded him and the *beis din* has reproved and rebuked him, he cannot be swayed, because his own inner life has been crippled. He can't even hear what you are saying to him. And the *ben sorer u'moreh* is, by definition, a child of 13 years old (until 13 and 3 months). If he is younger or older than that he cannot be considered a *ben sorer u'moreh* (*Sanhedrin* 69a). Imagine a child of 13 years so spiritually crippled!

I agree with the educator who said that a child constructs his picture of the world through the experience he has with his mother. According to whether the mother is loving or unloving, the child will feel that the world is loving or unloving. When he is not loved, he fails to learn to love. Such children grow up to be people who find it extremely difficult to understand the meaning of love. They enter into all human relationships in a shallow way. Show me the hardened criminal, the juvenile delinquent, psychopath, or misanthrope and in almost every case I will show you a person resorting to desperate means to attract the emotional warmth and attention he failed to get, but so much wants and needs. Aggressive behavior, when fully understood, is in fact nothing but love frustrated. It is a technique for compelling love, as well as a means for taking revenge on a society that has let the person down, leaving him disillusioned, deserted, and dehumanized. The best way to approach aggressive behavior in children is not by aggressive behavior toward them, but with love.

If you find rebels in society today, it is because they were never given proper love. Most of them don't know what love means. When a mother caresses her child, gives him hugs and kisses, and shows her affection, that love is transmitted to the child and forms his inner world. It is remarkable how a little baby feels and absorbs the tender care of his mother. The rebellious child never had his mother's love. A caring mother who feels happy with her child and whose child feels happy with her is creating an individual who will grow up to be a loving person destined for greatness. He will understand what goodness and love mean. We have today a crippled world, a rebellious world, because children are not being given proper care.

Regarding the *ben sorer u'moreh,* Rabbi Shamshon Raphael Hirsch points out that if either parent was flawed in a way that might affect his or her capacity to give the child proper care, the rebellious child might, over time, be cured (see his commentary on *Devarim* 21:18). He is only a *ben sorer u'moreh* when all the parents' facilities are in proper shape, showing that although they were able to do the maximum, they still could not change him. He is then considered an ingrate that nothing in the world will ever cure.

Contemporary society is one in which permissiveness and lack of morals prevail. And yet people are unhappy. It isn't poverty that is the cause; even those from well-to-do homes are filled with feelings of guilt, frustration, and disappointment. They have all they can wish for, but there is nothing in their lives that makes them happy. Love, graciousness, and goodness are what give a person the unequalled spiritual contentment that nothing in the world can ever replace. It isn't the physical dimension of life, the animalistic life that brings happiness. It is the spiritual life, the *neshamah* life that heals. I once said to a prominent psychiatrist, "You don't believe in the *neshamah,* but the very word *psyche* is Greek for *neshamah.* You don't understand the *neshamah,* so how can you cure the ailments of the *neshamah*?" All these mental ailments are due to the *neshamah.* I asked him, "Can you explain guilt feelings? Why should one get a guilt complex that plagues him to the point of taking drugs and worse?" The answer is that the *neshamah* yearns for something spiritual. Torah nourishes a person and gives him a certain gratification. And we in *Klal Yisrael* have that.

When Shlomo HaMelech married Pharaoh's daughter, his intentions were noble. In his estimation, the marriage would bring Egypt under Hashem's dominion and all the other nations would follow suit. Rashi in *Mishlei* says, "The night of his marriage, Pharaoh's daughter played music the whole night and he overslept." Since he was holding the keys to the *Beis HaMikdash*, no one was able to open it and people were afraid to wake the king. Our Sages tell us that his mother Batsheva reprimanded him. She said to him, "Everyone knows that your father, David HaMelech, was G-d-fearing. Now, seeing your conduct in life, people will say, 'This must be inherited from his mother Batsheva.' All the women of your father's household vowed and prayed that they should bear a son who would inherit the kingdom of David to become the future king but I vowed and said, 'May I have a son who is zealous and full of Torah knowledge'" (*Mishlei* 31:1-2, *Rashi*).

Batsheva prayed not just to have an heir to the throne, but to have a son who would be a Torah giant. "I prayed to Hashem that my son would be wise and fill his father's spiritual place," she said to him. "How in the world did you come to this?"

Shlomo HaMelech repented and admitted that she was right. He later wrote *Eishes Chayil* as a tribute to his mother Batsheva. If not for Batsheva, who knows what would have happened to him? Here you have a portrait of a mother who was responsible for her son even after he became great. This is the true Jewish *eishes chayil*, the mother who was responsible for the spiritual purity of her son, the mother who made sure that Shlomo HaMelech would remain Shlomo HaMelech.

QUESTIONS & ANSWERS

Q Does the *Rosh Yeshivah* say a parent should never hit his child?

A I can't give a blanket answer. In most cases, I always advise the constructive method as opposed to the destructive one. Hitting a child is not an effective way to punish a child. I always advise to give them prizes. When one child does something wrong, I would say to a second child, "Since you did not do that, you get a prize." I wouldn't *potch* a child who does not understand at all. Tell the child that the next time he will get a prize when he does not do the bad thing. A child emulates his father and mother, and punishing them only teaches them to be rough. Also, children get used to spanking and they don't listen. The positive way is much better. Give them a prize here and there.

There are other ways to get children to do things rather than spanking. You have to be careful with the hitting. You might cause a fear in the child that could be lasting or damaging for life. A better way of educating is to buy the child something nice. After 10 or 20 stars, for example, get him something he wants very much — something valuable. This accomplishes better results.

Q **May a parent rebuke a child in the presence of other members of the household if this causes the child embarrassment?**

A No, of course not. To cause embarrassment to a child is forbidden, since a child is very sensitive. Even one incident like this can cause lasting damage. Your emotional attitude to your child is much more important than your physical attitude.

Q **My children act so immature. Is that normal?**

A We expect too much of our children. Many of us have gone through hardships in life and we expect our children to act older than their age. Let them enjoy life and play around. Don't take the child's behavior too seriously and expect him to be what you are today. I myself was a somewhat mischievous boy. It does not reflect a fault in the child's character. As children grow up, they mature and settle down.

Q **If my child misbehaves, I hit him very hard and I get him under control. What's wrong with this?**

A You might get him under control but you could pay a very high price for this later.

Q **The *Rosh Yeshivah* said not to give children lollipops because sweets are not good. We stopped yelling at the children because "yelling is worse than hitting," and we stopped hitting them because the *Rosh Yeshivah* said not to hit. We give them lots of little prizes — where is the end?**

A Don't give them little prizes, for they will lose their value. Give them a big prize after 25 stars or so. If one child does not want to listen for a star, give the other child a star and he will see that after 10 or 20 or 25 stars the other child received a prize and he will also listen. But for very young children you do need to have some small prizes on hand because they don't have patience to wait for one big prize.

Q **Should the father also use the same reward system?**

A Definitely.

Q **The *Rosh Yeshivah* once said that he doesn't believe in spanking. Does this mean at all times?**

A Sometimes there is an emergency situation when you do have to hit a child. If a child does do something bad and you cannot reason with him at all and you can't overlook it, you should turn him around and give him a spank. Never hit him in the face, though, for you can develop a fear in the child that can be very costly. Hitting in the face can cause certain complexes that cause mental ailments. If you do it sensibly, a little spank without any fear is not so bad. But if you make a big fuss, it can create a fear. If you do have to give the child a spank in the buttocks, he should not see your face. You must be sure that you are not angry because you are not allowed to hit a child in anger. You must also be certain not to have an angry look on your face, in case the child does see your face, or an angry tone of voice, even if you are just making believe and are not really angry, because this could cause fears in the child. Likewise, yelling in a scary, fearsome voice can also cause fears.

Q **At what age should a parent insist that a child make *berachos*? Should I punish him if he doesn't?**

A You usually teach a child at the age of 3 to make a *berachah*; the *chiyuv*, the obligation, begins at 5 to 6 years. But don't push them. During these formative years, it is important for the children to develop physically and mentally into sound, healthy individuals. Let them live and enjoy their youth. If you pressure a child at the age of 5 or 6 he will become a mental wreck. Give the child a present when he does something good rather than slapping him and making him fearful of you. Many a time a mother is tired and lashes out at the child when he does something wrong, but it is wrong of us to do that.

What should you do with a 2-year-old child who starts to hit his mother?
Give him a kiss! He'll stop hitting her!

What if the child hits a younger baby?
This is a common question. This shows that the child is jealous. Shower him with as much love as you can. He doesn't understand that the reason the younger one gets more attention is because he needs it. He thinks you love the younger one and not him. Don't be alarmed — we were ourselves children and misbehaved and turned out to be *mentchen.* Have a little patience — we want our children to be like we are today, but that takes years! But of course protect the baby.

Should you hit a child for a lie?
You have to give him *chinuch* — I'm not saying to close your eyes and ignore it — but you have to be careful with the hitting. You might cause a fear in the child that could be lasting or damaging for life. I would rather not give them a smack and *b'ezras Hashem* when they get older they will be taught. *Chazal* say that these types of things have to be done in a wise way. A constructive manner is better for you and the child; if you lose control of yourself it is bad for both of you.

What are we supposed to do on Rosh Hashanah? Of course, as we see in the *Machzor*, we pray and beseech Hashem for all the good things we want in life: health, *nachas*, and a good income. But what does Hashem ask of *us*? Obviously, that we should do *teshuvah*, repent. The question is, in what way?

Every day in the *Shemoneh Esrei* we ask Hashem to help us repent: "Return us, our Father, to Your Torah, and bring us closer, our King, to Your service, and help us return in *perfect repentance* before You." Simply understood, this means that we want to come closer to Torah; we want to pray with a little more intensity and passion; and we want to come closer to Hashem.

We know that repentance is made up of three basic elements. The first is forgoing the sin, and the second is regret. We must feel sorry for any transgression we've committed, either against our fellowman or between us and Hashem. The third part of *teshuvah* is that we resolve to be more careful in the future, so as not to repeat the transgression. Without regret and a decision not to repeat the act again, there is no repentance.

What, though, is meant by *perfect* repentance?

R' Chaim of Volozhin explains that there are two ways to repent: out of fear of retribution, or out of love (*Nefesh HaChaim* 4:31). Repentance that stems from love of Hashem, he says, is what is meant by "perfect" repentance. This should be the fundamental reason motivating us to repent (and motivating us in many other ways, as well).

The story is told that Rav Yisrael Salanter, father of the *mussar* movement, once stuck his finger into a flame and then exclaimed, "This is only one-sixtieth of the fire of *Gehinnom*!" — just to sense what the fire of *Gehinnom* is like, to feel a measure of repentance done out of fear. Yet while there *are* penalties for transgressions, Hashem does not want us to do mitzvos simply to avoid punishment. He wants us to repent out of love. He wants us to do mitzvos not out of coercion, but motivated by love, just as we fulfill the wish of a friend — not because we have to, not because we will be punished for not doing so, but because we love to!

How can we accomplish this perfect, true repentance motivated by love? R' Chaim of Volozhin answers: only by occupying ourselves with Torah. Without Torah, we will not be able to repent out of love because we will not understand what Hashem wants. Only when we study Torah and understand its meaning deeply will we be able to do His mitzvos because we *love* to, not because we *have* to.

Hashem loves us. He gave the holy Torah, which is a unique and special gift, to *us*, His beloved children. And deep within us, we have the consciousness of this love. Say, for example, that a person has a son who went off the path, and this parent can't tolerate him now. At the same time, he has a wonderful student whom he loves as he loves himself. If a fire were to break out in the middle of the night, whom would he dash to save first — the student or his son?

The son! Why? After all, he hates his son, he can't even look at him, and he loves his student.

The answer is that *emotionally* — before he gets to the rational and reasoning part of himself — emotionally, it is his son who is his flesh and blood, his son to whom he feels closer.

In the same way, when a child loves his parent, he will fulfill the wish of his mother or father not because he *has* to, but because he would feel pain for his mother or father if, *chas v'shalom*, he didn't behave properly. These are emotions, not rational thoughts.

When we repent out of love, we feel as close to Hashem as children feel to a father. We say, "our Father, our King" — yes, Hashem is the King, but He is also our Father, our heavenly Father, Who feels for His children. Likewise, we should feel that we are His children, and this feeling is obtained through the medium of Torah. The Holy One, Blessed be He, the Torah, and Israel are one inseparable entity. A person who studies the holy Torah becomes closer to Hashem and feels toward Hashem as a child would feel to his parent, and he won't do anything to hurt that parent. Therefore, says R' Chaim of Volozhin, repentance out of love can only be obtained through the medium of Torah.

How, though, can a woman involve herself with Torah? Of course, supporting Torah and living a life of Torah is the basic way. Yet there is another aspect, an additional way a woman can connect to Torah.

After the Midianites committed a criminal act against the Jewish people that caused the death of 24,000 Jews, Hashem told Moshe Rabbeinu, "Execute the vengeance of *Klal Yisrael* on the Midianites, and afterward you shall be gathered unto your people" (*Bamidbar* 31:2). Hashem commanded Moshe to take vengeance against Midian. It was a great mitzvah, after which Moshe would die. Our Sages tell us that Moshe could have delayed the revenge against Midian, thus delaying his own death, yet he was so quick to fulfill Hashem's Will that he gave up many years of his life to do so. Moshe immediately said to the people, "Arm from among your men for the army" (ibid., 31:3).

Now, Moshe was considered a king to the Jewish people, and, as the Rambam points out, the king as the commander-in-chief should be the one to lead the army to execute vengeance (*Hilchos Melachim* 4:10). Yet Moshe tells *the people* to execute vengeance. The *Midrash Tanchuma* asks a question: If Moshe was obligated to do it himself, why did he send others instead?

The answer given is that Moshe was raised by Pharaoh in Egypt and then fled to Midian. Because he once lived in Midian, he reasoned that it was unjust for him to take vengeance on Midian and cause trouble to the place where he lived for many years.

Hashem had told Moshe to do it himself — *you* select an army. But Moshe answered: I cannot raise my arms against the place where I was a guest; it would be ungrateful. Raising and leading the army is the obligation of the king, and Moshe should have done it, but he was a grateful person, and thus he was exempt. Herein lies an astonishing revelation: It seems that Hashem's command was on one side and Moshe's emotions were on the other. How could Moshe decide which should take precedence?

In *Bircas HaMazon* we ask for "*sechel tov,*" good understanding. Why single out "good understanding"? The answer is that there are certain situations where proper understanding is dependent on knowing outside factors. For instance, in this incident, Moshe realized that the Torah did not specifically command "you and *only* you." It depended on the individual circumstances. If you, Moshe, feel you cannot wage war, Hashem was saying, you don't have to.

The Torah is the source of everything. But, as we see here, only a *good understanding* of the Torah can bring us to a correct decision. This is why halachic questions cannot be answered by just anyone. They must be brought to a halachic authority, for his understanding of the depth and scope of the Torah might produce a different answer than what one might think.

Without Torah, we have nothing. Torah is always first and foremost and all solutions come through it. But in order to understand Torah, one needs to consult a *gadol b'Torah* — not just on matters of *kashrus*, but on questions of "Where should I go?" or even, "Should I go?" And although emotions sometimes should be taken into consideration, they can often override reason and people may end up doing what they *want*, instead of what they *should*. Questions need individualized answers — one can't rely on someone else's *psak*. Without knowing the background, the people, and the issues involved, a *psak* can be misinterpreted. Only a *gadol* can give an answer that is according to the Torah, and not just what rationalizing might tell a person to do.

This then is a further way that a woman can involve herself with Torah: by making her home one in which questions are brought to a *gadol* so that decisions are made according to Torah. Once Hashem's Will is known, she can then fill it wholeheartedly and so draw close to Him in perfect repentance, through love. We are Hashem's beloved and He is ours and, as we become one with Him through Torah and do what He wishes us to do, He will reciprocate and make our wishes His.

Moshe Rabbeinu's "good understanding" of the Torah brought him to refrain, out of gratitude toward them, from personally executing vengeance against the Midianites. Often, the basic cause of *shalom bayis* problems is lack of gratitude. People complain about their spouses, but often overlook all the gratitude and indebtedness they should feel for the good things their spouses do for them. Gratitude goes a long, long way in solving many *shalom bayis* problems. Of course, there are always two sides. People have different mentalities, they come from different homes and different backgrounds. Yet, as one *gadol* wisely noted, two right shoes don't make a pair — you need a right *and* a left. The man and the woman *together* make a team. (I always tell husbands that it pays to listen to what their wife has to say because she may be right. That I have a yeshivah today is only because of my wife.)

Gratitude begins with honoring one's father and mother. Who doesn't understand the importance of honoring parents? Yet we don't really understand. It is a fact that we often overlook what our parents have done for us. We take it for granted. We do not understand how grateful we should be — until we ourselves have children.

Some people say, "We know that people want to have children. They yearn and pray for children, even if only to have that wonderful feeling of having a child. If their motivation is selfish, why then are we required to honor them?" Yes, they may have had ulterior motives, they may have had selfish reasons, but that doesn't override the fact that in the end, we are here today, *baruch Hashem*, thanks to them.

If you are a parent, be grateful to Hashem that He gave you a child! Of course, raising children is not always easy. I often tell parents that there is nothing abnormal if a child sometimes breaks a dish or is a little wild. That is normal behavior. Many parents want the child to be an adult. They take it for granted that this is the way it should be. But we need to remember that we ourselves were once children. We too were mischievous. So be grateful to Hashem that

He gave you a child. Don't complain to Hashem, saying, "Why in the world did I have such a child?" Remember to be grateful.

Gratitude is a tremendous virtue that can overcome many problems in your life. Many people nowadays find it hard to earn a living. Every day people tell me that although they have been trying for years, they have not been able to establish themselves. "Why in the world am I being punished?" they ask. They have complaints against Hashem. But they fail to have gratitude to Hashem for what they *do* have.

Money comes and goes; it doesn't stay in one place. And wealth doesn't necessarily mean happiness. Be thankful to Hashem for whatever you have. Be grateful to Hashem for opening your eyes. What a wonderful feeling! Be grateful to Hashem that you are here, be thankful for what you have, and pray for more. When said with a feeling of gratitude, your prayers will be different.

Remember, on Rosh Hashanah when we say, "our Father, our King," it is not "King" alone. It is to our Father in Heaven that we pray — and not just because we have to. We should feel that He worries about us more than we worry about ourselves.

We say in *Hallel*, "Please, Hashem, bring us success now." We want success in life, but why don't the prayers stipulate in *what*? There are so many areas in which we can ask for success: livelihood, *nachas*, children, health — why doesn't the *siddur* specify?

The answer is that we really don't know what success is. We tend to think that if we were rich we would be happy. Not necessarily! Hashem knows better than we do.

We should always be grateful to Hashem for what we have, for it could be our real success. For instance, a person who is poor will pray with much more heartfelt intensity than someone who is rich, so his poverty is the biggest benefit he could have. There was a family who, when they lived downtown near us, were observant Jews. Over time they became rich, tried to keep up with the Joneses, moved up to Fifth Avenue ... and completely left *Yiddishkeit*! So wealth is not necessarily a virtue.

Is poverty a big handicap in one's life? Not necessarily. Hashem will provide for you somehow. You will have your basic needs met, even if with difficulty. But imagine your prayers! They will be an outpouring of the soul. True, we have fulfilled our obligation to pray even if we only mouth the words. But when you need something badly, your prayers become a supplication to Hashem. So poverty is often not a disadvantage, but a means to achieving a higher level.

Gratitude is a foundation of Judaism, and the most important basis of peace between neighbors and between husband and wife.

Only Hashem knows what is in store for us, so remember to learn to be grateful to Him. Whatever we have is the best for us. It might not be what we think is the best, but we don't know what is best for us. If we were a little richer, perhaps we would become spoiled. We might not pray as profoundly as we should because we wouldn't feel the need as badly. Gratitude is the basis for everything.

QUESTIONS & ANSWERS

Q Do women have to hear all 100 sounds of the *shofar*?

A No, just 30.

Q What parts of the *davening* should a woman busy with a young child say on Rosh Hashanah?

A The main part would be just as on a weekday. You just substitute the *Shemoneh Esrei* of Rosh Hashanah for the weekday *Shemoneh Esrei*. If you *daven Pesukei D'Zimrah*, or if you don't, follow the same pattern. You don't have to say the *piyutim*, just the *Shemoneh Esrei* of Rosh Hashanah.

Q Must a woman with small children go to shul with the children for the *tekiyas shofar* before Mussaf and stay in shul with her children for the entire *davening* or should she stay home?

A Take care of the children first. The whole matter of *tekiyas shofar* is not really imperative for women. It's only a *minhag* that became an obligation because the women took it on themselves. A woman is not obligated to hear *tekiyas shofar*, which is a time-related mitzvah, since women are not obligated to fulfill time-related mitzvos. Since it's customary, it is similar to an obligation nowadays, but it's not as important for a woman as it is for a man. Do not neglect child care because of hearing *shofar*. If your child is well-behaved and you can take him to shul and *daven* and hear the *tekiyos*, wonderful. But if a child doesn't behave properly, makes noise, and disturbs the peace of the shul, do not take the child to shul. Stay home, and you'll hear the *tekiyos* later. All communities arrange for mothers who cannot hear *tekiyas shofar* during the day to hear them later.

Q **Does one have to be inside the shul or can you hear the *tekiyos* from outside?**

A One can listen from outside.

Q **Is it important to eat meat on Rosh Hashanah?**

A Yes. It's a mitzvah to eat meat, because it's a Yom Tov.

Q **We know we are supposed to think about Hashem and be close to Him. Does this mean that when I have a problem I can, after speaking it over with Hashem in prayer, trust my own judgment about the answer I feel I'm getting? Or is it only through the Sages that we can get any answers?**

A Prayer is supplication. We pray and beseech. But the purpose of the prophet was for us to consult him for advice. The Vilna Gaon says that today the *gedolim* are the ones we should consult because they know the *daas Torah*. When Rivkah Imeinu felt the battle of two children within her, she went to the study hall of Shem. Can we presume to be more knowing and intuitive than Rivkah Imeinu? If she went to seek guidance, why shouldn't we?

The Gemara tells us that one who partakes of a festive meal the day before Yom Kippur is rewarded as if he has fasted for two days (*Berachos* 8b). Why is this so?

One of the most significant accomplishments a person can achieve in his lifetime is atonement for all his sins. I heard from the *mashgiach* R' Yerucham of Mir, *zt"l*, one of the great *mussar* masters, that the last of the 15 times we say "*dayeinu*" in the Passover Hagaddah is for the building of the *Beis HaMikdash* to atone for all our sins, to teach us that atonement is the greatest gift Hashem has given us. The Ramban writes in *Shaar HaGemul* that even all the tribulations that Job suffered here on earth would, had he suffered them in *Gehinnom,* not have been enough to atone for even the smallest transgression of one person. So it is the utmost privilege to have a Day of Atonement when one can rid oneself of the contamination of one's sins and transgressions. There can be no greater joy in a person's life than the knowledge that his sins have been forgiven. And the outward sign of this great joy is the festive meal we make on erev Yom Kippur, when we show our great elation that the day of our atonement has arrived. When a person is able to show such elation at the arrival of the day of his atonement, he is rewarded as if he has fasted for two days.

We all know the importance of Yom Kippur. When our Sages say that it is the most important of the Festivals, they are telling us that it is greater than Shavuos, when we received the Torah, greater than Pesach, the basis of our faith, and greater than the joy of Succos, which is called in the *siddur,* "*zman simchaseinu,* the time of our happiness."

A person who does not understand the mechanics of *teshuvah,* repentance, might say that one would become gloomy and guilt-ridden if he dwells on all the sins he committed the previous year. But this is not so.

The Gemara tells us that *teshuvah* is among the seven things created before the creation of the world (*Pesachim* 54a). Hashem wanted to create the world through the Attribute of Justice but He saw that such a world would not survive. A world created solely through justice would be a world in which people received immediate punishment for transgressions. A world created through the Attribute of Mercy, as is our world, is just the opposite. Punishment is not meted out immediately, with the full force of the law, but is delayed and applied with mercy.

We might assume that *teshuvah* is a dimension of mercy, but it is not. It is a separate entity, a gift to cleanse us from transgression.

When a person disobeys Hashem's Will, impurity is imprinted upon his soul. Hashem, likened to a *mikveh,* which cleanses impurity, cleanses the person's soul, washing away the flaw caused by his transgression. This is a concept we can readily understand. But what if through the sin someone was killed or a *mamzer* was born? In such instances, the sin has concrete results. How is rectification accomplished?

This is a difficult concept that can be understood more easily through an analogy: If a person wishes to be released from a vow, he must go to a Torah scholar and have it absolved. On what basis is the vow absolved? The person is asked: "Did you realize what you were doing when you made the vow?" If the answer is no, then the person is asked, "Do you now wholeheartedly regret having made this vow?" If the answer to this question is yes, then we assume the person's faculties were not working when he made the vow. He somehow slipped into it hastily, without thinking. He was perhaps a little angry, a little disturbed, and so he made a vow he would never have made otherwise.

The scholar, in asking the person if he had full cognizance of what he was doing when he made the vow and whether he now fully regrets it, in effect allows the person to uproot the will behind the vow. Similarly, rooting out the will behind transgressions is considered to be rooting out the essence of the act itself. Although the fact is that a person was killed, the perpetrator of the deed, by realizing that he did something wrong and by wishing wholeheartedly that he had never done the bad deed, feels pain in his heart and avoids doing the sin again. This roots out the will that prompted the act, and removes his sin entirely.

The Attribute of Mercy is not sufficient to accomplish this. Mercy can come into play for forgiveness of a sinful act, but not for forgiveness of an accomplished fact. This can only be eradicated by *teshuvah*, and this is the essence of *teshuvah*. *Teshuvah* is the rooting out of the will of the action so that it is as if it were not done at all. Then there is no sin at all and the person need not feel guilty.

It is a big job to do *teshuvah* properly. The laws and details of *teshuvah* are substantial and Rabbeinu Yonah wrote a whole *sefer* on this subject. Special *sefarim* have been published listing all the sins one can think of. All of us go over the *Al Chet*, and in some form we have committed almost all of the sins mentioned. Usually, as we go through the *Al Chet* on Yom Kippur, we do regret having transgressed certain sins and not having fulfilled Hashem's Will by doing the mitzvos we were supposed to. And we take it upon ourselves to do better in the coming year.

Basically, as our *Rishonim* have told us, after we distance ourselves from the transgression, there remain two further conditions for *teshuvah*: *charatah* and *kabbalah*. *Charatah* is regretting what you have done; *kabbalah* is taking it upon yourself not to do it again. *Teshuvah*, though, works efficiently only if there is sincere regret. If a person does not completely regret what he did, he does not merit *teshuvah*. He should say to himself, "I didn't want to do it. Some inner force prompted me to do it. My will was not in it," for if there was no will behind this action, then there is no punishment — and there should be no guilt feelings.

But *teshuvah* must be done wholeheartedly. One should not fool oneself. It is a remarkable comment on human nature that in the *Shemoneh Esrei* of Maariv immediately following Ne'ilah we say, "Forgive us for we have sinned." If all sins were forgiven on Yom Kippur, when was there time to sin?

Under the pressure of the last chance for forgiveness at Ne'ilah, a person is intent upon *teshuvah* and no thought of sin enters his mind. But the minute the pressure is off, unwanted thoughts may come to him.

The great *mussar* masters kept a notebook in which they recorded their deeds so that they could scrutinize and analyze all of their actions daily. They mentally reviewed their speech and thoughts, for they were determined to correct any actions that seemed to trigger sin. The purpose of this scrutiny was not to cause excessive introspection and brooding, but to enable them to do better in the future.

We should always strive to correct negative traits. If a person has a bad temper, there are positive things he can do to correct himself. He can promise to pay $10 every time he has a temper tantrum. He can even raise it to $25 — that will make him think twice before he gets angry! The serious person will find constructive ways to improve — ways that will not lead to depression.

No one is infallible. "There is no righteous man who does only good and never sins" (*Koheles* 7:20). *Teshuvah* was created for the righteous as well as for the wicked. It is a helping hand stretched out to guide a person to mend his ways. Don't feel guilty! Feel happy to have the opportunity to do *teshuvah*. We eat a special festive meal the day before Yom Kippur because we have merited reaching the Day of Atonement, when we can be granted a clean slate. It is an opportunity to cleanse ourselves of all the sins that have tainted our souls in the past year, and we can start anew.

It may surprise some people to hear that happiness forms the basis for *teshuvah*. A happy person will not sin as much as one who is unhappy. A person who is depressed will commit sins he otherwise wouldn't. A person who is happy will be more efficient in his work, for as we all know, a worker who is depressed will not do as good a job. This holds true for every aspect of life. The happy person will accomplish and achieve his goals much more efficiently than one who is unhappy.

If a woman is happy, it will be much easier for her to fulfill her purpose in life. If she's not happy, it will be that much harder for her. What gives a woman happiness?

What will make the woman who is intelligent, well-versed in Torah, and wants to do Hashem's Will happy?

Each of us has his or her goal in life. And one who accomplishes his goal feels happy, for he has done what he was supposed to do. When a woman feels she is accomplishing her purpose in life, it makes it that much easier for her to carry on with her tasks. But what is this purpose? What should be the top priority for her to accomplish so that she will feel that she has fulfilled her purpose in life?

Shlomo HaMelech says: "Women's wisdom builds her home" (*Mishlei* 14:1). The Vilna Gaon notes that the verse begins in the plural, *women's*, but continues with the singular, *her*. This alludes to the fact that not every woman understands that her goal in life is to build *her home*. Which home? Her permanent home in the next world.

Many people build homes but they are only temporary, not everlasting. For instance, people who marry for financial considerations or because of superficial attraction do not build homes that are everlasting. As we know, love is blind. They may be happy for a year or two, but then the illusion wears off. Their love was a love dependent on outside factors, and when those factors vanish, the love vanishes as well. But if a home is built on spiritual values, it will be everlasting because spirituality never vanishes. As the Gaon says, this is a very basic foundation of building a home — not materialism or enjoyment. A foolish woman, who is only out for enjoyment, will not build an everlasting home.

Since it is a woman's goal to build her home spiritually, she must know what her goals are. Some women don't like housekeeping — they prefer to read or go to a lecture. They get a certain satisfaction, a spiritual lift. And if they don't get that satisfaction, they somehow feel that they're missing something in life, and some of them might even complain that they're not fulfilling their purpose in life. While activities outside the home may give her some fulfillment, a woman may fail to appreciate the importance of her real goal: creating an environment conducive to the development of a warm family life. A mother of young children should realize that when the children are a little older and can take care of themselves, she will have enough time to do whatever reading she wants. Right now, she has a job to do, one that is filled with much spirituality, even though it involves the physical.

A woman should not think that being a homemaker is just preparing meals, washing the floors, and keeping the house clean, although this is a basic part of the job. The Gemara says there are three things that expand a person's mind (*Berachos* 57b). One of them is a pleasant home. This means pleasant in all ways, materially, emotionally, and spiritually. What does "expand" mean? When a man has a home that is not clean, he can't even think! His mind becomes limited. If he comes from a nice home, where everything is taken care of, he feels so much at ease his mind expands. Now that is spirituality. The husband will accomplish so much more if he's happy when he goes out in the morning and if he finds a warm atmosphere when he returns home. It gives him *menuchas hanefesh*, peace of mind, to come home and find the children taken care of and a meal prepared. All of these together build a wonderful feeling — and it is the woman who can create such a home that expands the mind.

A woman's ability to build a home isn't something secondary. It is an intrinsic capacity ingrained in her by Hashem. If she fulfills her purpose, it will bring out the beauty in life. If she doesn't, she will perceive herself to be a failure. She might succeed in other areas, but that won't make her happy, because she won't feel the great satisfaction that comes with fulfilling her purpose in life. For true satisfaction, she must use not only her emotions and intellect in creating a home, but all her capacities. She will then create a home that allows for the growth of all of its members. This is not a matter of drudgery but one of spirituality!

The *Eishes Chayil* sung on Friday nights begins, "*Eishes chayil*, who can find [her]?" (*Mishlei* 31:10). The Ramban explains that by definition the word *chayil* means being diligent and knowing how to run the home (ibid., 18:28). This might sound shocking to you. This is an *eishes chayil*? It is true that an *eishes chayil* is a *tzadekes*, a pious, righteous woman of good deeds. But the *eishes chayil* is also the woman who is diligent in homemaking. Far from degrading the woman, this points to a woman's greatest accomplishment, one that uses all her powers. If she fulfills her purpose and builds a home, this is spiritual.

And it all begins with *chesed*. You can't learn Torah or be an *eved Hashem* without *chesed*. For instance, the obligation to pray to Hashem must be done with your whole heart. If one has ulterior motives for praying to Hashem, that is not the ideal level of *tefillah*. *Tefillah* has to be only for *kavod Hashem*. I beseech Hashem because He is the only One Who can give me anything. Strengthening your trust in Hashem is the purpose of prayer. So if you *daven* just to get something for your own egotistical purposes, that's not the purpose of prayer. You have to give your whole heart to Hashem to fulfill your obligation of prayer. And doing so is *chesed*.

Similarly, to study the Torah wholeheartedly, seeking the truth, requires so much energy. One can study superficially, but that is not what Torah is supposed to be. Studying Torah has to be done with total devotion. One's whole mind and heart have to be put into the study to see the truth of the Torah. And that too is *chesed*.

Many times a woman will cry, "I can't take it anymore! I

can't stand it!" She often feels physically fatigued and mentally exhausted. How different she would feel if she recognized that she was achieving her goal! This will automatically enable her to do mitzvos with a better spirit. Women sometimes feel that they have no strength to *daven*. It's all mental exhaustion, which has a negative effect on the body. But if they worked in a better frame of mind, they wouldn't be so tired.

Let the joy of knowing that you are a wonderful woman doing an important job be the foundation of the *simchah* that will enable you to do true *teshuvah*. In doing so, you will have much more confidence in yourself. You will feel happier seeing that things are going smoothly. And your family will also be happy.

If you resolve to make *simchah* your basis for *teshuvah*, next Yom Kippur you'll look back and see that you had a much better year. I am confident of this — everything will go smoothly. Your husband will be happy, your children will be happy, and your own life will give you fulfillment.

So we approach the erev Yom Kippur feast with great happiness. We review our past actions, not morbidly, but with a positive feeling that we can mend our ways. The motivated person can learn to improve his spiritual standing.

Let us be happy that we are fortunate to have a Day of Atonement, and look forward to the year following this unique day as a year of forgiveness and compassion.

QUESTIONS & ANSWERS

Q What should I do if I am trying very hard to be careful about *lashon hara* and someone comes to my house and insists on speaking *lashon hara*?

A You should say nicely, "My dear friend, you are not supposed to be saying this, it's *lashon hara*." If the person continues, go out of the room. If you can't leave the room, then follow the advice of the Gemara that says that Hashem gave us index fingers so that we could use them to close our ears when necessary.

Q If someone is pouring out her heart to me in pain, do I also have to insist that she not speak *lashon hara*?

A The Chofetz Chaim asked that question and said that in general it is forbidden and that you should not listen — not at the expense of hurting another person. Tell the friend not to say the name of the other person. But there are exceptions. If someone is troubled and the listener's intent is to ease the speaker's pain so that the matter can be straightened out or dropped, then sometimes it is a mitzvah, maybe even an obligation, to hear the story, even if you have to hear the name. When the intention of the speaker is to speak *lashon hara*, then you are not allowed to listen.

Q **If you tell yourself that you're not accepting what you're hearing as *lashon hara*, is it okay?**

A You still shouldn't listen.

Q **Is it *lashon hara* if I am trying to bring someone closer to Yiddishkeit and I have to talk it over with someone else?**

A Must you mention the person's name? If it is for a purpose, you can talk about him without mentioning his name. But if it's necessary to mention the name, then you can.

Q **Sometimes we read about a Jewish person in a high government position who has done something terrible. What should our attitude be toward such a person?**

A I wouldn't speak about this fellow at all. Why not speak about the Chofetz Chaim? Remember, we can never tell what this individual might turn out to be a few years from now. Speaking about evil is an *issur* in itself, says the Chofetz Chaim, even without *lashon hara*. We should speak about good things and then we will become good as well. If we speak about mean things, we automatically are mean.

Q **Does a woman have less of an obligation than a man does to improve her *middos*?**

A No. A woman definitely has to control her anger, but there are certain complications when you haven't slept the night before and your nerves are on edge. But generally, of course, a woman is obligated to improve her *middos* just like a man.

Q On fast days I am usually weak, and stay in bed all day. I feel I am setting a bad example for my children. Would it be better for me to fast or not?

A Who says staying in bed is a bad example?

Q Do I have to fast if I recently had hepatitis?

A This depends on which fast day it is, and also on your condition. Ask your doctor and consult with a halachic authority. You may need to eat small amounts at certain intervals.

Q What should a woman in her first three months of pregnancy do on Yom Kippur?

A When there are any doubts, a rav and/or doctor should be consulted before the fast. Sometimes it is advisable that a pregnant woman should remain in bed the whole day. You can *daven* in bed — there is no need for you to go to shul or stand up — and you needn't feel bad about this. Your husband should remain home to take care of you and the children, and this is a big mitzvah for him, so you needn't feel guilty. Sometimes it is necessary to eat and drink less than a *shiur*. In that case, you should eat and drink healthy and energy-giving foods. Sometimes it is even necessary to eat regularly for part of the day or even for the whole day.

Q I read that during the Ten Days of Repentance one should try to be more stringent with his actions. But sometimes this is very hard, and after Yom Kippur, we usually drop whatever we have taken upon ourselves. This sounds hypocritical!

A Let me explain this to you. It is not hypocritical because you are doing something special, out of the routine, to become closer to Hashem. Doing *teshuvah* means going out of your way to do His

Will. You have to do this by special actions during the Ten Days of Repentance. When you do something you ordinarily don't do, that in itself brings you closer to Hashem, and the effect remains with you after the Ten Days of Repentance as well.

Q **Does a child who is allowed to eat on Yom Kippur have to make Kiddush?**

A No. There's a *machlokes*, a dispute about it, but we don't make Kiddush.

Q **On Yom Kippur, if you feel that you can *daven* much better sitting down and everyone else is standing while the *Aron Kodesh* is open, can you sit?**

A It is a *minhag*, custom, to stand while the *Aron Kodesh* is open, but if you have a good reason to do so, you may sit.

Q **To keep my children happy in shul, I usually pack a bag of sweet treats. But what should I do on Yom Kippur?**

A Why can't you do the same thing? If you can keep them quiet with a cookie, wonderful!

Q **In what way is the washing of children limited on Yom Kippur?**

A Where it is a matter of washing dirt, you are allowed to wash. However, for *negel vasser* or other purposes, wash only up to the knuckles. One may not wash for pleasure.

Q **If someone refuses to speak to you, how can you ask for *mechilah*, forgiveness?**

A You should use a third person, preferably a friend of that person, as an intermediary. You are obligated to try three times.

Q **If someone dies within that year how can we ask *mechilah*?**

A You must go to the *kever*, gravesite, with a *minyan* to ask *mechilah*.

Q **Should one ask for *mechilah* from *ketanim*, children?**

A I would. But do it in such a way that the child does not lose respect for the parent.

Q **How should one approach the laws of *teshuvah* — especially the part about not doing the transgression again — when we know that in the end we will probably end up doing it?**

A The Rambam says that if a person does *teshuvah* honestly, then Hashem will help him. He must be serious. But *teshuvah* does not end on Yom Kippur. The *mussar* masters say that it is a good idea to make *kabbalos*, resolutions. For instance, if one does *teshuvah* for speaking *lashon hara*, then after Yom Kippur he should resolve that each time he catches himself speaking *lashon hara* he will pay a fine. He should continue to remind himself of this *teshuvah* throughout the year. During *Shema Koleinu* is a good time. This usually works effectively.

Q **If one knows that he cannot possibly learn all the halachos dealing with *teshuvah*, how can he do proper *teshuvah*?**

A The answer is simple. It says in *Avos*: "All those whose deeds are greater than their wisdom, their wisdom is sustained." If a person says to himself, "I don't know much but whatever I learn I will keep, whatever I learn I will perform wholeheartedly," then this person is given a reward even for things he has not yet learned. The main thing — even beyond one's knowledge — is the wholehearted desire to perform.

Q Could you please tell us which transgressions on the part of a parent can cause illness in his child? If a child becomes seriously ill, about what should a parent do *teshuvah*?

A A parent should not think in these terms. He should do *teshuvah* but he should not go about blaming himself for his child's illness. It could cause terrible guilt feelings and emotional upset.

But I will tell you that one should be very careful about making a *neder*, vow. Always say *bli neder*, and if you say that you are going to do something, then you should be careful to do it.

Q If someone wants to do *teshuvah* and he wants it to be a complete *teshuvah*, how far back does one have to go?

A As far back as a person remembers his sins.

Q How can you do *teshuvah* on anger? Can you ever do complete *teshuvah*?

A The most difficult *teshuvah* is on *middos*. The *sefer Erech Apayim* is helpful in overcoming anger. There are certain situations that trigger anger. If you were to learn not to take things to heart, you would overcome anger. Something pushes a person and he feels he can't stand it. I say, take it easy, relax. As Shlomo HaMelech says, the words of the wise are listened to when they are spoken *b'nachas*, in a peaceful manner. I know you are talking intelligently when you talk to me in a calm manner. I know that your mind is functioning then. But when you come at me in anger, it's just your emotions at work. You'll always be wrong when you're angry. You'll never accomplish your mission. Later you'll regret what you said when you were in a state of anger. Make a habit of repeating, "*Divrei* *chachamim b'nachas nishmaim*, The words of the wise are heeded when they are said in a peaceful manner" (*Koheles* 9:17), a few times every day. Just as you say *Modeh Ani* every day, repeat this five times a day, every day, in a low tone. You'll see a change in yourself. You'll never come to a person in anger. You'll feel wonderful, and you'll see how well you will accomplish your missions.

13 BRINGING LIGHT INTO OUR LIVES

Many miracles happened on Chanukah: The strong were vanquished by the weak and the many by the few. But the most important miracle of Chanukah, our Sages tell us, was that of the jar of olive oil. All of the jars of oil had been made ritually impure. When the Chashmona'im defeated the enemy, they found only one jar with the seal of the Kohen Gadol on it showing that it had not been defiled. Although there was just enough oil in this jar to last for one day, it burned for eight days. This is the miracle that we celebrate every Chanukah, adding a candle each day until we reach eight.

To us, this does not seem to be a bigger miracle than the others, yet our Sages had a deeper understanding of what is really important. By looking at the life of Yaakov Avinu, we can gain more of an understanding of the Chanukah miracle and how it should affect our own lives.

Of the three patriarchs who built *Klal Yisrael* — Avraham, Yitzchak, and Yaakov — the one who had the most difficult life was Yaakov. Avraham had wealth and prestige and was acknowledged by all. Yitzchak also had all that one could hope for. Why did Yaakov, who our Sages tell us was the choicest of the *Avos*, have the most difficult life.

Another important question concerning Yaakov Avinu is why he waited so long to get married. The Midrash tells us that Yaakov was 84 when he married, whereas Esav was 40 (*Bereishis Rabbah* 68:5). I do not have to tell you the importance of getting married. As we say, "at 18, to the *chuppah*," meaning that this is the right time, when one is able to shoulder the responsibility. If so, why did Yaakov Avinu postpone marriage until he was 84?

The above Midrash tells us that Hashem will sometimes delay the marriage of *tzaddikim*. The commentaries explain that Yaakov Avinu could not have reached the level required of him by Hashem while suffering the stresses and strains of raising children. Hashem pushed off this stage of life for Yaakov so that it would not interfere with his spiritual growth (ibid.).

We might think it better for Yaakov to have married young. Think how many children and grandchildren he would have had studying Torah earlier. Isn't that more important than his own Torah? To us it would seem even more important than for Yaakov Avinu to become great himself. But we must remember that Yaakov merited children who became *bnei Torah* only *because* he was the symbol of Truth — and it took him many years of toil to reach this level. By then, he had achieved spiritual greatness and thus was able to pass this trait on more effectively. It was worthwhile for future generations that Yaakov Avinu marry later.

When we had the *Beis HaMikdash*, the Kohen was allowed to sacrifice the offerings even if *Klal Yisrael* was ritually impure. Why, then, when the Chashmona'im came to rededicate the *Beis HaMikdash* couldn't they use the defiled oil? Since it was a *korban tzibbur*, a public offering, it could be used even when defiled. The answer is that this is exactly what Chanukah comes to teach us — about the *purity* of the oil.

The fight between Hellenism and Judaism was a fight between Yefes and Shem. Both sons of Noach embodied a path toward a spiritual life. Yefes embodied external beauty. He bestowed upon the world music, art, and poetry. A spiritual dimension was included in what he offered, but only if it appealed emotionally. Shem, however, exemplified truth and morality, a beauty that is not only external.

Chanukah comes to teach us about the fight between Hellenism and the Jewish people. The Greeks tried to uproot Judaism. They tried to teach the Jews about the external beauty of life and its pleasures. They defiled the oil, as if to say, "Your purity is not purity." They wanted the Jews of that time to choose a life of externalism. So even though the Chashmona'im could have offered the impure oil, even though doing so was halachically permissible, they wanted only what was pure, for even if what is pure is only a drop, it will go a long way.

The *Chovos HaLevavos* says that "a little bit of truth will conquer a lot of falsehood, just as a little bit of light dispels a lot of darkness" (Ch. 5). As we say in our Rosh Hashanah prayers: "Sanctify us with Your commandments and grant us a share in Your Torah; satisfy us from Your goodness and gladden us with Your salvation. And purify our hearts that we may serve You in truth. For You are the true G-d, and Your word is true and endures forever." Purity, truth, is the highest level, and should be our goal in life.

The Yaavetz, R' Yaakov Emden, in his introduction to his commentary on the *siddur* writes that the continued existence of *Klal Yisrael* is a bigger miracle than the miracle of the Exodus. How is a small, poor, weak nation, out of all the nations in the world, able to survive? Every day there are miracles because we are a nation of truth, the truth of Torah, and truth will always conquer. Falsehood has no legs to stand on but truth will always prevail.

This is the lesson of Chanukah. Just as we begin with one candle and add on, so is it with each individual's growth. We grow a little each day, adding a little more truth, until we reach the level with no more falsehood, a place where there is no room to speak *lashon hara* or to embarrass someone. At this spiritual level, all such things disappear. We all do foolish things, make mistakes at times, but is this any reason to slander a person and hurt him? Of course not. All the troubles we have today come from falsehood, *lashon hara*, and *sinas chinam*, baseless hatred, which are all due to a lack of truth.

Yaakov Avinu's life was a difficult one but always an honest one. Although it takes long years of toil to reach this level, we must strive for it. One of the *baalei mussar* notes that the *Shulchan Aruch Orach Chaim* begins with "S*hivisi Hashem lenegdi samid*, I place Hashem before me always" (*Tehillim* 16:8), because it is such an elevated level. For a person to merit this takes a long time — it must be a gradual process, one candle at a time — but the aspiration has to be there now. Whatever you say should be truth without trying to fool anyone; this is purity. Chanukah is not just about remembering the miracle of the oil. It is a lesson in the purity of Judaism. A little purity can overcome all forms of darkness in one's life.

The Gemara tells us about the dispute between Beis Shammai and Beis Hillel regarding how the Chanukah candles are to be lit (*Shabbos* 21b). Beis Shammai says that on the first night we should light eight candles and on each ensuing night, light one less. Beis Hillel says the opposite, that on the first night we light one candle and continue adding candles as the nights go on. The Gemara explains the reason for this dispute: Beis Shamai maintains that the miracle of the entire eight days should be expressed on the first day, thanking Hashem for all eight days of Chanukah on the very first day. On the next day, seven candles would be lit, thanking Hashem for all the days that remain, and so on throughout Chanukah, taking into account all the coming days.

Beis Hillel's reasoning is that the outgoing days have more importance. Each night (which in Judaism marks the beginning of the new day) a candle is lit for the miracle of the day that has passed.

At first glance, Beis Shammai's argument seems very sound. It does seem plausible to thank Hashem for the eight days of Chanukah at the very onset of the holiday. What is Beis Hillel's reasoning that we should thank Hashem for the days that have passed?

When we read the verse, "*Tefillah l'Moshe ish haElokim,* Prayer of Moshe, man of G-d" (*Tehillim* 90:12), what do we expect Moshe Rabbeinu to ask Hashem? We would probably assume his prayer to be in reference to Torah and mitzvos. Yet Moshe Rabbeinu asks Hashem, "*Limnos yameinu kein hoda,* Tell us the counting of our days" (ibid.). The Ibn Ezra explains this as a request for an understanding heart to be able to know how long we have to live. When we know how long our lifetime is, we will start to appreciate our days.

Realizing the importance of time is what makes a person outstanding. It is not so much the accomplishment, but using one's time to the utmost. The Vilna Gaon says that we will have to give a reckoning not only of what we did or didn't accomplish, but of what we did with the time allotted to us. Did we utilize our allotted time to its fullest? Can we justify every moment of our lives? Moshe Rabbeinu is asking Hashem to grant us an appreciation of time by knowing how long we will live. When a person thinks life is endless, he wastes time. Moshe Rabbeinu knew that we would automatically accomplish what we have to, if we knew how many years we actually had.

Beis Hillel argues that we kindle the lights not in anticipation of the forthcoming days but because of the outgoing days. In my opinion, we follow the position of Beis Hillel because in order to appreciate life, we have to look at the past, for only in that way can we be aware of the future. When we count, for instance, two days gone by, we think, "Two whole days disappeared from my life! What did I accomplish in those two days? Did I achieve anything worthwhile for *Klal Yisrael*, for my family, for my neighbor? Will my accomplishment light up my life and make me happy?" If so, then the next light will glow more brightly, for we know that we have fulfilled our purpose in life. To appreciate the value of life you have to count the past, not just look to the future.

The Gemara says that after 120 years we will be free of our obligations in Torah and mitzvos, but while we are living every second counts (*Shabbos* 30a). The Chofetz Chaim says on the verse, "Who is the man who is *chafetz chaim*, who desires life?" (*Tehillim* 34:13), that it is the man who is *ohev yamim*, who loves his days and fills them with good deeds, knowing they will all appear before him after 120 years. What we fail to realize is the significance of our each and every action.

The Torah tells us that when Reuven wanted to save his brother Yosef, he told his brothers not to kill Yosef but to throw him in the pit, thinking he would rescue him later. What is the purpose in telling us that Reuven planned to rescue Yosef later if he did not actually accomplish this?

The Midrash says: Had Reuven known that this would be written in the Torah, he would have carried Yosef on his shoulders to their father Yaakov (*Yalkut Shimoni, Bereishis* 37:4). Reuven's mistake was that he did not appreciate how great the deed would have been and so did not carry it out fully. The Torah wants to teach us that when we do a mitzvah, it should be done wholeheartedly, b'simchah. The Midrash continues: Had Aharon known that it would be recorded that he was happy when he went to greet his brother Moshe, he would have gone to greet him with drums and tambourines. Had Boaz known that it would be recorded that he fed Ruth roasted kernels, he would have fed her fatted calves. Our Sages point out these incidents as examples of people not realizing the lasting importance of their acts while doing these mitzvos.

The ben Torah is utilizing his time fully only when he davens, learns Torah, or does any other mitzvah he has an obligation to fulfill; any other time is wasted. Busy housewives, though, don't waste time and could always use more of it. They are fulfilling mitzvos galore, and their task is to recognize the lasting significance of each mitzvah and every act of chesed.

The Gemara says that one who kindles Shabbos and Chanukah lights will merit to have children who are Torah scholars (Shabbos 23b). Rashi explains this by citing the verse, "Ki ner mitzvah v'Torah or," which means that lighting the candles of Shabbos and Chanukah will be rewarded with the light of Torah.

Our Sages teach us that the good deeds of the righteous are likened to light, while the actions of the wicked are compared to the darkness of night (Bereishis Rabbah 1:6). The fifth verse of the Torah states: "G-d called the light 'day,' and the darkness He called 'night.'" The Midrash says: "In the beginning of the creation of the universe, Hashem anticipated the deeds of the righteous and the wicked" (Bereishis Rabbah 2:5). In the second verse, tohu refers to the confused deeds of the wicked, which are likened to darkness. The deeds of the righteous are likened to light. In the fourth verse, Hashem differentiated between light and darkness, day and night — between the deeds of the righteous and those of the wicked.

Or, light, is always associated with goodness. Our Sages therefore likened the deeds of the righteous to light, for the very essence of Torah is light. Light is life itself, and lighting candles helps us understand what life really means. A mitzvah is likened to a candle, whereas Torah is likened to a big fire, to a torch, a beacon of light. Just as mitzvos and Torah are associated with light, they become the very essence of life and the only things that truly make a person happy. A good piece of cake gives only a temporary, sensual fulfillment. Torah, *l'havdil*, is a positive *simchah* that we call a *neshamah simchah*, a joy to the soul. The *neshamah* does not enjoy earthly, materialistic desires. This teaches us that in the kindling of the menorah and appreciating the light brought out by the mitzvah, we will merit Torah.

Mitzvos themselves also provide light to a certain extent, but it is not enough. Our goal is to reach the big light of Torah. We learn from this that it isn't just the kindling of the lights but the realization and appreciation of what light means that are important. Our task is to attain and achieve light to the degree that we feel it in our bones.

The Gemara relates that one time a matron saw R' Yehudah the son of R' Il'ai, whose face shone. She asked him: "Do you lend with interest?" implying that if so, then he had no worries about money and so that must be the cause of his radiant happiness. He answered her, "No. It is the study of Torah that makes me so happy" (*Berachos* 55a).

The message we should take out of Chanukah is to bring the pure light of Torah, which is truth, into our lives, for there is nothing else that can give us such happiness.

QUESTIONS & ANSWERS

Q Is it proper to give Chanukah *gelt* or does this come from non-Jewish customs?

A No, it does not stem from the non-Jewish world. It is an old custom, so why not give it to the children if it makes them happy?

Q Can you give children toys for Chanukah?

A You can give children toys the entire year. We don't give them just for Chanukah, but we can give them toys then to give them satisfaction, because Chanukah is a happy time.

Q What is a woman not allowed to do while the Chanukah candles are burning?

A She should not do housework, mending, sewing, washing clothing, ironing, and the like. Cooking is permissible.

Q If one has olive oil that does not have a good *hechsher* regarding *orlah,* can one still use it to light Chanukah lights?

A Some are lenient and some are stringent. You can use it if you have no other oil.

TRANQUILITY OF MIND

14

It is surprising that, especially in communities where the husbands are established with well-paying jobs, people want to know how to acquire *menuchas hanefesh*, tranquility of mind. They are not suffering from the pinch of inflation, and their homes are filled with all the latest luxuries. Why, with all this, don't they have tranquility of mind?

Regarding the sin of Adam HaRishon, the Sforno explains that the snake symbolizes the *yetzer hara*, the evil inclination (*Bereishis* 3:1). Just as snake venom can be used as a cure, although it is extremely poisonous, so too, the evil inclination is of some benefit, yet its potential for damage is great.

Although we seem to know the halachos of what is forbidden and what is permitted, we manage to sin anyway. The Sforno explains that this is due to physical lust being a product of fantasy. Chavah was overwhelmed by the appealing look of the *eitz hadaas*, the Tree of Knowledge. It was so beautiful and so enticing, to the point that her emotions overpowered her intelligence. She knew very well that it was forbidden to eat from the tree, but emotion overpowered logic and she was carried away by fantasy — and thus she stumbled.

This battle of emotion versus logic, according to the Sforno, is the tool of the *yetzer hara.* If a person would logically analyze whether or not he should do a wrong deed, of course he would not do it. But when one is carried away by his emotions, at that moment he loses his knowledge that the act is forbidden. He finds a pretext for doing what his feelings tell him to do, and he makes a mistake. As our Sages say, "A person doesn't sin unless *ruach shtus,* a spirit of folly, enters his mind" (*Sotah* 3a), causing him to fabricate some sort of pretext permitting him to perform the forbidden act. It is this *koach hadimyon,* this fantasy, that lets his emotions carry him into a dreamland and causes him to lose contact with reality and logic.

Having peace of mind necessitates getting beyond emotion, because emotions are only temporary. A person suffering from an ulcer may eat something temptingly delicious, knowing he will suffer from it later. Why does he eat it? Because he is carried away by his *taavah,* his desire. At that moment, he has lost contact with reality; he does not pay the consequences now but later he will. This is the reason for sin.

All of us can picture to some extent the *dor hamidbar* who received the Torah on Har Sinai. There is a shocking statement made by this *dor de'ah:* "We remember the fish that we ate in Egypt free of charge; and the cucumbers and the melons" (*Bamidbar* 11:5). Rashi asks: Did they really eat it for free? They had to work very hard for it! How could the generation that lived with the *Shechinah,* the *Ananei HaKavod,* Clouds of Glory, and Moshe Rabbeinu, speak in such a manner?

The verse continues with their complaint that all they

see is the manna and they boast about the cucumbers that they used to have. What does all this mean?

The obvious meaning is that *Klal Yisrael* didn't care about the nourishment provided by the food; what they missed was the variety. As the saying goes, "Variety is the spice of life." They wanted something different. When life appears to be a drudgery, human nature, which prefers excitement, will look for adventure and change. It is a matter of emotion versus logic.

In *Tehillim*, the manna is described as the *"lechem abirim,"* the food of the angels, with great spiritual richness (*Tehillim* 78:25). The Gemara points out that the manna would take on any taste they wished it to have (*Yoma* 75a). We cannot find a food like that today. *Klal Yisrael's* problem was that the manna was not visually appealing. Human nature loves adventure as opposed to the monotony of life. When a person's desire for adventure and excitement carries him away, his rational state of mind is overpowered. At that point, he is not using intellect and logic to look at life in its reality. The Torah picked this generation, with all its greatness, to illustrate the point that even when a person is spiritually on the highest level, he can be swayed by his emotions into making such a mistake as to mourn over cucumbers and melons.

Peace of mind can be acquired only if we know how to use our minds. Immediate and temporary satisfactions do not give peace of mind. One may have a full refrigerator but this does not necessarily guarantee peace of mind. Peace of mind is achieved when the mind is down-to-earth and ruled by logic. This makes a person happy, because intellect is all-inclusive: It takes not only the present into account but the future as well. A person who follows the dictates of his emotions will be carried away by impulse and instinctive desire without weighing the consequences.

Torah is the basis of truth. Our holy Torah is not merely 99 percent true but 100 percent true. It is all-encompassing, with everything taken into account: the present, the past, and the future as well. The older Torah scholars get, our Sages tell us, the more *menuchas hanefesh* they have. This is because as people age, passions die out and intellect alone remains. People who devote their lives to a Torah life have the wonderful sense of having accomplished a goal.

Evildoers, though, become more and more upset the older they get. They become confused and embittered when they look at the past, for they have left nothing behind. There is nothing to show for their lives; at best someone will have to be hired to say Kaddish for them.

A working man was once asked, "Why do you work so hard?" He answered, "I work so that I can make a living," to which he was asked, "But when will you *live*?"

Women who live a Torah life should not at all envy the adventurous lifestyle encouraged by contemporary society. Its excitement is only temporary. When parents get older, they look back and worry more about whether or not they gave their children the right Torah education. If their decisions were made on the basis of fleeting considerations, parents will feel guilty and will blame themselves. They will bemoan their shortsightedness and the damage they did to their children by stressing the wrong values rather than encouraging a Torah lifestyle.

There are all kinds of tranquilizers nowadays, but the best pill of all is *bitachon*, faith. What is lacking today is what the manna symbolized — the peace of mind that we acquire through faith in Hashem. Prices go up and we become a little shaky — how will we be able to meet the bills? But Hashem will take care of that too. It is all in His hands.

We can learn a further lesson in faith from Tu B'Shevat.

Tu B'Shevat, the 15th of Shevat, is the Rosh Hashanah of the trees. On this day judgment is passed upon the trees as to whether or not they will produce fruit. It is advisable to pray at this time for a beautiful and kosher *esrog*.

The 15th of Shevat or, according to others, the first of Shevat, was chosen as Rosh Hashanah because, according to the Gemara, by this time the greatest amount of rain has already fallen and, as Rashi explains, it is then that the trees start blossoming (*Rosh Hashanah* 14a). But why should this Rosh Hashanah fall in Shevat? Why should Shevat, the coldest month of the year, be the time when the trees begin to blossom? We might think that a sunny, warm season would be a more appropriate time, rather than the cold weather with its snow and ice. The answer brings an important message to us.

In the Torah portions relating the Exodus from Egypt, the Torah tells us that Pharaoh, who had leprosy, bathed in the blood of Jewish babies. The Jews suffered under the Egyptian bondage and cried out for salvation. Their supplications rose to Hashem and He answered their prayers and took them out of Egypt (*Shemos* 2:23). We then read an outstanding fact: After they left Egypt, Pharaoh decided to chase after them to kill them or bring them back. As the Jews saw Pharaoh getting closer, *u'Pharaoh hikriv* (ibid., 14:10), they saw that they were surrounded by the threat of death. Trapped on all sides, they couldn't run away. What did they do? They cried to Hashem and prayed that He save them. He answered their prayers and Moshe Rabbeinu said in Hashem's Name, "Hashem will fight for you. You shall remain silent" (ibid., 14:14). Hashem said to Moshe, "Why are you praying so much? Tell Israel to proceed" (ibid., vs. 14-15), and in the merit of their forefathers, I will save them (*Rashi*). Our Sages explain that *u'Pharaoh hikriv* means that Pharaoh brought them closer to repentance and caused them to cry to Hashem.

To what is this compared? Reb Yehoshua ben Levi says it is like a king who came upon a princess being attacked by robbers. Hearing her cries to be saved, the king rescued her. A few days later, the king decided that he wished to marry the princess. He wanted to talk to her again and hear her voice once more but she refused to talk to him. What did he do? He arranged for the robbers to chase after her once more. This time too, she cried out to the king, who saved her as before and said, "I had wanted to talk to you again but you refused. Now I am happy that I can talk to you once more" (*Shemos Rabbah* 21:5).

The Jewish people cried to Hashem when they were enslaved in Egypt and He heard and saved them. Now He wanted to hear their voices again but they did not cry out to him, so he brought Pharaoh closer, which caused them to cry out and beseech Him. This is compared to a dove that is caught between the rocks and can't get out, and cries for help. Similarly, *Klal Yisrael* cried to Hashem and He rescued them (*Shir HaShirim* 2:14, *Rashi*).

Sometimes a doctor will say, "There is nothing more we can do to help. Only prayer and faith can help now." Such situations might appear to us as simply part of the natural order of the world, but this is not so. They are brought about by Hashem because He wants a person to become introspective. He wants the patient to cry out to Him and ask for His help with the realization that no one else can help but Hashem.

Hashem could have brought the Jewish people to Eretz Yisrael in a very simple manner, without any trouble at all. But, according to the Rashbam, in order to acquire full trust and faith in Hashem in all difficult situations, it was necessary for them to see the miracles of the splitting of the sea. Then they feared Hashem and believed in Him, trusting that He would provide for them even in the desert. We see the greatness of *Klal Yisrael*, as they left Egypt with no food, with nothing in sight, having faith in Hashem. Hashem said to Moshe, "The merit of their faith is enough of a merit to save them from the Egyptians and have the sea split for them."

Tu B'Shevat teaches us that even in the cold of winter, the earth's strength is renewed so that it can bring forth produce. In the most severe, freezing weather, the Creator has the beautiful ability to create fruit. So too, we see that sometimes Hashem brings a person to situations in life where he cannot imagine being able to find help. There are times when a person seeks help and can find it, but there are certain situations where help does not seem possible at all. And in those dark days to whom can we turn? Only to Hashem. This is the *bitachon*, the faith, that brings complete tranquility of mind.

QUESTIONS & ANSWERS

Q Do you wait six hours from when you start or finish eating meat?

A From when you finish eating, not from when you *bentch*.

Q Should we use separate burners for *milchig* and *fleishig* on the stove?

A It is advisable but not obligatory, as long as you take care that nothing spills on top. If it does, you must wash it off. On erev Shabbos, you might want to use them all for *fleishig* which is okay according to halachah.

Q If hot oil in a *fleishig* pan (but there was no meat in the pan) splashes on a cold *milchig* frying pan, is the *milchig* pan *treif*?

A No, wash it out and set it aside for 24 hours.

Q I have one oven and I would like to cook both *milchig* and *fleishig*. How can I do this?

A The best thing to do is to make sure to keep all pots covered when baking (even if a small amount of vapor escapes, it is still permissible). Then you have no problem at all. However, if you must cook *fleishig* uncovered, you must: (1) Clean out the oven well; (2) preferably wait 24 hours; (3) turn the oven to its highest possible setting; when it reaches the hottest temperature it can get, leave it on for about half-an-hour.

Q **I put a bag of *unkashered* chicken livers on a plate and blood dripped into the plate. Does the plate become *treif*?**

A Well, it all depends on how much blood and how long it stayed on the plate. A drop of blood doesn't mean anything. It only becomes *treif* if there was a great deal of blood on the plate and it stayed there for at least 24 hours. Ask a *shei'lah* if in doubt.

Q **Are there any rules about when to ask a *shei'lah* on a chicken because of broken bones?**

A In general, most breakage of bones in chickens today is not problematic because usually nowadays the breakage of bones is due to mass production, where the bones are shattered in the machines. The exception is if you see a black-and-blue mark, which indicates that the break occurred when the chicken was alive. Then you must ask a *shei'lah*.

Q **Does dishwashing liquid need a *hechsher*?**

A If it is not edible then it does not need one. Anything that is not fit for *achilas kelev* is not *treif*.

Q **If the detergent says "kosher for Passover" without a *hechsher* can you still use it?**

A Yes.

Q **Does regular tea need a *hechsher*?**

A No, but flavored tea can sometimes be a problem.

Q **What about the spots we find in eggs. Are they considered blood?**

A Brown spots are not a problem. The only *shei'lah* is when the spot is bright red. But we are usually lenient even with the red spots, because they are not what we call embryonic. Only eggs with a potential to hatch into a chick can present a problem of what we call "*dam rikum*." Today, because roosters and hens are caged separately, almost 99 percent of the eggs are okay even if they have real blood.

If you want to discard the egg, you can, but it's really enough to remove just the spot and use the egg itself. It is certainly permissible to use the vessel.

Q **If you cut off the head of an onion and peeled it, can you leave the onion overnight to use the next day?**

A You have to use it the same day. If you leave the head or the peel on, then you can leave it overnight.

Q **Do I have to check sweet paprika?**

A You do have to check sweet paprika. Take a handful and spread it out to see if there are worms or bugs. It should then be stored in the freezer.

Q **How should I check chickpeas and other beans?**

A Sometimes from the outside it is not possible to see the worms so you must open each one up before you eat it.

Q **Is it true that when checking for bugs only what the eye can see is considered forbidden?**

A Yes, but that applies to something like vinegar, which is full of bacteria. But with something like chickpeas, you do not need a microscope to see. The problem is opening them up; it is not the size. You can see all insects with a strong light.

Q If you buy food in a restaurant that has a good *hechsher*, can you assume that the food was also checked for insects properly?

A The *hechsher* does not necessarily cover the checking. However, if you can speak to the *mashgiach* about it and he seems reliable, then you can assume it was properly checked.

Q If you find worms in a pot in which you cooked, is the pot *treif*?

A No, no matter how many worms you find.

Q Can we rely on lettuce or cabbage checked by someone else?

A If the person has good eyesight and knows how to check, then he can be relied upon.

Q What is the *din* of *tevilas keilim* for a toaster oven?

A According to some opinions, one can be lenient and not *tovel* it. However, if the parts that touch the food are removable, *tovel* just those parts.

The best thing is to *tovel* the whole appliance. Before using it, make sure to let it dry out completely to prevent a short circuit. Before *toveling*, check with an electrician to make sure that no permanent damage will occur to the appliance.

Q At what age should a child begin waiting between milk and meat?

A Six, 7, or 8 years. But for children or anyone who needs the milk, such as a pregnant or nursing mother, an hour is sufficient. She should clean her teeth after the meat.

Q My young children eat meat at 2:00 p.m. Can I give them a dairy supper at 6:00 p.m. so that they can go to sleep on time?

A Yes, if it is necessary for the child.

Q Is it enough to give a year-old baby only a drink of juice between chicken and milk?

A Even that is not necessary for such a young child, meaning, up to the age of *chinuch*.

Q Until what age do the leniencies with *hechshers* apply?

A Any permissible leniencies with *hechshers* are not just for infants. I would say it's even for 6, 7, and 8-year-olds.

Q My daughter is 8 and knows all about *hechshers*. She always gives the man in the grocery store a hard time about the different *hechshers*. Is this okay?

A It is not usually her place to give any storekeeper a hard time, especially in public. It is also not modest.

Q If I am stringent about using only certain *hechshers*, can I be lenient with my children and let them eat food with a less stringent *hechsher*?

A A child does not have to fulfill all the mitzvos like an adult. According to halachah, the child is not a *bar onshin*, liable for penalty, before the age of 13 (a girl from the age of 12), so he has more leniencies than his parents, if necessary. We don't give him *treifos*, though.

But a parent must weigh his actions carefully, taking into consideration his child's character. If the parent makes a point of allowing the child to eat food with what he considers a less stringent *hechsher* and the child is a bright child, he may reason that he is not as obligated as the parent. This might lead him to take the whole subject of *kashrus* lightly, which is a serious problem. In such a case, you should be more careful.

So it really depends on the child

15 INTOXICATION OF THE MIND

Our times bear a similarity to the times of Mordechai and Achashverosh. The *Megillah* says that at that time the Jewish people *kiyemu v'kiblu*, affirmed and accepted the Torah (*Esther* 9:27). Our Sages relate that this acceptance was the reconfirmation of the receiving of the Torah at Har Sinai. Then, the Jewish people had no choice. Their acceptance was not voluntary but came after Hashem raised Har Sinai over them and warned them: If you will accept the Torah, well and good; if not, today you will be buried.

Our Sages comment that this opened the way for arguing against punishment for wrongdoing. After all, we could just say that we didn't want the Torah but were forced to accept it (*Shabbos* 88a). But in the times of Achashverosh, our forefathers voluntarily reaccepted the Torah, making it an unquestionable obligation forever after.

The question is raised: What moved them to do this? Our Sages answer: It was Achashverosh removing his signet ring and giving it to Haman.

Our Sages further state that this act was more effective than all of the 48 prophets and seven prophetesses (*Megillah* 14a). This is very surprising, for included in this count of all the prophets is Moshe Rabbeinu and the giving of the Torah on Har Sinai! Why was nothing able to move them like the removal of the ring?

Many people are under the impression that people today are less religious, that they don't study Torah as well as they once did. Why do they think this is so? For the simple reason that today people don't see the *Elokus*, the G-dliness, that previous generations were privileged to see. "Were the Vilna Gaon alive today to guide and inspire us, how devout we would be," they claim. "If Abaye and Rava were our contemporaries, we would be great Torah scholars." "Were Moshe Rabbeinu our leader, we would all become *gedolei Torah!*"

Our Sages refute this false argument. We see that until the time of Achashverosh, all the prophets and prophetesses had not moved the Jewish people sufficiently. Could it have been a lack of seeing G-dliness, the greatness of Hashem? Not at all. The Ramban says that the Jewish people at Sinai were shown that Hashem is the *Elokim*, that He alone rules the world and is Supreme. The giving of the Torah at Har Sinai removed all questions of faith and belief until everything was crystal clear and without a shadow of a doubt. Yet the Torah says, "It was given in order to test you [the Jewish people]" (*Shemos* 20:18). Hashem wanted to test the Jewish people to see if they would follow in the path of the Torah. But what kind of test could it be if they had just seen everything revealed so clearly and vividly? They knew without a doubt that *"ein od milvado,"* there is no reality in the world other than the sovereignty of Hashem. They knew that Torah was absolute, so why was this a test? The

Ramban explains that the test was a test of their willingness to sacrifice of themselves to fulfill the mitzvos.

As we know, fulfilling the mitzvos requires selflessness to a certain extent. One who is selfish will find it too hard to perform mitzvos. The test for the Jewish people was not whether or not they would search for more G-dliness or more faith in Hashem. The test was rather to see how much each person was willing to sacrifice himself with the total dedication required for the observance of all mitzvos.

A person who is a little lazy and wants some more sleep will not get up to *daven* on time. Observing Shabbos today, *baruch Hashem,* isn't so hard — but at one time, getting a job without being forced to work on Shabbos was an ordeal. People used to have to give up their jobs because of Shabbos. *Kashrus* also requires *mesiras nefesh*; it means giving up one's pleasures of life. This test, then, is not a matter of finding out more of the existence of *Elokus* but a matter of giving up physical pleasures.

Our Sages say that the Jews in the time of the Purim story were punished with all the evil decrees of Haman because they enjoyed themselves at Achashverosh's feast (*Megillah* 12a). The food he served was kosher, but the event itself was forbidden to Jews. In the *Megillah* we read of the luxuries and wealth that Achashverosh produced and showed off to the world (*Esther* 1:6). This evoked in the Jews a love for materialism equal to the extent to which they enjoyed the banquet. And this is what brought about their punishment, Achashverosh's decree that they be destroyed. Queen Esther's advice to save the Jewish people was that they refrain from eating. Fasting, in and of itself, demonstrates a willingness to sacrifice one's physical pleasure for a higher goal.

But it was even more than that. Our Sages have

likened earthly life to the night. Just as nighttime has as its prime element darkness, so too is this world a world of darkness. The *Mesillas Yesharim* explains that darkness can produce two errors: One can either see things in the darkness that do not actually exist, or one can fail to see correctly that which does exist (Ch. 3). We might think we see something in the dark when it is actually nothing, or we might be deceived into thinking that a man is a pillar or a pillar is a man. We might misconstrue falsehood for truth and truth for falsehood. These mistakes are a product of the darkness that is night and of the darkness that is the world we live in. We see people groping in the darkness. They ask, "What is religion?" They don't even know what it is! But we also see others who misinterpret and claim that Reform or Conservative is the true Judaism. And even in the Torah world there can be mistakes made due to the darkness that living in this earthly existence produces.

Some people are drunk even without wine. A drunk is a person who has lost his mental clarity and cannot think straight. These are the people groping in this world, searching for the truth. Remarkably, we can note that the whole miracle of Purim came about because of wine. Queen Esther ordered a wine party that caused Haman's downfall. We are therefore told to drink wine on Purim to the point of intoxication, a mitzvah unlike any other. Our Sages say that one has to drink until he is at a stage where he can't tell the difference between *baruch Mordechai* and *arur Haman*, blessed is Mordechai and cursed is Haman, like a drunk who cannot think (*Megillah* 7b). What is the reason for this strange practice?

The answer is that we all live in a state of mental intoxication similar to the intoxication caused by drinking wine. The mental confusion of the Jewish people in those times was as much of an intoxication as if they were drunk. On Purim we are commanded to drink wine and reach a stage of intoxication where we cannot differentiate between what the two lives, Mordechai's and Haman's, meant. When we later recognize what drunkenness can do, we will realize that one can be mentally drunk as well. We will then be motivated to get our faculties of mind working properly so that we can understand the reality of the value of life. We will be able to appraise life in its true sense. With evildoers, though, the older they become the more confused they are. We can all see this clearly. The youthful, adventurous years are a time when people do not think realistically or stop to ask themselves, "What am I accomplishing in life?" Such a person will not stop to think whether or not he is being carried away by emotion. He is mentally intoxicated. But when he gets a little older and his desires wane and disappear, he doesn't enjoy life. He has spent his life pursuing physical pleasure and when that is gone, what's left? Nothing! His life is empty and now he thinks back on how much he could have accomplished but didn't. As he looks back over his wasted lifetime, guilt sets in. Many people can't overcome their guilty consciences and find themselves in trouble, either with psychiatric problems or drugs or worse.

The drunkenness of Purim comes to teach us that one can be drunk even without wine. This realization is what enabled the Jews in the time of Mordechai and Esther to reconfirm their acceptance of the Torah. They successfully passed their test, which was not to see if they lacked faith, but to see if they were willing to give up their earthly pleasures for the sake of the Torah. Not only was their fasting a form of self-sacrifice, but it gave them a chance to look at life soberly.

Overindulgence clouds our vision. When one is fasting, though, his mind becomes sufficiently clear to see what life is all about in its truest sense. He can realize what is expected of him. Our Sages therefore tell us that it is only on Purim, after the Jewish people left all of these worldly pleasures, that they were able to look at life realistically. They saw with their own eyes what comes from pleasures: The signet ring was given to Haman! This was the very reason why it was more effective than all of the 48 prophets. The prophets merely *told* the people that their pursuit of pleasure was not the proper thing to do, but their warnings had no sense of immediacy for the people. However, when the Jews in the time of Achashverosh lived through the fear of death, they were able to see for themselves what their pleasures caused them.

We should also examine our lives and think realistically about what exactly life has in store. It says in the *Megillah*: "The Jews had light and gladness and joy and honor" (*Esther* 8:16). Our Sages say that *light* is Torah, as it says, "*Ki ner mitzvah v'Torah or*, For a mitzvah is a lamp and the Torah is light" (*Mishlei* 6:23). It is Torah that enlightens us and enables us to see reality clearly. The light of Torah dispels the darkness, revealing life's meaning with striking clarity. That insures *gladness and joy*, for one who leads a life of Torah will have true happiness.

A materialistic life with overindulgence in the comforts of life is not the Torah way. Fulfilling our goal and mission by living the Torah life is what brings the greatest contentment. We have tranquility and peace of mind, and we don't feel guilty at all. What did our *bubbies* and *zeides* have 70 years ago in Europe? What did the yeshivah *bachurim* in my era have for supper — a piece of bread and a potato! Yet they were happy and content. Contentment, coming from peace of mind, is a spiritual feeling that the body doesn't understand. It is only when one is content that he can enjoy life, and the soul is only content when we observe Torah and mitzvos. The Chofetz

Chaim says that Torah is likened to bread. One can enjoy all the delicacies of the world and not be content unless he eats bread, which is filling. So, too, one who studies the Torah, which is likened to bread, feels gratified and satiated (*Nidchei Yisrael* 12).

We can now see the beautiful message of Purim: One will not find happiness in life through intoxication of the mind. Having all the physical pleasures in life does not bring enjoyment. It is only when you have the *orah* — the Torah — that there is *sason v'simchah*, gladness and joy.

QUESTIONS & ANSWERS

Q How does one know if he is looking at things through his emotions or his rational mind?

A Pause for a little while and take a breather. Think things over. The *yetzer hara* tells a person to do things in haste. The whole sin of the *eitz hadaas* came about because Chavah was so enticed and motivated by her emotions that she did not stop to think whether she was doing the right thing. So, too, if you want to use your mind, remember: Don't be carried away by your emotions to the point that you forget to think. An alcoholic drinks because he is carried away by the desire for schnapps; people still smoke even though doctors say that with every cigarette smoked one loses precious minutes of his life. I keep telling people not to smoke, but for some the desire is so overwhelming that they think they cannot stop. The main thing is: Stop! Think things over and don't rush, because when you rush, emotion take over and you'll regret it. *Sechel* always functions in a quiet, calm way, with a slow reckoning.

Q Can a weak woman eat or drink before hearing the *Megillah*?

A Yes, she can drink. *Bish'as hadchak,* if it is really necessary, she can even have a light snack.

Q If we send *mishloach manos,* the mandatory Purim gifts of food, as a family, have we fulfilled our obligation?

A No. You should not send as a group. Women should send to women, and men to men.

Q Which should you give more of, *mishloach manos* or *matanos la'evyonim,* charity to the poor?

A The halachah explicitly says to give more *matanos la'evyonim.*

Q Can you give *mishloach manos* to someone who will not say a blessing over the food?

A If you are not sure about this, you can send the *mishloach manos.* But if you know for sure that he will not make a *berachah,* then it's better not to, unless it will cause enmity between you and the person.

Q Is it forbidden to do work such as cleaning and laundry on Purim?

A On Purim we don't do any *melachah* that is not necessary for Purim.

Q I hate it when my husband gets drunk on Purim. Is it wrong for me to ask him not to get drunk?

A It depends on the person. He should consult his rav and be careful not to upset anyone with his behavior. If he gets drunk and vomits all over the carpets, that's terrible. If he wants to get that drunk let him stay in a room by himself.

Q Is it proper for girls to wear short skirts or pants on Purim?

A We don't allow it. It's not proper.

Q What is the *Rosh Yeshivah's* opinion on scary Purim masks, such as monster faces that frighten young children?

A People should not wear scary masks that frighten children. Why not emulate Avraham Avinu instead?

16 ESTHER'S UNIQUE VIRTUES

We all admire the greatness of Queen Esther, whose courage and virtues made her the queen of the world. But we have to delve deeper to understand why she was chosen to be Queen Esther. As we know, she had a poor complexion and she did not wear cosmetics when going to the king. And yet, she had a certain *chein*, an inner beauty that was, of course, a G-d-given gift.

Shlomo HaMelech makes an astounding statement: "One man in a thousand I have found, but one woman among them I have not found" (*Koheles* 7:28). Shlomo HaMelech sought the perfection of the individual. He found one man among a thousand, but none among the women. Some of us misunderstand this statement. We take it as a slight that belittles women. Why does he say, "one woman among them I have not found" when we know that there were so many righteous women throughout our history?

The Yaavetz, a great and renowned Kabbalist, explains this when he discusses the individual's aspiration to greatness: "Most people remain consonant with their basic natures." In other words, they use their natural capacities. They were born with certain physical traits, and that's how they remain. Their nature was, of course, decreed by Hashem, yet most people don't work on changing any part of themselves. A person who has a tendency to get angry easily remains that way. Only very few people change their basic nature. All the people in Shlomo HaMelech's time were on a very high spiritual level. So what does the verse mean? It means that he found only one man out of a thousand who was able to refashion his personality — and since it is very difficult for a woman to change her nature, in most cases she will remain with the nature with which she was born.

For example, the Gemara says that Rabbi Akiva, before becoming such a great *talmid chacham*, hated *talmidei chachamim* to such an extent that he wanted to tear them to pieces (*Pesachim* 49b). What made Rabbi Akiva change to become the great *tzaddik* we know him as? Our Sages say that one day Rabbi Akiva noticed a stream of water flowing onto a rock, carving a hole as it flowed. This caught his attention and he was astonished that such a thing was possible, that even the soft substance we call water could carve a hole into something as hard as a rock (*Avos d'Rabbi Nassan* 6:2). Rabbi Yisrael Salanter said that this hole was formed only because of a steady flow of water. Every drop of water does make a dent, but it is only after a long period of time, when many drops flow over the same place, that the hole is carved (*Ohr Yisrael HaShalem*, letter 10).

Rabbi Akiva derived from this phenomenon that if this can happen in the physical world, it is certainly possible for the Torah, which is likened to water, to vanquish a stony heart, which is made of flesh. He also realized that this is something that takes time, that it's not a matter of just one drop of water, a one-day occurrence, but it is a lifetime aspiration. Rabbi Akiva is the prototype who shows that one can change, refine, and perfect his nature. But we have to remember that it is a slow, gradual process.

Queen Esther is the perfect woman who personifies this great lesson. When we delve into the life of Queen Esther we see that she had a dual relationship: She was married to Mordechai, as our Sages tell us, for the word *l'bas* is really read *l'bayis*, denoting marriage (*Megillah* 13a); and she was also married to Achashverosh, the non-Jewish king. This sounds like fiction! Who would undertake such a marriage? Certainly it wouldn't be an outstanding woman who was a prophetess and married to Mordechai, whom our Sages have compared to Moshe Rabbeinu! (*Esther Rabbah* 6:2).

But Queen Esther was imbued with the spirit of a courageous prophetess, and she knew what was in store for the Jewish people. Her task was to change her soft-natured familiarity with her husband Mordechai and to live instead as a good-natured wife catering to the evil Achashverosh. It took an endless amount of courage and power but that was the greatness of this woman — she was able to overcome her nature when circumstances demanded it.

Rabbi Akiva became a *talmid chacham* because he saw the moral lesson of the water and the rock. It wasn't easy to become a Rabbi Akiva. He had to invest a lot of spiritual energy. Every one of us is created in the Divine image and we all have invested in us that greatness to change our personality if need be. That is the greatness of Queen Esther that all of us should admire.

And yet, we have to read between the lines. The prayer Queen Esther repeated continuously was: "My G-d, my G-d, why have You forsaken me?" (*Tehillim* 22:2-3). This is a beautiful song depicting the exile of the Jewish people. The psalm continues: "Why so far from saving me, from the words of my cry. O my G-d! I call out by day, but You answer not; and by night, but there is no respite for me."

Queen Esther pleads with Hashem, "Why have You forsaken me? I cry and beseech You in the morning and night and You don't answer me." Our Sages tell us that this "morning and night" allude to the reading of the *Megillah* in the morning and at night (*Megillah* 4a). Esther was praying steadily to Hashem to help her through the terrible predicament in which she found herself. "You, Hashem, are holy and dwell amidst the praises of Yisrael, and our forefathers trusted in You and You saved them. To You they cried and they were saved."

In my opinion, it was Queen Esther's outstanding *middah* of *bitachon*, her trust in Hashem, that enabled her to act as courageously as she did. It was due to this *bitachon*, knowing that everything was from Hashem, that she was able to save the Jewish people. And it wasn't just a one-time prayer; there were many tears, but all accompanied by *bitachon*, never giving up hope. Queen Esther accepted her task as a courageous soldier, and all understood that the trials were *min haShamayim*, Heaven-sent.

But why did it have to be Queen Esther, a woman, and not a man like Mordechai? Our Sages say that in all our exiles, the women have played an important role in the salvation of the Jewish people. They were instrumental in the past and will be so in the future as well (*Midrash Zuta, Ruth* 4:11). This is because women have a virtue in which they are greater than men, and that is the matter of *bitachon*.

Woman, as a rule, understand the *middah* of *bitachon* simply and literally, even though they might not be as learned as the *talmid chacham*. Women accept what Hashem says as the unshakable truth; this has been the virtue of the righteous women in our history. Our Sages tell us that these women merited to raise generations of good and worthy people because they had what is called "*emunah p'shuta*," pure, unshakable faith.

We can therefore understand the necessity of Queen Esther possessing this great virtue of *bitachon*. This is what helped her through the terrible predicament in which she found herself. It was her courage, along with the *middah* of *bitachon*, that gave her the strength to withstand all the pressures that were put on her. When Queen Esther cried to Hashem, she did not give up hope — and in the end she won.

This was the greatness of Queen Esther. She showed us that a woman can change her nature as long as she has the *bitachon*. We just have to remember that it is a slow, gradual process. One has to have a lot of strength to overcome one's personality. It is a very difficult task, but if you have the *bitachon*, Hashem helps you along. We must think: Today might not have been so bright, but tomorrow, *b'ezras Hashem*, will be a sunnier day. It is these thoughts that will help us succeed.

From this great lesson, women can learn how to fill the gap in their lives. Many women are fed up with the drudgery of housework; they are fed up with changing diapers, even though this in itself is a big *chesed*. Our goal is to study our personality. We must think: "Today I am a little softer"; "Today, I'm more good-natured"; "Today, I did more *chesed*." That in itself is changing one's nature, which is the greatest accomplishment in one's life.

Many times, though, we lose ourselves in trying to achieve this great ambition, because it is, after all, a very hard task. Rav Yisrael Salanter says that to change one's nature is harder than learning the entire Gemara, which we know is a very difficult accomplishment.

It is possible to do, though, as we see from Queen

Esther's example. We see that we can have the courage to overcome all the tribulations that we encounter, as long as we have *bitachon*, steadily praying to Hashem. This great power of prayer is so very important in one's life. David HaMelech, the author of *Tehillim*, always found himself in terrible times and awful plights. Before he became king, he was constantly being pursued, and we can imagine his fear of being caught at any moment and killed. But he did not let this in any way diminish his spirit. The *Tehillim* he wrote helped him survive those hard times, and these very same *Tehillim* keep the Jewish people going even today. We gain so much hope from saying one chapter of *Tehillim*, and, of course, the real value lies in our believing what we say.

This is the lesson of Queen Esther. Every woman can become a great Jewish woman and an outstanding figure in her very own home. You are the one responsible for your children becoming great *talmidei chachamim*. But this takes patience.

Women often ask me, "What should I do? My child doesn't behave and he gets on my nerves."

I answer, "Sing while you work and do not despair." If you rely only on your natural feelings, you will give up. Our task is to overcome these feelings and form that spirit of resolve in ourselves that will keep us going. Singing helps you overcome difficult situations but, of course, it has to be accompanied by *tefillah*. If you do this, I can assure you that you will always accomplish, and you will become a Queen Esther in your own home.

QUESTIONS & ANSWERS

Q What should you do if your child starts to cry when you're in the middle of *davening Shemoneh Esrei*?

A If a child is crying you may go over and give him something to quiet him, and then resume *davening* again. Anything necessary for *tefillah* is not called a *hefsek*, interruption. However, you are not allowed to talk in the middle of *Shemoneh Esrei* unless it is a life or death situation, *chas v'shalom*.

Q If you don't have time to *daven* Minchah before candlelighting should you light with a *tenai*, condition, and then *daven*?

A This is a *machlokes*, dispute. It is better not to make a *tenai* but to later *daven* two Maarivs. We only make a *tenai bish'as hadchak*, since a woman usually accepts Shabbos upon herself with candlelighting.

Q If I am in the middle of *Pesukei D'Zimrah* and am interrupted, may I talk?

A It depends on the interruption. If a child cries terribly and you need to quiet him by telling him something, if there is no other way, definitely. And then continue where you left off.

Q

A

What is the *chiyuv* of women in *tefillah*?

An organized woman has time for *tefillah* and is obligated to *daven*. This means two *tefillos*, Shacharis and Minchah, and even on Friday. If you want to leave things out you must look at *Mishnah Berurah simanim* 52 and 70 to see on which *tefillos* you can be lenient. The first verse of *Shema* and then continuing from *emes veyatziv* and *Shemoneh Esrei* is very important to say. It is a halachic dispute whether *Birchos HaShachar* and *Pesukei D'Zimrah* must be said and in some cases you can be lenient. In the morning, though, you must say the *berachos al netilas yadayim*, *asher yatzar*, *Elokai neshamah*, and *Birchos HaTorah*.

Q

A

What if you are not organized? Should you *daven* and let the children scream?

Chas v'shalom. If you cannot help yourself, then you are exempt from *tefillah* like a *shomer choleh*, one who watches over an ill person. This is because one engaged in a mitzvah is exempt from another at that same time. A child who is screaming needs attention. He has to be fed or taken care of, and you become exempt. It's better to be organized and get up to *daven* a few minutes before the baby wakes up.

Q

A

Can you answer the phone or otherwise talk after having gone to bed and said *hamapil*?

It is better not to unless it is very urgent.

Q

A

Is it better to *daven* with a clean house or to *daven* early while the kids are sleeping and the house is dirty?

You are allowed to *daven* before the house is cleaned up, but if this bothers your *kavanah*, then clean up first. Probably, you can *daven* better when the children are sleeping, so take advantage of the situation and *daven* before they wake up. Some women don't *daven*. I'm not condoning the fact but it's a hard task to raise children. Sometimes the situation can come up where she is exempt from *davening*. She cannot help herself and therefore is exempt.

Are women also obligated to go to shul to *daven*?
We go to shul to *daven b'tzibbur*, from which women are exempt. Tending to children is a big mitzvah during which you are exempt from *tefillah*. The Chofetz Chaim says the woman taking care of children is like one tending an ill person. A wise woman will organize her life to find time for a *tefillah* here and there but she shouldn't feel bad at all if she is staying home to care for her children. It's a big *chesed* for the children and a double mitzvah if you take care of the chidren and *daven*.

If I missed Minchah Friday afternoon, should I *daven* Maariv twice?
Yes, you should *daven Shemoneh Esrei* twice.

Can we say *Tehillim* at night?
Based on the Kabbalah, we do not say *Tehillim* at night unless it is necessary, such as for a sick person, etc.

Is it a *segulah*, a formula for success, to *daven* at the *Kosel* for 40 days in a row? Is it of any proven benefit in getting a *shidduch* or having any other prayer answered?
I haven't seen it in halachah, but the *minhag* certainly claims that there are benefits. If you can go, it's wonderful. One of the best *segulos*, the Chofetz

Chaim says, is to learn and support Torah.

Q **After the story of Purim was over, why did Esther continue to live with Achashverosh?**

A It is obvious that she could not have left him. If she had, Achashverosh would have killed all the Jews.

SHIRAH

17

When the Jewish people were delivered from the Egyptians at Ya*m Suf*, they sang a beautiful song to Hashem. It is remarkable that among the statements sung, no mention is made of the sufferings they endured while in Egypt. What is outstanding in the beautiful song are the praises defining what Hashem meant to them.

Klal Yisrael said, "Hashem is a Master of war, *Ish milchamah*, and *Yud-Kei-Vau-Kei* is His Name" (*Shemos* 15:3). This Name, though, denotes *rachamim*, compassion and graciousness. How does this correspond with *milchamah*, meaning the battles of war? How does battle correspond with compassion? They seem to be opposites. If we would have compassion, there would be no wars at all. Only human cruelty does not let people live together. Where there is compassion and kindness, there are no confrontations, for the atmosphere is always peaceful.

There are many explanations for this question. Rashi explains that even when Hashem does battle and exacts vengeance from His enemies, unlike earthly kings, He exercises His quality of mercy. Although Pharaoh and the Egyptians deserved the penalty they received, Hashem did not punish simply for the sake of revenge. Hashem had compassion for them at the same time. When the Egyptians were drowning in the sea, the *Malachei HaShareis* wanted to say *shirah*, as they did every day. But Hashem said to the angels: "Those whom I created are drowning in the sea. Can you say *shirah* at this moment?" (*Shemos Rabbah* 23:7).

No, they could not say *shirah*. The Egyptians deserved the justice they received but, at the same time, the attribute of mercy prevailed. Hashem is the Master of war, but within the war, there was so much compassion.

Klal Yisrael sang this beautiful melody of *shirah*, expressing their feelings by saying, "This is my G-d and I will adorn Him" (*Shemos* 15:2). *Adorn*, our Sages tell us, also means that we should emulate Hashem's virtues. Just as He is compassionate and merciful, so should you be.

This is the only way a person can sing *shirah*. One cannot sing *shirah* without compassion. The embittered person will always seek revenge, and these vengeful feelings will ruin his personality and destroy him. It is the compassionate and gracious person who loves other people, who is always *b'simchah* no matter how hard he works or how hard it is at times to do *chesed* with others, who can sing *shirah*. While at times it may be tiresome and tedious to do a *chesed*, those who do so are full of happiness and joy at being able to help another person. So *Klal Yisrael* say in this *shirah*, "This is Hashem and I will adorn Him by emulating His virtues, by being merciful and compassionate."

This is a big leap. How can a person say he will be like Hashem? Can we in any way emulate His attributes?

The answer is yes, for there is a reservoir of spirituality within us. Each member of *Klal Yisrael* possesses a *neshamah*, soul, and our Sages tell us that this *neshamah* is part of Hashem. We are called children of Hashem, and a child has something in common with the parent. We are children of Hashem because we have a part of that greatness within us. We can at least partially transcend our physical limitations and our natural inclinations in order to elevate ourselves. We can emulate Hashem because we are a part of Him. *Klal Yisrael* sang *shirah* only after they realized that if we emulate those *middos* of Hashem, then we are in a state where we can say *shirah* to Hashem. If one does not possess that graciousness and compassion, that feeling for other people, one will never say *shirah*.

It takes a lot of courage to conquer the *yetzer hara*. All of us have instinctive inclinations, lusts, desires, anger, etc., to a certain degree. Greatness comes from not following these inclinations but from rising above them.

Yet there are even higher levels. For example, people who bear insult and do not try to take revenge by insulting in return are compared to the sun shining at its full strength. Physical desires, such as lust and greed, are not easily conquered, but still greater is the one who suffers reproach without taking revenge. This is because refraining from vengeance is a spiritual matter. The hurt which one suffers causes pains to the soul, and conquering the desire for revenge is harder than conquering physical desires.

All in all, we must know that the only time we can say *shirah* is when we can say, "This is my G-d and I will rise up to emulate Him, to do the things He wants me to do."

Today we live in a world of luxuries, but 70 or 80 years ago in Europe, the poverty was terrible. In the Mir Yeshivah, there were many poverty-stricken families. One yeshivah *bachur* I knew was a real powerhouse, who, when his suit wore out, turned it inside out and wore it with patches. Even getting water was difficult. At times, the temperature would drop to 20 degrees below zero and the wells would freeze over. But people were happy and enjoyed life. Just compare those times with our times today, with all our riches. People are wealthy but they go around with bitter faces. They are unhappy with themselves, unhappy with their children, and unhappy with their jobs, totally unhappy. You seldom find an individual with a smile on his face or a person who will say he's happy. People try to make themselves happy but they often do not succeed.

The difference is that in previous generations, doing a *chesed* for someone meant so much more than it does today. They enjoyed doing the *chesed* and that enjoyment, that *simchah*, brings out *shirah* in a person. A person can have all the wealth in the world and not enjoy it because he does not possess within himself the compassion and *chesed* that gives one that *simchah*.

A person is allowed to eat meat or drink wine, which give a person *simchah*, even when he is sitting *shivah*, but he may not study Torah because it brings *simchah*. What is the difference between the two? The answer is a simple one: Eating meat and drinking wine give only a physical type of *simchah* that will not dispel the mourning; he is still a mourner even while eating the meat. However, when one studies Torah, he is so full of *simchah* that he is on a level of singing *shirah*. How can he mourn when he is in the mood to sing *shirah*?

Emulating Hashem's virtues means that we are compassionate and kind not only when we feel like it or when the person deserves it. Even if someone has slighted us or reproached us, we should forgive the person and not reply negatively.

It is not so difficult to be merciful and compassionate when we feel the other person deserves it. But emulating

Hashem means that even when the person really deserves justice and punishment, we do not forget the compassion and *chesed*. When we are slighted and hurt, when someone has said *lashon hara* about us, what should we do? We are in such pain! The answer is to emulate Hashem. Forgive and forget, have mercy and kindness. We all sometimes do foolish things, but we can do *teshuvah*. Maybe the person who hurt you will come at some time to say he's sorry and ask *mechilah* from you.

Our Sages tell us that in a certain year of drought, Rabbi Eliezer stood before the Ark and said 24 blessings for rain but received no answer. Then Rabbi Akiva arose and said, "Our Father, our King, we have no King but You," and it began to rain. The renowned Rabbi Eliezer, who was Rabbi Akiva's rebbe, had beseeched Hashem for rain but received no response at all, whereas Rabbi Akiva uttered just a few words and was immediately answered. Having witnessed this scene, the disciples were shocked. Was Rabbi Akiva greater than his rebbe, Rabbi Eliezer? Just then a heavenly voice came forth and declared: "It is not because one is greater than the other, but rather that one ignored any slights done to him by his fellowman while the other didn't" (*Taanis* 25b).

When a person is *oveir al midosav*, ignoring slights, he will overlook and forgive the insults of others. He does not pursue the way of *middas hadin*, the attribute of justice, the strict method according to which the sinner must be punished immediately for his sin. Instead, he strives to maintain in himself the attribute of compassion, which means forgiveness, overlooking evil, and giving people a second chance. Our Sages explain that Rabbi Eliezer was not answered because he would not have lightly forgiven a person who had slighted him, a great teacher of Torah, whereas Rabbi Akiva would have overlooked and forgiven the same act.

Rav Yisrael Salanter makes a remarkable comment on this. Why, he asks, couldn't Rabbi Eliezer have followed this way as well? Certainly if Rabbi Akiva had attained that virtue, his own rebbe could have achieved it as well. We find the same difference of opinion between Shammai and Hillel. Shammai is thought to be the strict, firm, stern individual, while Hillel is considered the humble person who always forgave. Here, too, Rav Yisrael Salanter asks the same question: These people were like angels. Couldn't Shammai have become as humble as Hillel? Why did he remain strict? Why didn't he change his nature?

Rav Yisrael Salanter explains: It wasn't that strictness was a facet of Shammai's nature or one of his character traits; it came from a decision made by him in his *avodas Hashem*. Shammai believed in pursuing the strict path, for if one is too lenient, people will continue to sin and will not, for example, respect the bearers of Torah. We find that Hashem wanted to create the world only according to the attribute of justice, but since the world would not have been able to exist with so much immediate punishment, He created the world through the attribute of mercy. The commentators say, though, that on an individual basis one should still strive to attain the level of *middas hadin*, for this is a path of absolute truth. Shammai agreed with and lived by this preferred opinion. Hillel, on the other hand, was the humble person, who shunned the path of sternness in *middas hadin*.

The difference of opinion between Shammai and Hillel and between Rabbi Eliezer and Rabbi Akiva was one and the same. Rabbi Eliezer was known as a disciple of Shammai, while Rabbi Akiva was a disciple of Hillel, each following the path of his own rebbe. From these two possible paths of life, we learn an important principle: According to the way one acts toward his fellowman, so does Hashem act toward him. Rav Yisrael Salanter explains that Hashem accepted the prayers of Rabbi Akiva because Rabbi Akiva emulated the attribute of mercy.

Concerning an *ir hanidachas*, an entire town that had turned to idolatry, the Ohr HaChaim mentions a wonderful thought (*Devarim* 13:18). The Torah commands that the whole city be destroyed and its memory expunged. Although the people were obligated to destroy the town in its entirety, nevertheless, in doing so they ran the risk of becoming *achzarim*, cruel and mean-spirited, through this brutal act. But the Torah assures us that Hashem promised to have pity on the people. Which people? The Ohr HaChaim answers: those who were merciful. He explains that Hashem will have pity on these people by protecting their wondrous lifesaving attribute of compassion, ensuring that it not be warped by their performing the necessary mitzvah of expunging evil. This is consistent with what we have learned: that Hashem has mercy only on a merciful person.

One who lives according to the attribute of mercy will be judged with mercy. To acquire this attribute, to make it a part of you, is not easy — but it is very important. We ask Hashem for many things and sometimes we wonder, "I asked so often and cried so much, why weren't my prayers answered?" One reason is that it depends on how we act toward others.

We all have the attribute of mercy. The trouble is that we lose our compassion when we are slighted or hurt. Being overly sensitive is a major cause of trouble in our lives. It prods us to bear a grudge and take revenge. Let us resolve not to take things to heart, not to make a fuss, and to forgive the person who hurts us.

How wonderful it would be if we were to merit the attribute of mercy! Not only would we merit many good things from Hashem, but we ourselves would feel so much better. The Gemara brings the story of Binyamin

HaTzaddik, the chief trustee of the charity fund (*Bava Basra* 11a). During a famine, he was approached by a woman asking for aid. When he told her the funds were exhausted, she replied, "If you don't give me food, my seven sons and I will die." Binyamin HaTzaddik then gave her money from his own personal funds. A short time later, he fell ill and was about to die. The angels said to Hashem, "Binyamin HaTzaddik saved a mother and her seven sons. Why should he die?" The decree was immediately revoked and 22 years were added to his life. He was called Binyamin HaTzaddik, but all his other acts of righteousness could not have saved him from *middas hadin* — only the attribute of mercy saved his life, for "Charity rescues from death" (*Mishlei* 10:2).

Let us resolve to pursue compassion and mercy with our neighbors, spouse, and friends, and in that way we will merit that Hashem will treat us with these attributes.

QUESTIONS & ANSWERS

Q What time should women *daven* in the morning?

A Get up a few minutes earlier and *daven* before you have to get started with the children, if possible. Or, if the children leave for school by 8:00, you can *daven* then but if you don't have time earlier, you can *daven* until *chatzos* [halachic noon].

Q Are women *yotzei* with their husband's Friday night Kiddush if they did not *daven* Maariv?

A Yes, although some authorities, like the *Magen Avraham*, rule that it is better that she *daven* herself. The problem is that since the husband already *davened* Maariv, his Kiddush is *d'Rabbanan* while her obligation for Kiddush would be *d'Oraysa*. Then the question would arise whether by hearing his Kiddush she has fulfilled her obligation. The best thing is for the husband to have the intention during Maariv not to fulfill his *chiyuv d'Oraysa* in case his wife did not *daven* Maariv.

Q Can a woman make Havdalah herself if her husband is not home?

A Yes. She can make Havdalah herself. She doesn't have to drink the wine; someone else can drink it.

Q If one finds a piece of food between his teeth after he has made a final blessing what should he do?

A It is preferable to take it out of one's mouth.

Q Does a woman have to wash *mayim achronim*?

A Yes, especially if she dishes out food and gets her hands soiled with grease. In this case, according to all opinions, she has to wash her hands. She even has to wash her hands if they are soiled before making the *berachah borei pri ha'etz* on fruit, or any other *berachah* at any time. The same way she wouldn't shake hands with dirty hands, it is not dignified to say Hashem's Name with dirty hands, and therefore this *takanah* of our Sages applies to women as well.

Q Regarding *mayim achronim*: Can you wash your hands under a faucet instead of pouring water over them from a cup?

A Yes.

Q Must one wash one's hands every time one touches young children's upper arms and legs, or is this necessary only during a meal or every time one has to make a *berachah*?

A One may be *meikil* and needn't wash the hands after touching very small children, who are handled continuously, if they are bathed every day, unless they perspire freely.

Q While washing *netilas yadayim* in the morning, if a child holds the cup the wrong way and sticks his thumb into the water, does the water become *tamei*, halachically impure?

A Some are stringent, so if you have other water, change the water.

Q Is it permissible to use a basin that is normally used to wash dishes for *negel vasser*?

A Yes. But afterward, make sure there is no *negel vasser* left.

Q After going to the bathroom, does one have to wash with a cup?

A Preferably yes, but the faucet is sufficient.

Q Can you make a *berachah* in the presence of a child who is undressed?

A Not if the child is a girl over the age of 3, or a boy 9 years or older.

Q Can you say half of Hashem's Name in order to teach a child to say a *berachah*?

A At the age of *chinuch* you can even say the whole Name, but under the age of *chinuch* you cannot.

Q What *berachah* is made on fruit pie at the end of a meal? There is crust on the top and bottom and it is loaded with fruit?

A The whole *shei'lah* of making *berachos* on cake at the end of the meal is only if you're not fully satiated. If you're not full and you still have room for the cake, there is no need for the *berachah*. If you are full and have no room for the cake, then you have a *shei'lah*. But the Chayei Adam offers an idea to avoid the *safek*. When you make the *hamotzi*, have the cake in mind, and then you need not make a separate *berachah*.

ENJOY THE SEDER

In former times, wealthy people who had large houses also had many servants who did their every bidding, while poor people, who could not afford servants, lived in small homes of one or two rooms. The pre-Pesach chores of the rich were performed by their servants, while the poor, who had only their one or two rooms to clean, a few pieces of furniture, and a minimum of utensils and clothing, took care of their needs themselves. In those days, cleaning was hard work. Tables were made of raw wood, requiring that they be scrubbed or even sanded to ensure that no pieces of food were left hidden in the cracks. Earthen or wooden floors also needed to be thoroughly cleaned and scrubbed.

Today we seem to be caught in a trap. The average modern home is larger than ever. Furniture, utensils, and clothing are much more plentiful. Yet, while the average home today is comparable to the more affluent homes of previous generations, we do not have the servants they had, so that today all the chores fall on the housewife. At the same time, she still feels obligated to clean and scrub as they did in former times, even though the wood of her furniture is finely finished and her floors are acrylic, marble tiled, or carpeted, making this type of cleaning unnecessary.

As a result, the pressure of pre-Pesach cleaning has reached unnecessary and overwhelming levels. Housewives feel pressured, and the stress makes them unable to enjoy Pesach as they should.

Pesach, like every other Yom Tov, must be enjoyed by every member of the family, including women. This is an obligation clearly defined in the Torah as explained by our Sages (*Mishnah Berurah* 529:15). Pesach is to be looked forward to and anticipated with joy. Every woman should be well rested, relaxed, and alert at the Seder table so that she can fulfill all the Torah and Rabbinic obligations and follow the Haggadah with the rest of the family. Clearly, the performance of her pre-Pesach duties must be balanced against her Pesach obligations.

Pre-Pesach cleaning is required to avoid transgressing any Torah or Rabbinic prohibition of having *chametz* in the house on Pesach, but the cleaning need not be excessive.

It is not the intention here to abolish *minhagim* that have been passed down by *Klal Yisrael* from generation to generation. Nevertheless, some practices adopted by contemporary women in their Pesach cleaning are not an actual continuation of the old *minhagim*. For example, if a person does not sell his *chametz*, of course it is necessary to check his utensils and wash off any *chametz* left on them, or render the *chametz* inedible. But if the *chametz* is sold, then washing the pots, pans, and dishes that are going to be locked away is not necessary. One might be tempted to insist on doing the extra work anyway, to be *machmir*, stringent. Also, many women like to do more cleaning than the bare minimum, often incorporating general spring cleaning into the required pre-Pesach chores. However, by putting so much effort into cleaning, far above and beyond what is called for by the Torah, a woman runs the risk of coming to the Seder too exhausted to properly observe the Seder.

In general, all property and possessions must be cleaned and checked to make sure that they are free of all *chametz*, except in the following cases:

a. If, during the year, *chametz* is not brought into a place, that place does not have to be cleaned out or checked for *chametz* (*Orach Chaim* 433:3 and *Mishnah Berurah* 17).

b. Any article that is not used on Pesach does not need to be checked for *chametz* provided it is put away properly and the *chametz* in it is sold.

c. Crumbs that have been rendered completely inedible to the extent that they are not fit to be eaten by a dog are not considered *chametz* (*Orach Chaim* 442:2).

d. The general obligation to check for and destroy crumbs does not apply if the crumbs are less than the size of an olive, what halachah calls "*kezayis*," and are dirty or spoiled enough to prevent a person from eating them (*Mishnah Berurah* 442:33, and *Shaarei Teshuvah* 12).

e. The household cleaner used must spoil the crumbs to the extent that people would refrain from eating them.

f. It is customary that an item to be *kashered* should not be used for hot *chametz* for 24 hours prior to *kashering*, in order that it should not be a *ben-yomo*.

Practical applications are as follows:

(1) *Clothes Closets:* If there is a significant possibility that they contain *chametz*, they should be checked for edible *chametz*, and also for crumbs (*Mishnah Berurah* 442:33, and *Shaarei Teshuvah* 12). If the probability that *chametz* entered these places is remote, a rav can be con-

sulted to clarify the conditions under which they do not have to be checked (*Orach Chaim* 433:3 and *Mishnah Berurah* 17). This includes chests, dressers, basements, and all other similar places.

(2) *Floors:* In our times we don't have earthen floors with deep cracks in them. It is sufficient for tiled or covered floors to be swept and washed with a household floor cleaner. Cracks and spaces between tiles do not have to be checked if the cleaning solution reaches into them.

(3) *Food Cabinets:* If the cabinet is not going to be used on Pesach, then you just have to lock it or seal it in a manner that will remind you not to use it on Pesach, and sell it with the *chametz*. If the cabinet is going to be used on Pesach, take out all the food, and wash it with a rag soaked in a household cleaner. Be sure the cleansing agent reaches into all the cracks and soaks into any crumbs that might be left there. The usual practice is to line the cabinets (*Orach Chaim* 442:2).

(4) *Refrigerator:* Take the food out, and wash the refrigerator with a rag soaked in a household cleaner. The racks are usually covered. (It is advisable to leave holes for air circulation.)

(5) *Kashering sinks:* (a) Clean the sinks well. (b) It is customary that no hot *chametz* be poured into the sinks for 24 hours before *kashering* them. (c) Pour boiling water into them and on their sides. (d) Some people pour bleach down the drain followed by boiling water. (e) One should line the sinks (e.g. with a plastic insert or contact paper).

(6) *Faucet taps:* Cleaning, without any other *kashering* procedure, is sufficient.

(7) *Marble and stainless steel counters:* If they were used for hot *chametz* then (a) they should first be cleaned well. (b) Next, preferably (if this will not ruin the countertop) pour boiling hot water on them (see *Sinks* (b)). (c) The

counters should be completely covered so that nothing for Pesach touches them.

(8) Tabletops: Wash them with a household cleaner. The usual practice is to cover the tables.

(9) **Kashering** *the stove:* There are many different types of stoves and ovens and it is not within the scope of this talk to discuss all of them. The following are the general guidelines. If you have any questions or doubts consult a rav.

Stovetop: Wash the top and side surface areas with a rag soaked in a strong household cleaner. Clean the knobs well. If you do not have a set of grates for Pesach then the grates can be *kashered* by first cleaning them very well; then put them back on the stove, light the burners to the maximum, and cover them with the Shabbos *blech* (a piece of sheet metal). [Be careful that the knobs don't melt.] This spreads the heat over the whole top and intensifies the heat on the grates. Let them heat for 10 minutes. Before *kashering*, it is customary to let 24 hours pass after the last use of cooking *chametz.* After you have *kashered* the grates, cover the top with aluminum foil (being extremely careful not to block the air inlets around the burners and on the back of the stove, as this could create poisonous fumes in the room).

Oven: (a) *If it is necessary to use the oven,* first clean it well with a chemical oven cleaner, making sure that it reaches into all the cracks and around the screws. It is customary to let 24 hours pass after the last use of cooking or baking *chametz.* Then heat the inside of the oven by turning it on to its highest temperature for about one hour (*Mishnah Berurah* 451:32). If possible, line the entire inside surface of the oven (including the door) with thick aluminum foil. If a closed oven insert is available, this would be preferable.

(b) Do not use the *chametz'dik* oven racks for Pesach. If this is difficult, then one can *kasher* the racks with the same procedure as for the oven, placing them in the oven as close as possible to the heating element. Afterwards, if possible cover them with aluminum foil.

If the oven is not going to be used: None of the above is necessary. Just make certain that there is no edible *chametz* inside, tape it closed well and see below #10.

(10) **Pots, pans, dishes, silverware:** Whatever is not going to be used for Pesach should either be locked up, or put away and sealed in a manner that will remind you not to use it on Pesach. If there is a possibility of actual *chametz* in them, the *chametz* should be sold, following the general rule that any article not used on Pesach does not need to be checked for *chametz* provided it is put away properly and the *chametz* in it is sold. If you do not sell *chametz*, then they should be either washed or soaked in a household cleaner; it is not necessary to scrub them (*Mishnah Berurah* 442:33, and *Shaarei Teshuvah* 12). (Concerning *kashering* utensils for Pesach, consult a rav.)

(11) **Food processor or mixer:** One should have separate bowls, beaters, and blades for Pesach. Clean the outside base and the inside motor area where *chametz* can reach.

(12) **Dishtowels:** It is customary to have a set of dish towels especially for Pesach. However, if one does not have a Pesach set of dishtowels, then regular dishtowels may be used if they are washed with a detergent and no food remains attached to them.

(13) **Pesach tablecloths:** These can be ironed with the same iron as is used during the rest of the year.

(14) **Clothes, blankets, pockets, etc.:** If they have been washed in detergent or dry-cleaned, then there is no need for them to be checked, following the rule above that the general obligation to check for and destroy crumbs does not apply if the crumbs are less than the size of an olive, *kezayis*, and are dirty or spoiled enough to prevent a person from eating them. If they haven't been washed, they need to be cleaned and checked thoroughly by brush-

ing or shaking them out well. However, if there is a possibility of crumbs between the stitches or in a hidden crevice that cannot be shaken out, then they must be wiped with a rag that has been soaked in a detergent (*Orach Chaim* 442:2; *Mishnah Berurah* 442:33, and *Shaarei Teshuvah* 12). Clothes that will not be worn on Pesach do not have to be checked, but they should be put away and the *chametz* in them sold.

(15) **Siddurim, bentchers, sefarim, and books:** If there is a chance that they contain *chametz* crumbs, then they should either be put away and sold with other *chametz* utensils, or cleaned and checked well.

(16) **Toys:** If there is edible *chametz* on the toys, then it should be either removed or rendered inedible. There is no need to scrub toys.

(17) **Tahinah and other kitniyos:** These may be used after the house has been cleaned for Pesach. They should not be cooked in utensils that will be used on Pesach, and certainly not on Pesach itself (according to the Ashkenazic *minhag*).

(18) **Checking the rooms:** If it is too difficult to check all the rooms on one night, then the work may be divided and done on other nights (according to all the laws of *bedikas chametz*). No *chametz* should be left in any room that has been cleaned and checked properly. Since the blessing is not recited before the night of the 14th of Nissan, therefore, at least one place that had *chametz* should be left unchecked. Then, the mitzvah of *bedikas chametz* can be performed with a *berachah* on the night of the 14th in that area. If the whole house had already been completely cleaned before the 14th, then the 10 pieces of *chametz* that are customarily hidden and found should be hidden by someone else so that a proper *bedikah* can be made.

(19) **Food that falls** onto a chair or onto the floor on Pesach should be washed off for hygienic reasons. The

item does not become *chametz* even if the food is hot.

(20) **Last-minute preparations:** Last-minute preparations such as setting the table should be done early enough in the day so that that the woman of the house will be able to rest. The Seder should be started immediately after Maariv to ensure that the children won't fall asleep at the Seder (*Orach Chaim* 472:1).

(21) **Enjoy Pesach!** Try to make the Pesach chores easy for yourself. Don't do unnecessary hard work. Don't do unnecessary cleaning. You can be like a queen and you must enjoy your Pesach!

Some women have a habit at the Seder of taking a bite of matzah then running back and forth to the kitchen, taking a few more bites in between. This way it takes them too long to eat the matzah and they do not fulfill the mitzvah properly. You have to be careful to eat a *kezayis* matzah at the Seder within 2 to 4 minutes. If this is impossible, 5 to 6 minutes is also acceptable. At the most, it should be within 9 minutes.

The wine preferably should be drunk in two swallows. If this is difficult, then up to 4 minutes is acceptable. If necessary, even up to 5 or 6 minutes. If you can't drink wine at all, you may use grape juice. If you can't drink grape juice, then *chamar medinah* can be used. What is considered *chamar medinah* varies from country to country so consult your rav.

The mitzvah of eating the *kezayis* matzah is *d'Oraysa*, so be careful with it. The mitzvah *d'Rabbanan* of drinking the four cups of wine, and eating the *maror, korech,* and *afikoman* are special mitzvos for this night, so do not leave the table until you have finished eating and drinking the required amount. Sit like a queen! Relax and be calm while eating and drinking the matzah and wine within the time limit. The cooking can be checked after completing the mitzvos. Remember: These are mitzvos that can be done only once a year, so enjoy them, and enjoy the whole Seder.

QUESTIONS & ANSWERS

Q Is ridding the house of *chametz gamur* a basic obligation or a stringency?

A There is a *chiyuv* of *biur* and *bedikas chametz*. You don't have to do the whole *bedikas chametz* on the last night. You can check and close off rooms beforehand. Leave one room or one place in a room unchecked. Then the actual *bedikah* should not take very long. If you wash the floor with detergent, you don't have to worry about crumbs. Then, you only have to check for pieces of *chametz* that are the size of a *kezayis*, which is quite large and easy to find and get rid of.

Q Can one actually sell *chametz gamur*?

A The Vilna Gaon didn't want to resort to this sale because it seems like a fictitious sale. According to the halachah you may.

Q Is there any reason to scrub *chametz* pots when I clean for Pesach?

A No. If you are not going to use them for Pesach, just sell the *chametz* on them.

Q If you wash a pot with soap and the dirt doesn't

A come off, is it still considered *pasul*?

Of course. Any detergent that you would use would probably make it *pasul*.

Q How do you clean every crack and crevice in a closet that held *chametz*?

A If you are not going to use it on Pesach, you don't have to clean it. You can just lock it up and sell it. But if you are going to use it, clean it and squeeze some liquid detergent into the cracks and corners.

Q Should you put out 10 pieces of bread?

A This is the *minhag*. Someone other than the one who is making the *bedikah* should hide them.

Q Do you have to check children's toys?

A If you wipe them well with a rag and detergent then you don't have to check them because any possible *chametz* will have been spoiled.

Q Can I use regular perfume on Pesach?

A If the perfume is made from grain alcohol, it would make it non-kosher for Pesach. But if the alcohol is a synthetic one, you can use it. If you don't know for sure, sell it and use perfume that is kosher for Pesach.

Q If I make sure throughout the entire year not to bring *chametz* into a room, when cleaning for Pesach can I assume that there is no *chametz* in it?

A Yes, the halachah is that a place into which *chametz* is not brought does not need to be checked. The same holds true for *sefarim*. If you are sure that the *sefer* contains no *chametz* inside or outside, it is enough to wipe off the shelf.

Q Are we supposed to go to the Kosel on Pesach?

A It is a good practice but you are not obligated to do so.

Q

I'm worried about cleaning for Pesach. How much do I need to do?

A

Our women aren't enjoying Pesach. They are falling flat on their faces from overwork. Many women have been overwhelmed by the stresses and pressures of Pesach preparations. Pesach should not be a Tishah B'Av. Many women have taken upon themselves *chumros*, things that are not according to the halachah. The vast majority of the cleaning being done is unnecessary and just self-torture.

A woman asked me, "If one is very tired, how much Pesach cleaning should one do?" She's already tired before she began! How can she clean properly if she's tired?

I said to her, "Sit down and enjoy a cup of tea. If you listen to me, there is very little cleaning that needs to be done."

Places where you do not enter with *chametz* don't have to be cleaned. Places you don't use on Pesach you can just close off and sell. You can put away all the *chametz* dishes. You don't have to scrub them. Even if you don't sell your *chametz*, just wash the dishes or soak them in detergent to *pasel* the *chametz*, then lock them up in a room, and there you go. If you do sell your *chametz*, put all the items to sell in the same room. You can save yourself hours of tedious work that is not necessary at all. If the house is properly cleaned, the actual *bedikas chametz* can be done within half-an-hour.

Scrubbing the burners on the stove is entirely unnecessary; it is enough to wash them. There is no *chametz* there; if it's burnt to a crisp, it doesn't have the din of *chametz* anymore. However, the grates upon which the pots rest must be cleaned well. Then put the Shabbos blech over the burners for 10 minutes, turn up the fire full force, with the heat concentrated on the burners. All these preparations shouldn't take very long. That's all you have to do. It is recommended to put a little aluminum foil on the open areas. This doesn't take long.

As for the refrigerator, there's nothing that can make the refrigerator *chametz*, unless there is a piece of actual *chametz* there. Remove any actual *chametz* and wash out the refrigerator; that is sufficient. The racks are usually covered with some paper for Pesach. That's more than enough. It won't take that much time at all.

Regarding the sink, wash it out. Pour a kettle full of boiling water on the sink and line it, (e.g. with an insert or contact paper or heavy-duty aluminum foil). How long will that take you? Some people pour bleach down the drain; afterward they pour boiling water down also.

The same principle applies to the floors. Just sweep them and go over them with a wet mop soaked in detergent and there's no need for any more cleaning. For *bedikas chametz*, glance here and there and that's all. Even if there's *chametz*, it's *nifsal me'achilah*.

If you just want to get the house clean, okay, but there's no need for it. You don't have to do work that is unnecessary, and get yourself sick and come to Pesach falling on your face! Instead you can be a queen and enjoy Pesach.

By the way, if you have children, prepare the table before the afternoon. Have it all set. Don't wait till after Maariv when you may be tired. You should even take an afternoon nap! When Maariv is over, you should start the Seder right away so the children won't be too tired to enjoy the Seder.

Q What should we do about pockets?

A If you have children, there might be a sandwich in the pockets, so look through them. What you should be careful about is *sefarim* you use on Shabbos. Sometimes you find crumbs in the pages of *zemiros* Shabbos. Put these away with the *chametz* things that you will not use over Pesach.

Q Do I have to clean each page of my cookbooks, or can I just put them away with the *chametz*?

A You can just put them away and sell them.

Q Do we also have to be careful about places where we don't usually eat but where food may have been brought in?

A The Sages suspected such places. In those days, people had what was called a wine cellar. During the meal, a person might go down there with a sandwich or a piece of challah to bring more wine and inadvertently, food might have been left there. There is an obligation to check those places because large pieces (the size of a *kezayis*) were brought there. But as for crumbs, *al pi din* there's no obligation to check at all. The *minhag* is to be *machmir* on crumbs that are edible. It all depends on each family to know where *chametz* might have been brought.

Q Is putting children's clothes in the washing machine sufficient to clean them for Pesach? Even if clothes are washed in the machine, sometimes there are still some crumbs in the pockets.

A It's definitely sufficient. Even the pockets get clean with machine washing. Since detergent was used, people won't eat any crumbs even if they may find them during Pesach, so it's okay. It is best to pull the pockets out when you put the clothes in the machine.

Q **If you sell a cabinet that may have** *chametz*, **does it need to be checked?**

A No, just put a sign or reminder on it to remind you not to use it and tape it closed.

Q **Can one use the same dishtowels for Pesach as for the rest of the year?**

A Yes, if you use a detergent to wash them. But it is better to have special ones for Pesach.

Q **If a child puts his toys, which are always with** *chametz*, **on the Pesach table, what should I do about it?**

A Since they were wiped off well before Pesach, you can just sit back and sing *zemiros*! There's nothing to worry about.

Q **If I have no clean clothes during** *Chol HaMoed*, **may I wash clothes?**

A Prepare enough clothes not to have to wash on *Chol HaMoed*.

Q **If an adult's clothes constantly get dirty because of children, can they be washed on** *Chol HaMoed*?

A No, because adults are considered capable of taking measures to keep their clothes clean, even if they are caring for children.

Q **Can children color, paint, cut and glue on** *Chol HaMoed*?

A If the child has reached the age of *chinuch*, I would not recommend these things because they are *melachos*. However, if it is like a toy or game to him, in which case it would be considered a *maasei hedyot*, non-skilled labor, then he would be allowed.

Q I am studying in Israel. I plan to live here, but I'm going to visit my parents in America for Pesach. How many days of Pesach should I keep?

A This is a very common question. The American boys and girls who have their affiliations in America, their friends and family, in most cases will eventually go back there to live. To help them decide how many days of Pesach to keep, I ask the boys this question: If a girl would come along with all of the virtues you are seeking, the only condition being that she wants to live in America, would you marry her?

Once you resolve to live here permanently no matter what happens, through hardships, etc. — unless, of course, for some reason you have to go back — then this is your home and you're a one-day girl or boy. Going back for a visit does not change your status.

But if you have not made up your mind to stay, or for instance, if a *shidduch* or a job came along and you might go back, then you're a two-day boy or girl. To keep only one day, you've got to resolve that "this is my home" come what may, just like a Yerushalmi who was born here!

Q How does the *Rosh Yeshivah* personally feel about living in Eretz Yisrael as opposed to living in America?

A When I came to Eretz Yisrael I felt at home, that I belonged.

Q What are one's obligations toward non-religious parents coming for Pesach?

A You must respect them as much as you can and try to draw them closer. But if you keep only one day, you can't conduct a second Seder for them; they must conduct it for themselves. If they don't know how, help them join someone who is making a second Seder.

Q **Can one do work in front of these parents on the second day of Yom Tov?**

A Of course. Only outside of Eretz Yisrael we don't.

Q **There are Haggadahs that are printed for non-religious people and these may have pictures that are immodest. May one give such a Haggadah as a present to someone who will not appreciate or understand the Orthodox Haggadah?**

A No, you should not give it to them.

Q **Which foods are *kitniyos*?**

A Rice, beans, and peanuts are some examples of *kitniyos*.

Q **Is one allowed to eat tahina, ground sesame seed paste, on Pesach?**

A No, it's *kitniyos*.

Q **I am due to give birth Pesach time. Could the *Rosh Yeshivah* please explain the bare minimum I must do for Pesach cleaning?**

A Stay in bed. Let your husband do the *bedikas chametz* and that's all.

Q **Can a person who is converting to Judaism through an Orthodox rabbi attend the Seder?**

A He may, but if he hasn't converted yet, he shouldn't touch the wine.

Q **How much of a hand matzah is a *kezayis*? How much of a machine matzah?**

A There are conflicting opinions about a machine matzah. Some hold that half is a *kezayis* and some hold that it is two-thirds. One should eat hand matzos for the mitzvah of matzah.

For the hand matzos, it depends on the thickness of the matzah. I usually say just fill up your mouth with matzah as much as you can. And remember — do not feel pressured when you eat the matzah. Sit back and eat slowly. The time for eating the *kezayis* is not from when you begin to chew but from when you swallow. So break the matzah into small pieces, fill up your mouth as much as you can, then chew calmly, and swallow the whole *kezayis* at one time if possible, as the halachah requires. Then you will have fulfilled the mitzvah according to all opinions.

Q After I clean the *chametz* dishes before Pesach, before putting them away, my husband checks them over. Usually he finds *chametz* stuck to them here and there. What should we do?

A Just wash them with detergent as well as you can. Then, even if something is still stuck on, it's no problem at all — even if you are not planning on selling the *chametz* on the plates. Just put them away with the other *chametz'dik* dishes and don't worry about it.

Q Is there any detergent other than strong ammonia or bleach to make unreachable food in the category of "not edible to a dog"?

A Any detergent that makes it abominable is fine.

Q Can a food processor that has a plastic bowl and metal blades be used for Pesach if it was only used for potatoes?

A Yes, you can use it if it was used only for potatoes, but only if you were careful never to use it for *chametz*. A juicer may be used for Pesach if *chametz* never came in contact with it.

Q If you have a separate Pesach plastic bowls and beaters and separate blades for a mixer, can you use the same motor?

A Yes, if you clean the base well and you change the parts that touched the *chametz* and thoroughly clean out the inside motor area, where *chametz* can reach.

Q I have a stove with a self-cleaning oven. May I use the oven on Pesach?

A A self-cleaning oven's mechanism *kashers* the oven.

Q Can you iron tablecloths that you are going to use on Pesach with an iron that was used for *chametz* tablecloths?

A Of course.

Q If I have a room that I do not want to use for Pesach and I know there is no *chametz* in it and it is basically clean, do I have to check it?

A No. If you are not going to use that room for Pesach, just lock it. You don't have to check it or clean it at all. Just sell it.

Q If the house is cleaned for Pesach a week before Pesach, may you cook *kitniyos*?

A Yes, you may, but do not use your Pesach pots for *kitniyos*.

Q Do pots need to be *kashered*?

A Yes, used pots have to be *kashered* if you want to use them for Pesach. A new one does not have to be *kashered*. You need only *tovel* it.

Q If toys are thrown into the bathtub with cleanser, how thoroughly do you have to clean them?

A You don't have to scrub them. The soaking is enough for the toys.

Q If food falls on the floor or on a chair during Pesach what should I do? What if it's hot?

A Just wash the food off. It is nothing, even if it's hot. The floors were clean. There is also no need to wash fruits and vegetables before Pesach. Of course, you rinse them for hygienic reasons.

Q Do you have to *kasher* and cover the faucets?

A No, this is not necessary. But some pour boiling water on them.

19 BEING HONEST WITH OURSELVES

When we read about Yisro, one of the most surprising things we see is the reaction of the nations of the world to the great miracles done for Israel. They were shocked and seized with trembling, fear, and dread upon hearing the awesome and terrifying events that G-d brought about in Egypt. Yet only Yisro was moved to join the Jewish people. The Torah says, "Yisro heard" (*Shemos* 18:1), and our Sages ask, "What did he hear?" Rashi tells us that Yisro heard of the splitting of the Red Sea and the war with Amalek. These two events so moved him that he left everything behind and came out to the desert. The question is why was Yisro different from the other peoples of his time? They must have also believed, because if they thought the events were mere accidents of nature, they would not have been shocked and filled with fear.

Yisro was a famous priest in his day. We are told that after these events "he came out to Moshe in the desert where he was encamped" (ibid., v. 5). Rashi explains that the mention here of Moshe

Being Honest with Ourselves ☐ 247

being in the desert, a fact already stated elsewhere, emphasizes what Yisro gave up. He sacrificed everything — fame, his way of life — to come to the desert, a place of utter desolation, to hear the words of the Torah. Others who heard and trembled may not have had as much to lose, so we certainly could have expected them to come. But they did not possess Yisro's greatness.

What was the greatness that made Yisro merit that a *parashah* in the Torah is named after him? The answer is that Yisro was a thinker, a philosopher who understood life. He had worshiped all the idols in the world and was familiar with every type of idol worship — and he knew that there was nothing of value in them. Yisro was not a pleasure seeker. His thinking was objective, removed from all selfish motivations. He had analyzed every form of worship and had come to the conclusion that only Hashem is G-d. Yisro freed himself from all egotistical inclinations, lifted himself above his natural inclinations, and saw the truth.

It is the constant searching for the truth that makes one a practical, realistic person in this universe. Yisro analyzed all the idolatrous cults in the world and came to the conclusion that Hashem is the G-d of truth, for he saw that the Egyptians were punished with exactly the same type of torture they inflicted on Israel. By the very thing which they inflicted were they punished. By the truth of the events, Yisro came to the conclusion that Hashem is the G-d of truth.

The non-thinker doesn't take the truth into consideration. Esav, for example, was actually a great man, a genius with an even greater mind than Yaakov Avinu. Yet he denied G-d and sold his birthright because he saw only what was before him. He lived only for the present, saw only his own generation, and did not have the foresight to see future generations. This was precisely the "eat, drink, and be merry, for tomorrow we may die" approach of the Epicurean philosophers. They didn't worry about tomorrow; only today was important. It takes the objective thinker to analyze the past and the present, and then project into the future. He who sees only the present will never recognize the truth, because truth encompasses not only the present but the future as well.

Yisro recognized that truth is everlasting. When we believe in the eternal nature of Torah, then we know that all these Epicurean ideas like Reconstructionism and Reform Judaism are false. As the Rambam states in the *Ani Ma'amin*, the Torah is eternal, and only that which is eternal is true (*Peirush HaMishnayos, Sanhedrin*, Ch. 10).

The Ramban says that if Adam had not eaten from the Tree of Knowledge, he would have lived forever (*Bereishis* 2:17). With his action, he effected a flaw in man's material being that causes it to disintegrate. Man's spiritual being, though, is everlasting because it is true. "The signature of G-d is truth" (*Shabbos* 55a). A check isn't worth much without the signature, which signifies the truth of what is written. G-d's signature is absolute truth.

"Who is wise? He who sees the future." Why does the Gemara use the term "*sees* the future" (*Tamid* 32a) and not "*knows* the future?" There is a basic difference between just knowing and actually seeing. There are many people who believe in the World to Come, but if you ask them if their deeds are consistent with this belief, they would have to answer in the negative. They do not pursue those things that will merit them the World to Come, like learning Torah, doing mitzvos, and performing good deeds. We see from this contradiction that merely knowing, having a theoretical understanding, is not enough. A person will act upon his knowledge and understanding only when it becomes a part of him, when it becomes a living reality, a basic part of his very being. This is what is meant by the opening passage in *Mesillas Yesharim*: "A man is required to clarify for himself and verify for himself what his obligations are in this world." A person can do this only by linking the past, the present, and the future as one. This means actually seeing the future as a necessary outcome of the past and present until it becomes a living reality for him.

The future is hidden, as our Sages say, but a person would never commit a crime or transgression if he fully understood the connection between the past, present, and future. A person commits a transgression only when a spirit of folly overtakes him. At such times, the living reality vanishes. Its momentary disappearance gives the person an opening to commit a crime, for during that moment he doesn't see the connection between the present and the future. But a person who clearly sees both present and future can't separate the two, for truth is inseparable.

Yisro was fully aware of the connection between the present and the future. This is evident in the advice he gave to Moshe Rabbeinu about judging the people. Yisro saw that in judging the people alone, Moshe had taken upon himself too great a burden, and he felt that the situation could not continue. "You will surely wither away," Yisro tells Moshe (*Shemos* 18:18). Yisro's greatness lay in this ability to analyze the present and to see the future. It was this ability to see the present and future as an inseparable unit that made Yisro leave everything and go out to the desert to join the Jewish people. While other nations saw only the present, and the miracles they saw were forgotten in a week, Yisro saw the truth.

In all areas of life a person must take the future into consideration if he is to succeed, just as a businessman must take into account his total investment, projected yearly profit, and the estimated inflation. Otherwise, he will go bankrupt in half-a-year.

Shlomo HaMelech says that we should seek Torah "as if it is silver and search for it as if for hidden treasures" (*Mishlei* 2:4-5), for only "then will you understand the fear of G-d." Why does the verse use the term "understand the fear of G-d?" Isn't "fear of G-d" the result of understanding? But Shlomo HaMelech wants to emphasize what is involved in seeking the fear of G-d. Like the business venturer, or the diver seeking pearls, a person must take into consideration all the problems and hazards he may encounter. The diver must take into account the dangers involved in his going down and coming up again. If you seek it like "silver or a treasure," then you will understand what is involved in the fear of G-d.

In the same manner, one should take everything into consideration in seeking Torah. Some people see only the present, but a smart person will look ahead 50 or 60 years from now. Even if he amasses millions, what will it mean to him? He will have sleepless nights and restless days trying to gain another million and yet another. But he will have no real satisfaction from all this money. He may build a magnificent mansion but he will only live to enjoy it for 70 or 80 years.

If we scrutinized our deeds, would we find that we have fulfilled our obligations? Usually, this is not the case. One should analyze his situation as a reliable businessman analyzes a business venture. As the *Mesillas Yesharim* advises, the question "What are my obligations in this world?" is the inner core of everything. Look to the future, to 10, 20, or 30 years from now. How will you look at life then? The appetites will vanish and disappear. You will no longer enjoy a charcoal-broiled steak. Chocolate will not have the same appeal. You may develop an ulcer and will not be able to indulge in elaborate foods. You won't be able to run around like you did when you were young. What will remain then?

We are obligated to be honest with ourselves. We can learn from a good businessman. He keeps his accounts and records the profits and deficits year after year. He looks ahead. A person should not waste time. We are here for only a few years. Take full advantage of time by looking ahead.

So let us learn this lesson from Yisro. The nations were shocked, but nothing moved them. The realistic, practical person is the person who thinks about the purpose of life. Day by day, think about what the real purpose of today is, to get as much spiritual attainment from the present as you can.

Look at the example of Yisro. A non-Jew looking realistically at events made a spiritual goal for himself and merited to assist Moshe Rabbeinu and have his name appended to a *parashah* in the Torah. We, too, can think and look realistically at life. Look to the truth. Do not cheat and fool yourself. May G-d, Whose seal is truth, enable us to achieve our true goals in life, the life of Torah, and be proud of ourselves and our children in this age of darkness.

QUESTIONS & ANSWERS

Q Should we invite non-religious relatives for Shabbos in order to draw them closer to Judaism?

A Yes. You can and should invite non-religious relatives for Shabbos. This befriends them and shows them the beauty of Shabbos, and you will be surprised to see that they might come back to Judaism.

There was a man whose father wasn't religious. I told him to try to draw his father closer. He succeeded and his father later became religious.

Q How should we react to a convert who does not want to remain Jewish?

A If it was a proper conversion, she remains a Jewess whether she wants to go back or not. It is our obligation to encourage her. She is just like any other Jew who will be punished for all her transgressions, so we must strengthen her.

Q How does one react to a non-*tznius'dik* advertisement at a bus stop?

A Don't look, that's all!

Q Can a *ben Torah* watch TV at his widowed moth-

A er's house to keep her company and make her happy?

No, it will cause sins. The *yetzer hara* mixes non-kosher with kosher. She doesn't need his company when she watches TV; she has the TV. He can keep her company at other times, or she can shut it off when he comes. There are many bad things on TV and we should not expose ourselves to it.

Q Is it better not to rebuke someone who will not listen?

A This principle applies only if you are 100 percent certain they won't listen. If they might listen, it is better to give them *mussar,* but consult a halachic authority for other details involved.

Q If you have an English name, how important is it to be called by your Hebrew name? And if you have two Hebrew names, should you be called by both?

A You should change your name to go by a Hebrew name. The Hebrew names are beautiful, denote something, and have meaning. As to being called by both names, many times it is too hard to say both names and you can use only one. But in a *misheberach* or on a *kesubah* both names should be used.

20 BNOS TZELAFCHAD

The daughters of Tzelafchad — Machlah, No'ah, Choglah, Milkah, and Tirtzah — came to Moshe Rabbeinu to clarify an issue. "Our father," they said, "died in the wilderness. He was not among the company of those who gathered themselves together against Hashem with Korach — he died of his own sin — and he had no sons" (*Bamidbar* 27:3). They wanted to know why they should lose out on a portion in Eretz Yisrael just because their father left no son.

All those who came out of Egypt were entitled to a portion in Eretz Yisrael. When a person passed away, his male successors were to inherit their father's portion. Tzelafchad's daughters argued that they should not lose out, since their father's whole spiritual future rested with them. Moshe listened to their arguments and asked Hashem for a decision as to the truth of the matter. Hashem responded that their claims were correct and that they should receive their father's inheritance along with the rest of *Klal Yisrael*.

Our Sages comment that it seems strange that the whole matter of inheritance laws was brought out through the daughters of Tzelafchad. Wouldn't it have been more fitting for Moshe to present these laws? After all, he received the Torah and was the one who transmitted it to *Klal Yisrael*. Since we know that *"Megalgalin zechus al yedei zakkai*, Meritorious deeds are done through those who have merit" (*Bava Basra* 119a), Tzelafchad's daughters must have had a certain merit that made them worthy of having the inheritance laws introduced through them.

Our Sages go on to tell us that at the time of this event all of the daughters were over the age of 40 and were still unmarried. They would eventually marry men from the tribe of Yosef and also have children.

Why did they delay marriage? And why were they so privileged that Hashem looked upon them with favor and made miracles for them?

Tzelafchad's daughters wanted to get married but had not found anyone suitable. They were called *nashim tzidkanios*, *chachmanios*, and *darshanios*, righteous, wise, and seekers of truth. They were looking for a spiritual standard in marriage and would not lower their expectations. Desperation could have influenced their thinking. After all, the years were rolling by and time was running out. But they were not prepared to compromise their spiritual standards.

The daughters of Tzelafchad recognized the importance of their virtues, not in a conceited way but in a realistic way, and it seems that this was their merit. They knew that they were righteous, wise, and seekers of truth. They were learned, intelligent women who had brought a scholarly argument to Moshe, one with which Hashem agreed. That they would not marry someone below their standards teaches an important point: Arrogance is wrong but, at the same time, a person must recognize his virtues.

For the daughters of Tzelafchad, nothing was greater than Torah. Women today, knowing that their special qualities are meant to be used for Torah, should also place spiritual values first. Of course, each individual should ask her rav about her specific situation. And as Hashem helped the daughters of Tzelafchad find their true mates, may all women today be so worthy.

QUESTIONS & ANSWERS

Q
A
Can you say "No" to a *shidduch*?
Why not? If he is not good for you why can't you say "No"? If your heart is not in it, don't accept the date.

Q
A
Is it permissible to lie about a *shidduch*?
No, always tell the truth in a *shidduch*. Never lie. It might invalidate the *kiddushin* and make it a *kiddushin b'ta'us*, because maybe he would not have married her if he had known that particular thing, and then they are considered as living together without *kiddushin*.

Q

A
If a person who is a *baal teshuvah* is on a date, does he have to reveal this fact right away?
At the beginning of a *shidduch* it isn't necessary to divulge the fact that you're a *baal teshuvah*. Only do so when you get to know each other better and the *shidduch* looks favorable. It is no disgrace to be a *baal teshuvah*. The Gemara says that even a saintly person does not come to the level of a *baal teshuvah*.

21 THE IMPORTANCE OF WOMEN TODAY

In the secular world today, and perhaps even in the Jewish camp, many people do not understand the woman's role or realize its importance — a role of such importance that the entire future of the Jewish people is resting on it. And it is the quality of *chesed* that enables a woman to fulfill this role.

We can understand the importance of *chesed* if we delve into the remarkable life of Ruth, from whom descended the kingdom of David.

Usually we attribute the greatness of Ruth to her self-sacrifice for Judaism. Clinging so steadfastly to Naomi, unwilling to say goodbye, Ruth said, "Wherever you go, I will go" (*Ruth* 1:16). She clung to the whole Torah with great strength of faith and belief in Hashem, and it is this that most people consider outstanding.

Our Sages say differently. True, Ruth was great because of her steadfast belief in Hashem, but her unique trait of *chesed* counted even more (*Ruth, Midrash Rabbah* 2:14).

Ruth lived with Naomi for 10 years.

She had the unique quality of self-abnegation, of giving herself to Hashem. Indeed our Sages say that a *baal chesed* is one who gives of himself completely, without any reservations or ulterior motives.

This is better understood through a Rashi on *Chumash*. We all know that Eliezer arranged a test to help him find the right wife for Yitzchak. The right girl would offer him water and even give water to his camels. Rashi comments that this girl would then be capable of becoming Yitzchak's wife because she would be a proven *baalas chesed* (*Bereishis* 24:14).

All of us know that the three pillars that support the world are Torah, *avodah* (prayer), and *gemilus chasadim* (lovingkindness). The verse says: "Give truth to Yaakov, *chesed* to Avraham." Truth, the symbol of Torah, was given to Yaakov, the yeshivah *bachur;* Yitzchak, who was brought to be sacrificed, was the pillar of *avodah;* Avraham was the *baal chesed.*

Which type of girl do you think Yitzchak Avinu should look for? I would say that he should look for someone who is similar to himself, who does his type of work. If he serves Hashem through *avodah*, she, too, should be on the same level as he. Avraham Avinu, who was completely devoted to *chesed*, who is identified as the pillar of *chesed*, should seek a wife who does *chesed*, as did Sarah Imeinu. And we find that this is what happened. The Midrash says that they both shared the same type of work: Avraham converted the men, while Sarah converted the women (*Bereishis Rabbah* 39:14).

Yitzchak, then, should have looked for a wife who excelled in *avodah*. Why was he looking for one who did *chesed?*

Rashi explains that Yitzchak's wife had to be worthy of entering into the house of Avraham, which was a home of *chesed*. But the question remains: True, Avraham is the pillar of *chesed,* but she was going to be the wife of Yitzchak, the pillar of *avodah!*

The answer is simple. You cannot serve Hashem without *chesed.* In order to be a wholehearted servant to Hashem you have to give of yourself. A person who is egocentric is not serving Hashem in the true way, because he is not doing it for Hashem's sake; he is doing it for his own ulterior motives. Our Sages say that the woman is the mainstay of the home and therefore must have within her the quality of *chesed.* Serving Hashem is definitely *chesed,* and therefore not only did Avraham need a wife who exemplified *chesed,* but so did Yitzchak. He, too, needed a wife who would care for the Jewish people through graciousness and lovingkindness, for we know that our holy Torah is entirely *chesed.*

So all of the *Avos* needed a wife whose outstanding virtue was *chesed.* Yitzchak, who represented *avodah,* prayer, needed a wife who was outstanding in *chesed* so that she could enter the home of Avraham and emulate the *middah* that is required for *avodas Hashem.* And that was the purpose of Rivkah Imeinu — to be a *baalas chesed.* You might think that the major component of her character should be other virtues; perhaps being a *tzadekes* or a *baalas middos* should be most important; but no, it was a *baalas chesed* that Yitzchak sought. And that *baalas chesed* would make him into Yitzchak Avinu. Sarah, Rivkah, Rachel, and Leah were all builders of homes that made our *Avos* great. Rivkah gave Yitzchak the opportunity to become an *eved Hashem,* and Avraham became great because he had Sarah to care for him. Being a great woman, an *eishes chayil* full of *chesed,* is spirituality. And women should appreciate this.

So while Ruth was great in her steadfastness to Hashem, the endless *chesed* she did by being a servant to Naomi and serving her as a devoted daughter was even greater. Marrying the elderly Boaz was also a great *chesed*. There is a chain of *chesed,* one link after the other throughout her story, and Ruth's spiritual elevation stemmed from this character trait of *chesed*. She gave of herself to her mother-in-law and this enabled her to give of herself to Hashem wholeheartedly, without any ulterior motive. She did what Hashem wanted and nothing stopped her. She was a true servant of Hashem in all respects, and this faith was the result of her *chesed*.

All service of Hashem requires *chesed*, not only in a woman's life but in the Torah world in general, and for the yeshivah student in particular. Without *chesed*, a person cannot be a true *ben Torah*. One who constrains his *chesed* will not study the Torah wholeheartedly and diligently. His study will instead be for honor or as a profession. Our job, though, is to rise above this minimal type of *chesed* to achieve *chesed* on a lofty level, the *chesed* of the spirit. In this way we emulate Hashem's attributes: "Just as He is merciful, so you should be also." This is the level of *Toras chesed* required, as we see with Avraham, whose *chesed* was unlimited. It is required by the *ben Torah* and the woman as well.

A mother of a several months old baby once asked me a wonderfully interesting question. "I have a child," she said, "who likes to eat. I am nursing and spend about one-and-a-half hours at each feeding. This adds up to endless hours during each day, and I am forced to neglect the home and the other children. Should I stop nursing and give the baby formula to enable me to accomplish more?"

This is a very practical question. This mother, of course, loved her child but she also wanted to take care of the other children and be a good housewife as well. By giving the child a bottle she could then care for him and even herself a little bit. But I said no, she should not stop nursing the child. Nursing is a wonderful, G-d-given way to feed the child. Why should we deprive the child of the *chesed* to which he is entitled at birth? I then explained to her on what I based my answer.

"Do you know how much *chesed* goes into the feeding of a child?" I asked her. "This is a very important phase in the mother-and-child relationship. In the first year, they develop a closeness through this suckling and nursing. The mother derives endless love and affection for the child and comes to understand motherhood. Hashem has put so much *chesed* into the mother for this child. Nothing will ever replace the motherly love that the child feels from suckling; nothing can substitute for that special *chesed.*"

Her question amazed me. Here is a mother who gives so much for her child — one-and-a-half hours at each feeding. The mother is this symbol of *chesed*; we see how much she cares for and loves the child. Yet she did not realize the importance of what she was doing, that it was the caressing, the closeness, that was giving her — and all mothers — a special gratification.

This is part of the lifelong motherly love Hashem implants within each mother. It doesn't exist only during the suckling period but throughout all the other phases of life as well: childhood, puberty, adulthood, and even after the *chuppah*. Who do children talk to when they have a problem? Who makes meals for them? Who makes Pesach? Motherly love for the child is an everlasting love, even when the children grow older.

We find that women do mitzvos with more alacrity than men. I attribute this to their *middah* of *chesed*. It is the sacrificing of herself that gives a woman the unique readiness to do Hashem's Will wholeheartedly.

Today we find great misconceptions about the importance of women. People understand that the husband and wife are one, but they attribute the important role to the man. It is obvious, though, that as far as the home and the raising of the children, the main responsibility is the woman's. She is the *baalas chesed* who gives of herself to her husband, their home, and their family.

A child is not built by the man but by the woman who spends most of her time at home and takes care of him. She looks after him, dresses and feeds him, and loves him. Mothers of years ago, as I myself experienced when I came to the United States as a child of 9, lived through many trying times. The raising and rearing of a child today might be hard, but we have it so much easier than women did 50 or 60 years ago.

Things then were much more primitive. There were no washing machines, and they had to wash all the clothes and diapers in a sink. You can imagine how hard a mother had to work to keep food fresh in the summer. She had to carry ice into the house because there were no refrigerators. Things were almost primitive. Yet it was all *chesed* — and they had something that we do not have today.

So enjoy the *chesed* that you do, and remember: Ruth merited becoming the mother of the kingdom of David only because of her quality of *chesed*.

QUESTIONS & ANSWERS

Q

A

Who taught Ruth, coming from Moav, to have such *chesed*?

Having a mother-in-law like Naomi, who had such a sweet pleasant personality, taught Ruth what *chesed* meant. Naomi was a great woman who was married to one of the great men of the generation. She was called *Naomi* because of her sweetness, and she possessed the *middah* of *chesed*. She advised Elimelech not to go to Moav, and later showed Ruth an example of what Torah really meant. Ruth then saw that a Torah life is a life of total *chesed* and she clung to Naomi. We see Naomi's greatness when she overcame her feelings and explained to Ruth that she shouldn't join the Jewish people because there would be no one for her to marry. Ruth was a great help to Naomi; had Naomi followed her natural feelings she would have asked Ruth to stay with her and help her. But Naomi cared for the welfare of others first, and so she told Ruth to think about what would be best for her. Ruth yearned to follow this unbelievable *chesed*.

Q

How much *chesed* should a person be ready to do?

A You have to want wholeheartedly to do *chesed*. Even if you don't think you have the ability to do unlimited *chesed*, you should always be ready. For your family, the *chesed* required is unlimited. For other people, it depends on your strength, because first you owe your time to your husband and family. There is so much *chesed* to be done in the home, especially with children, where it is unlimited. *Chesed* to others should also be unlimited but you cannot do it at the expense of your husband. You owe it to him first so that he will have the time to learn; that in itself is a *chesed*. But if you are not neglecting your home and you do have some free time, your *chesed* to other people should also be unlimited.

A person who does *chesed* will always be happy and content, just like Naomi, who had a wonderful, sweet face because she did *chesed*. Doing *chesed* gives a feeling of fulfillment. Who doesn't feel wonderful helping another person get back on his feet? Why then does a wife feel like she is sacrificing and can't take any more of her "hard life full of struggle"? It should not be that way. If she were to appreciate and realize what type of *chesed* she was doing in building her own home, her children and their future, she would feel proud and happy that she is accomplishing this goal.

We should look at the sunny side of life. We have to think as Ruth did when she saw the beauty of the life that she wanted to build for herself. She was not only happy but she had the courage to go on. Later, she realized the wonderful work she was doing was building the future for herself. This doesn't mean torture, but the opposite, knowing that you're building your future on a Torah basis. This is what makes for real, permanent happiness. That's how we should feel. If we felt that way, we would not want to give up.

We do sometimes become overwhelmed and tired of the daily routine of changing the diapers and cooking meals but there is a *geshma'ke taam*, a deep satisfaction, to all this work and Ruth felt it. Orpah, on the other hand, could not take it anymore and she turned back. But look what she gave up! *Chazal* tell us she became the mother of Golias and not David — all because Orpah was not willing to do a little more *chesed*.

Q I know that taking care of children is an important *chesed*, but still I would like to be out there doing really great things, like giving a lecture to hundreds of women, or being a great rebbetzin.

A Why should you feel that taking care of children is not a "really great thing"? Isn't that what Shifrah and Puah were praised for? The fact that they were midwives is in itself amazing. That certainly wasn't their job. These great women, Miriam and Yocheved, were prophetesses, who took on the job of being midwives in order to save *Klal Yisrael*, and they did this at great risk to their own lives.

Why then does the Torah call these princesses of the Jewish nation Shifrah and Puah? "'Shifrah,' because she washed the baby and straightened its limbs, and 'Puah' because she sang it a lullaby"! Wouldn't we think that the Torah should have given them names more befitting their great deeds? But it is exactly that small *chesed*, the one that goes unnoticed, which is so important to the Torah. It is the greatness of the individual that he can detect importance in very very small things and that was the greatness of Miriam and Yocheved.

Who wouldn't save a child from death if she could? But singing a lullaby to a little baby? I might think I have more important things to do and let him cry himself to sleep. But this is the Torah's message to all of you. You can't imagine the importance of taking loving care of your children, and these small acts are not really small at all. So be happy and thankful that you are doing the job that the Torah praises so highly, for every act that you are doing is building the Jewish nation.

Q **Our neighborhood has a lot of pigeons. Pigeons are known to carry diseases and we have been told that the only way we can get rid of them is to poison them. Is this allowed?**

A No. That would be *tzar baalei chayim*. If they are coming there must be a nest near by. You should put up a net to prevent them from coming to the nest.

Q **Should a woman say *Bircas HaGomel* after a miscarriage?**

A No, unless there was a life-threatening complication. An uncomplicated miscarriage is very common in the early months of pregnancy.

Q **Is it proper for a pregnant woman to attend a funeral?**

A A pregnant woman can go to the funeral parlor, but it is better to avoid the cemetery unless the person who passed away was someone very close to her and she really wants to go. There are many details concerning this and if the situation arises, a woman should consult a halachic authority.

Q **May a woman who is expecting look at deformities?**

A She may if she does not dwell upon them.

Q **What should you do if, when cutting your nails, one drops on the floor?**

A If you can't find it and pick it up, you should at least sweep to change its position since if a pregnant woman steps on it, it might cause her to miscarry.

Q **Does a woman have to bake *challos* for Shabbos?**

A This is an old *minhag*. It is a big mitzvah, but if you are pressured by having to take care of children, then you are in the category of "one who is busy with one mitzvah is exempt from another." Your first duty is to finish your housework so that your husband can learn, and to take care of your children so that they can go off to *cheder* clean and happy. These are important mitzvos so don't belittle them. Don't think that for *chesed* to be a mitzvah you have to do it for someone else. You are doing *chesed* right in your own home with your very own children.

Q **What can I do about being afraid of *chevlei Mashiach*, the birthpangs of the Mashiach?**

A Torah and acts of *chesed* save a person from *chevlei Mashiach*. Have your husband learn as much as possible and do acts of *chesed,* and you need not fear *chevlei Mashiach*.

22 GETTING RID OF HATRED

In considering the destruction of the *Beis HaMikdash*, we should use some introspection to think about *Klal Yisrael* as it is today. We should ask ourselves what our obligation is to at least alleviate, if not remove completely, the troubles prevalent today. The out-of-the-ordinary situations we have all witnessed must prompt us to ask ourselves what we should do in these critical times.

Our Sages tell us the causes of the destruction of the First and Second Temples. The destruction of the First Temple came about because of the three worst sins we can ever find among the Jewish people: *avodah zarah*, idol worship; *gilui arayos*, immorality; and *shefichus damim*, bloodshed. These sins are considered the most serious of all transgressions.

But what about the destruction of the Second Temple? These sins were not prevalent at that time. Furthermore, the people occupied themselves with Torah, fulfilled mitzvos, and busied themselves with *chesed*. Our Sages tell us that the cause of the destruction was the *sinas chinam,* hatred without cause, that existed then. This teaches us that *sinas chinam* is equal to the three terrible sins that caused the destruction of the first *Beis HaMikdash.*

Our Sages then tell us that there was another striking difference between the First and Second Temples. In the first *Beis HaMikdash,* where there was no *sinas chinam,* the people placed their trust in Hashem. Despite the fact that they were committing three serious transgressions, they nevertheless had *bitachon* in Hashem. At the time of the second *Beis HaMikdash,* despite all their mitzvos and good deeds, they had *sinas chinam* (*Yoma* 9b).

The Vilna Gaon elaborates on this point. We think that *sinas chinam* is hatred without any cause. We think that when there is just cause, when there is a good reason, one may indeed bear a grudge. A person would not hate some-one he did not know, but if someone were to slap him or do something to hurt him, then he feels he is allowed to hate that person. Why should this be called *sinas chinam* — there is, after all, a reason for the *sinah*!

The Gaon answers: This is not a reason for *sinah,* because the person who wronged him did not do it on his own. Of course, the hurtful act was criminal and a big sin on his part, but if we had *bitachon* in Hashem we would attribute all of these events to what we call *hashgachah pratis,* individual Divine Providence. We would think, "Since everything is predestined by Hashem, why should I hate the individual? It was not his mind behind it. Of course he will be punished for the act, but we must remember that it is all *min haShamayim,* ordained from above."

When Shimi ben Gera vehemently cursed David, David said, "Leave him alone because it is all *min haShamayim*" (*II Shmuel* 16:7). Thus, we should not hate one who wrongs us, because he is Hashem's messenger. Our Sages say that one does not hurt his finger in this world unless Hashem decrees it to happen (*Chullin* 6b). *Sinas chinam*, then, is a lack of *bitachon* in Hashem, for if a person had true *bitachon*, he would realize that all is decreed from on High. The reason for his *sinah*, then, was *chinam* — the wrong reason.

During the generation of the flood, *dor hamabul*, the world was corrupt, morally and socially. Yet, although the people of the time believed in Hashem and did not rebel against Him, they were destroyed completely.

In the generation of the dispersal, *dor haflagah*, on the other hand, the people stretched forth their hands against the A-mighty. Nimrod, the Babylonian leader whose name is related to the word *mered*, rebellion, was a mighty emperor who had conquered the world. This infamous dictator regarded himself as a deity, and his aim was to build a tower to the heavens to challenge Hashem. The Midrash tells us that the tower was so high it took a year to walk to the top. Nimrod was a rebellious individual who wanted to fight, and he led his people in the sin of attacking the very foundation of faith, Hashem Himself.

Yet we see that the punishment meted out to the generation of the dispersal was not as severe as that given to the generation of the flood, which did believe in Hashem. Rashi tells us that the former did not stretch forth their hands against G-d, while the latter did; yet the former were destroyed completely while the latter did not perish from the world (*Bereishis* 11:9). Why?

The people who lived at the time of the flood were robbers. There was corruption, they stole from each other, and there was strife among them. There was no *shalom* between them and therefore they were destroyed. In the generation of the dispersal, though, there prevailed a friendship, a closeness, and unity. They conducted themselves with love and friendship. They were of one language and one speech.

Hashem dislikes dissension and loves peace, *shalom*. And that accounts for the different punishments. Logically it would appear that nothing could be worse than the sin of denying Hashem, which touches the very foundation of belief. We might assume that in comparison to the matter of *shalom*, belief in Hashem would be more important. But "*gadol hashalom*, great is peace."

We regard *shalom* as peace between a person and his fellowman. But peace doesn't begin with our fellowman; it begins within each individual, with an inner tranquility based on *bitachon*.

The *Chovos HaLevavos* says that when a person has *bitachon* he has *menuchas hanefesh*, tranquility of the mind (Ch. 1). He does not worry about what tomorrow will bring. He does not worry about whether or not he will receive his pay, have *nachas* from his children, be able to marry them off, or anything else that can cross one's mind. The word *bitachon* comes from the word *batuach*, 100 percent secure. A person with *bitachon* will be able to do mitzvos without any worries. A person with many worries cannot dedicate himself and devote his mind to study Torah. Learning Torah requires complete tranquility of mind. If he is disturbed by some situation in his life and does not have peace of mind, his studies will not register.

People often mistakenly think that *bitachon* is only a means to fulfill the Torah and observe mitzvos. The Gaon says no. He says that *bitachon* is not the means, but the end (*Mishlei* 22:19). Our goal should be to merit *bitachon*. Furthermore, says the Maharal, whatever one's quantity of *bitachon* is here in the world, that will be his share in the Next World (*Nesivos Olam*, vol. I, *Nesiv Emunah*, Ch. 2). This means that the complete goal of one's spirituality is not how many mitzvos he has accomplished but the level of *bitachon* he has achieved. The Gaon in *Mishlei* summarizes this by saying that the main purpose of Torah and mitzvos is not *bitachon* as a means to an end but as an end in itself.

In the *tefillah U'va leTziyon* we say, "May He open our heart through His Torah ... Blessed is the man who trusts in Hashem, then Hashem will be his security." The connection between Torah and trusting in Hashem indicates that the purpose of Torah is to come to trust in Hashem. This, as our Sages explain, is the underlying difference between the times of the First and Second Temples. The main reason for the destruction of the Second Temple was the lack of *bitachon* that caused *sinas chinam*. This teaches us the importance of *bitachon*: The first *churban*, destruction, lasted only 70 years, while the second continues till this very day, until Mashiach's arrival.

If we had perfect *bitachon*, we wouldn't have to worry about anything. We would believe that all is predestined. There are so many bitter problems prevalent today — one person lacks a home, another can't pay his bills — yet despite all of these problems, if we would have the proper *bitachon,* we would not worry.

The Chofetz Chaim made a beautiful observation on this point (*Chofetz Chaim al HaTorah*, *Shemos* 15:12). In the Torah we are told of the Jewish people walking in the desert without water for three days. They then came to a place called Marah, so named because of its bitter waters. The people challenged Moshe Rabbeinu, asking, "What will we drink?"

The Ramban says that after Marah the Jewish people traveled to Eilimah, where there were 12 wells of spring water and 70 date trees (*Shemos* 15:27), which the *Mechilta* notes parallels the 12 tribes and the 70 elders. The Torah relates this incident to teach us that each tribe stayed near its well and each elder by his date tree, all praising Hashem Who had prepared this oasis for them in a land of dry wilderness.

The Chofetz Chaim notes that from Eilimah to Marah was a very short distance, less than a mile, and the Midrash says that all of these things had been prepared for the Jewish people since the six days of Creation. Why, then, did the people complain and argue?

This, says the Chofetz Chaim, shows how shortsighted people can be. Everything was already prepared for them, as we see in this remarkable Midrash, which tells us that Hashem created these springs and trees during the six days of Creation especially for this purpose. *Hashgachah pratis* takes care of everything — but people don't have the patience to wait a little while to understand that. It's a very short distance from Marah to Eilimah, yet the people were already complaining.

A man lives for 70 years and thinks that he can understand life's chain of events. He forgets that he cannot link together past, present, and future. The people put up a fight. "Where is our water?" they wanted to know. True, when you come to a dry land you have to drink, but if they had had the proper *bitachon* they would have known that water was just around the corner. All you need is a little patience and *bitachon*, for if something has to be done it is already predestined.

Shlomo HaMelech tells us that there is a time for everything, including a time for giving birth (*Koheles* 3:2). I am often asked about inducing labor. Sometimes it is only for the doctor's convenience; he wants to go on vacation and wants to get the birth over with. But what about the fear of endangering the child? We know that a person is born not because he wants to be born but because the time is decreed in Heaven. The child must first learn the whole Torah before he comes down to this earth. There is a predestined time when the child should be born. If the child is not in danger, why force the *hashgachah*?

If we had proper *bitachon*, we would not be disturbed

by events but would let everything take its natural, proper course. The impatience of the individual and his short-sightedness in not understanding the relationship between the past, present, and future, makes him wrongly assume that he knows what is going on. We need to remember that the picture we see is not complete.

We can therefore understand that *bitachon*, the key to all Torah, isn't just the means but the end. Of course we can't do mitzvos properly if we are full of doubts, always worrying, and lack peace of mind. Spiritual progress is not measured by the number of mitzvos and good deeds a person does but by his level of *bitachon*. That is the yardstick for measuring one's level of spiritual attainment.

Bitachon is essential, especially in our complex life today. If a person were to look back at a diary he wrote 10 years previously, he would see that many of the things he thought did not make sense, suddenly do. What might have seemed to him at the time the biggest loss, turned out to be a wonderful improvement, changing his whole life for the better. At the time, he was stunned and disappointed, maybe even depressed. Yet that was only due to his shortsightedness and failure to understand the power of *bitachon*.

Our goal in life is to apply the trait of *bitachon* to every single situation in life. The Jewish people spent 40 years in the desert just to acquire perfection in this trait. Hashem could have given them the manna once a year, yet He troubled them to gather it every day. This is likened to a king who gave an allowance to his only son once a year sufficient for the entire year. But when he realized this meant seeing his son only once a year, the king decided to give him food every single day. Hashem said, "I want *Klal Yisrael* to have *bitachon*. If they only show up once a year to collect their manna, they won't *daven* anymore. If they have to gather the manna every day, they will acquire *bita-*

chon in Me."

So, too, we have to beseech and supplicate Hashem every day. It's part of our goal of acquiring the trait of *bitachon*. We must realize that Hashem has everything prepared in advance for us. All of the situations we are put in are only so that we can gain *bitachon*. We must not bicker or challenge our *nisyonos*, tests, but take them as a *ben Torah* or *bas Torah* should. We must not have any doubts but rather we must be sure and secure in Hashem Who will help us through the situation, and thus we will acquire the trait of *bitachon*. Looking at things this way, we will become richer spiritually and our hard situation will not break us but make us. We must remember that we are put into such situations for this very reason. When we believe this, then all of the animosities we have toward each other and all of the quarreling and complaints we have against one another will vanish. There will then be no room for all this quarreling and bickering, for we will understand that all is Heaven-sent.

If we look at things in this way, our whole perspective on life will change. There will be no more *sinas chinam*, no more bickering, but only love. With this level of *bitachon*, if someone slighted us and hurt our feelings, instead of blaming the person, we would go back and ask Hashem to forgive *us* for our transgressions. We would realize that the wrongdoer will certainly be punished — but not through us. Believing that it was *min haShamayim*, we would understand that we deserved this punishment, for, as our Sages say: *Yissurim* atone for a man's sins. For the person full of *bitachon*, *yissurim* with *teshuvah* are an atonement.

With *bitachon*, look how many things would change drastically in one's life! *Yissurim* would show one how to do *teshuvah*. Trials and tribulations are only a signal from Heaven to repent and analyze our daily life and actions for any improper things we might have done. With this attitude, everything in life would automatically change, whether it is a personal character trait or a problem with our children. Whenever one has some trouble in his life he should beseech Hashem to help him through it, and not blame the one who wronged him.

If we want the *Beis HaMikdash* to be rebuilt, we have to remove the cause of the destruction, the *sinas chinam*. The Chofetz Chaim says that if it has not yet been rebuilt it is a sign that we still suffer from *sinas chinam*.

Let us all take it upon ourselves to work on our *bitachon*, whether it is a problem at home, with the children, or any other problem we may encounter in life. Of course we may seek advice — don't stifle yourself and shut off your mind — but don't blame other people. Turn to the proper address. Ask Hashem for help, for He is the only one Who can help.

It says in *Tehillim* 118:9, "*Tov lachasos baHashem mi'bto'ach bin'divim*, Better to take refuge, *lachasos*, in Hashem than to trust, *mi'bto'ach*, in nobles." What are the connotations of *lachasos* and *mi'bto'ach?*

Lachasos means "to take shelter." There is no direct promise. *Mi'bto'ach* refers to someone who makes a promise and has the means to keep his word, much like an insurance policy. If one were to get a monthly allowance from a Rockefeller, people would say the man is living on easy street. With a billionaire behind him who has the wealth to back up his promises, one has security all his life — or so one thinks. We should seek shelter — *lachasos* — under Hashem's wings, so to speak, although we have no private, direct commitment that He will give us anything (*Mishlei* 14:26). This is better than all the promises of the "nobles," the great philanthropists. After all, it isn't within their power to promise that things will remain as they are. So although Hashem didn't promise, we can feel secure in knowing that we will receive everything we need, for

Hashem is the Source of lovingkindness and the Father of mercy, Who wants to bestow good. The greater our *bitachon*, says the *Chovos HaLevavos*, the more we receive from Hashem; with less *bitachon*, we receive less.

We should constantly ask ourselves: Was I able to vanquish and conquer this difficult problem I faced? Was I able to remain unaffected by the situation? Did I have true *bitachon* in Hashem? We should put up a sign on the wall that says, "How's my *bitachon* today?" If you make this your dictum, you will see how much happier you will be.

Developing our *bitachon* will eliminate *sinas chinam*. And this will be our biggest contribution to building the *Beis HaMikdash*, which we all hope to see in our time.

QUESTIONS & ANSWERS

Q If the Jewish people had faith in Hashem during the time of the first *Beis HaMikdash*, how could they have worshiped idols?

A Their idol worship was a different type than what we imagine. The Rambam explains in *Hilchos Avodah Zarah* that they believed that Hashem had designated certain powers to the stars, using them as His agents. Such a belief is not only wrong, it is forbidden, because we know that Hashem is the sole existing Power — *ein od milvado*.

Q If the Jewish people learned Torah in the times of the second *Beis HaMikdash,* why didn't they have perfect faith?

A Rabbeinu Yonah tells us that if a person studies Torah as an intellectual exercise or to attain knowledge, but not for its own sake, there will be no spiritual gain from such study. Thus, even though the Jewish people learned Torah at the time of the second *Beis HaMikdash,* they did not have true *bitachon,* because they lacked spiritual growth. There are some outside the yeshivah world who teach Talmud as just another form of knowledge. They

may see it as a deeper knowledge than other sub-
jects but not as Torah Divinely given with the power
to transform the person who studies it. The *maskil-
im* who started the movement studied the Torah but
then turned away.

Q **If one is consistently insulted by an individual who
might not mean harm but is just careless in manner and words, is it correct to overlook this or
should we make the person aware of his or her
behavior, even though this might hurt their feelings?**

A Rebuke is a very delicate matter. One must be very
careful in the manner they rebuke or point out
faults.

Q **Should I go into debt to buy new household items
because others have criticized what I have?**

A The people who speak that way are doing the wrong
thing. You don't have to take their criticism so seriously.

Q **If I go into labor on Shabbos afternoon, how long
should I postpone going to the hospital so as not
to desecrate Shabbos?**

A Go to the hospital as soon as you need to and don't
be concerned about desecrating Shabbos. You are
doing what Hashem wants you to do and you should
be relaxed and happy about it.

Q **What does the *Rosh Yeshivah* think about inducing
labor?**

A We never advocate inducing labor if it's for the convenience of the doctors. Only if it's medically
urgent may it be done. Bringing a child into the
world prematurely is not good. Leave it to *hashgachah*, to natural labor. Induce labor only if there

is a danger to the child. Remember, many times there is a miscalculation. When you think you are two or three weeks overdue, it may not be true. Every second inside means a great deal to the child. Besides being more developed physically, his spirituality is involved there too. So in general leave things to *hashgachah*, unless it is medically urgent.

23
ONE FIG

When Yeshayahu prophesied the destruction of the *Beis HaMikdash,* one would have expected him to reprimand *Klal Yisrael* for the chaos in which they found themselves at that time. One would have expected him to state all their sins, when in fact he mentions only some.

Remarkably, Yeshayahu begins his reproof by saying, "The ox knows his owner and the donkey his master's crib, but *Klal Yisrael* does not know, my nation does not consider." What a terrible decline! They haven't even reached the level of the ox and the donkey. The prophet is saying that even these dumb beasts know their owner by the dedicated care he gives them. When their owner appears, they show him recognition and appreciation.

But the Jewish people had sunk below even this level. They did not recognize what Hashem did for them — and this is the strongest charge that could be made against them.

The prophet Yirmiyahu said in Hashem's Name, "What fault did your fathers find in Me? They have estranged themselves from Me and gone after emptiness." The commentators explain that this refers to ingratitude. The people had forgotten all about the graciousness with which Hashem had tended to them in their youthful years as a nation, leading them through the wilderness and bringing them to Eretz Yisrael. The prophet did not mention *Klal Yisrael's* lofty spiritual level or the fact that they were chosen as Hashem's nation to receive the Torah. He spoke in plain, simple language, giving Hashem's message: "Remember what I did for you in taking you out of Egypt." Hashem provided everything for them, from the manna to every necessity of life. How in the world could they have forgotten?

Yirmiyahu then enumerated seven sins committed by the Jews of that time, all the result of a lack of appreciation. With every breath we breathe we should praise Hashem — but do we? When someone who cannot breathe by himself comes off a respirator, oh, does he thank Hashem! Who is עָשִׁיר, *ashir*, rich? One whose עֵינַיִם, שִׁנַּיִם, יָדַיִם, and רַגְלַיִם, eyes, teeth, hands, and feet are all working well. Only when we visit a hospital and see invalids do we come out saying, "How thankful I am to You, Hashem, that I have my own feet and hands and vision."

We often fail to appreciate so much of the beauty and majesty in Hashem's Creation. The psalms in David HaMelech's *Tehillim* are full of praise to Hashem for the *chesed* of this beautiful universe we live in. They are a result of his recognition of what he received from Hashem. When we wake up in the morning, we are fresh, newly born people. We should be saying *Modeh Ani* with enthusiasm. But it has become routine to us, and we just rattle it off without feeling its meaning. People can go to sleep and never wake up. When we wake up in the morning we should dance for joy!

The Gemara says that one of the greatest of the

Amora'im, Rav, had a miserable wife. Whenever he asked her to cook something, she did just the opposite, to torment him. Shlomo HaMelech says, "A bad woman is worse than death." She's worse than death because you can only die once. When Rav was once asked why he didn't divorce her, he said, "I recognize what she does for me. I'm married, she raises the children. For that alone I owe her my appreciation."

Even when someone wrongs you, try to recognize the good in the individual and appreciate what he does do for you. If someone does something for you, acknowledge it with a warm "thank you." If your spouse does something for you, even if he or she may be wrong in many other ways, recognize the good he or she did and appreciate it. If there is a disagreement between you, even though you may be right, even though you may have a point, let it go for now. Talk about it some other time when you are both in a good mood. At the moment, soften up.

If we would recognize and acknowledge *chesed*, would there be a cause for *lashon hara*? Would there be a cause for *sinas chinam*, groundless hatred? No, because if you recognized the good that someone does for you, you would be very hesitant to speak *lashon hara* about him and hurt him that way. There are many times when we have to momentarily blind our eyes and shut our ears. If we do this, we save ourselves so many troubles, and our *avodas Hashem* takes on a different character.

When the Jewish people settled in Eretz Yisrael, they became obligated to take the first produce of the land, put it into a basket, bring it to Yerushalayim, give it to the Kohen and say: I am thankful that I have reached this destination, that I have come to Eretz Yisrael (*Devarim* 26:3-10). The Kohen took this basket and placed it before the Altar. The owner of the fruit then recited a special text which recounts the entire history of the Jewish people, beginning with the words "An Aramean [tried to] destroy my ancestor," and concluding with their entering Eretz Yisrael.

At first glance, all this seems superfluous. Why relate the whole history of *Klal Yisrael*, including what the Egyptians did to us, how they tortured us, how Hashem hearkened to our cries and redeemed us and finally brought us to the land, etc.?

And how much fruit must a person bring? Just one fig! A man went down to his field, saw a fig or pomegranate that had ripened, tied a string around it and said, "Let this be *bikkurim*" (*Bikkurim* 3a). Can you imagine? All that he is required to bring is just one piece of fruit. Maybe he should bring a truckload of figs or something valuable — but just one fig? This is *bikkurim*?

He places that one fig in a beautiful basket, brings it to Yerushalayim, places it before the Altar and says, "With this fig that I have brought, I am thanking You, Hashem, for having brought me to this land" — and thus he remembers Hashem's *chesed*.

We can learn from this that it isn't what the person brings but the spirit behind it that is important. The fig is only a token of appreciation for Hashem's kindness, and shows that the recipient is not ungrateful. The person bringing the *bikkurim* had to travel a long distance to bring this one fig as a token of his appreciation for what he merited to have in Eretz Yisrael. And the appreciation expressed is not only for the fruit of Eretz Yisrael. The fruit is only the climax of a long chain of Hashem's *chesed*. Therefore, the person goes all the way back to Lavan the Aramean and then to the Jewish people entering Eretz Yisrael, to show that so much is behind this one fig.

There is something very important about the first of anything. The Hebrew word for a firstborn son, *bechor*, has its origin in the word *bikkurim*. We all know the excitement that surrounds the birth of a firstborn son. So much has led up to the wonderful event; what pleasure there is in seeing the first produce of labor! "Ah!" a person says to himself, "I merited to see the first child, the first fig or date" — and with this he expresses the highest degree of appreciation and thankfulness to Hashem. Filled with this feeling of satisfaction, he gives over the first fruit to Hashem as a token of gratitude. But it isn't just the first fig or date that he brings — it's the whole history that went into the first fig. And if he were not to express this past history, all the facts and factors that went into it, he would not be fully thankful to Hashem.

When we read that "a new king arose in Egypt who did not know Yosef" (*Shemos* 1:8), the Midrash wonders how it could be that the new Pharaoh did not know Yosef when everyone in Egypt knew Yosef and what he did for the country. It was all historical fact. The answer given is that the new king did not want to recognize the *chesed* Yosef did for the Egyptians. It was as if he were saying, "We gave the Jews room and board in Egypt. Here they developed as a nation. Perhaps we did more for them than they did for us." This is a lack of gratitude. From here we learn that ingratitude leads to atheism, for when a person denies that *chesed* was done for him, it is as if he denies the existence of Hashem (*Midrash Tanchuma, Shemos* 8).

Some people do not believe in honoring one's father and mother. They say, "Why should we respect and be thankful to parents? They are the ones who wanted to have a child for their own personal reasons." Those who think this way will not be thankful to Hashem either, says the *Chayei Adam* (*klal* 67,2). "After all," they will say, "did Hashem ask us if we wanted to be created? He just created us. Why, then, should we be grateful to Him? Why should we be religious and serve Him?" Such are the words of the ungrateful person who will always belittle a *chesed* done for him and make nothing of it.

To such a person one says: Yes, you were created against your will and you will also die against your will — but when it comes to dying, you will do everything to remain alive. So if you did not want Hashem to create you, why do you want to live? You must be getting something from being alive since you yourself want to live and would give millions to save your life. You want to remain alive because you enjoy being alive. But isn't that enjoyment a result of Hashem's *chesed*? How can you deny that?

So a person can turn the biggest *chesed* — life itself — into nothing, so that he doesn't have to feel any reason at all for being thankful.

A person with this character flaw will fail to appreciate and recall the kindness of his or her spouse. He will remember the one or two faults or misdeeds but forget all the benefits bestowed.

When your spouse performs an act of kindness, acknowledge it with a gift, a kind word, a note — any small token of appreciation to express your gratitude. If someone performs a *chesed* for you, sincerely thank him for this. In this way, you will cultivate the trait of gratitude.

But this is just the beginning. If a person were to lend another $10,000, which the borrower then invested in a business that eventually brought in hundreds of thousands of dollars, we'd expect the borrower to be appreciative. But if he were to express thanks only for the initial loan, it shows that he has not cultivated the trait of gratitude to the proper extent. If he had, he would also express deep appreciation to the lender for the outcome of his venture — the profits he reaped, which were due to the initial loan.

The one fig of *bikkurim* represents an endless chain of Hashem's kindness for us from our very beginning as a nation. We cannot predict the results of a particular act of kindness, and so there is no limit to the amount of gratitude we owe a person who does us a kindness.

QUESTIONS & ANSWERS

Q Can children take a course in swimming during the Three Weeks?

A Yes, it's allowed, but during the Nine Days one should not.

Q Can one go swimming during the Three Weeks?

A I've heard this question many times and have found no halachic source to forbid it. For therapeutic reasons one may even go up to Tishah B'Av.

If it is a hot day and a person is sweaty and needs to remove the sweat, one may take a lukewarm shower, even during the Nine Days. Only showering for pleasure is forbidden. Likewise, staying in the shower for pleasure is forbidden.

Q Can one make the *Shehecheyanu* blessing on a new fruit during the Three Weeks?

A You may make it on Shabbos, but our *minhag* is not to buy new fruit unless it is urgently required.

Q May one give *fleishig* food to children during the Nine Days?

A If the child needs it for his health, then children up to the age of 8 or 9 years, and even pregnant or nursing women if they need additional protein, may eat chicken during the Nine Days. They should preferably not eat meat other than chicken.

Q **May one eat chicken left over from Shabbos during the Nine Days to avoid *baal tashchis*, needless waste?**

A No, but you don't have to waste it. Keep it in the refrigerator or freeze it.

Q **May one call someone to welcome them to Eretz Yisrael during the Nine Days?**

A Yes, a friendly, casual call is okay.

Q **May one give a gift during the Nine Days?**

A No, no valuable gifts may be given, but something trivial such as a pencil box for a child is permissible. Only something that brings happiness is forbidden, such as clothes.

Q **May one deliver gifts that one received in America to give to people in Israel during the Nine Days?**

A It is better to wait until after Tishah B'Av. But call the person and tell him that you have certain things for him.

Q **Is it permitted to wash something that one needs medically, such as support stockings?**

A All medical necessities are permitted. Anything pertaining to your *refuah* is permitted. Skin conditions of any nature may be cared for during the Nine Days.

Q **Do I have to make a *zecher lechurban* in a rented apartment?**

A You're not supposed to unless you ask the owner for permission. But you *should* ask him for permission.

24 TEACHING RESPECT

When Plato, the Greek philosopher, visited Yerushalayim after the destruction of the *Beis HaMikdash,* he met Yirmiyahu and found him weeping bitterly. Plato thought it was ridiculous and asked Yirmiyahu, "Why are you weeping over wood and stones?"

Yirmiyahu responded, "You are a philosopher. Do you have any questions?"

Plato answered, "Yes, I do, but no one can answer them."

Yirmiyahu said, "Ask, and I shall answer."

Plato asked his questions and Yirmiyahu answered all of them immediately. Plato was astonished. Like all other philosophers, he had had many unanswered questions for years and here Yirmiyahu rattled off the answers with no trouble at all. Shocked, Plato asked him for the source of his wisdom. Yirmiyahu answered, "It is from these stones and wood" (*Rema, Toras HaOlah,* brought in *Lev Eliyahu,* vol. I, *Shevivei Lev Avos* #155).

The wood and stones of the *Beis HaMikdash* were sanctified. As the Rambam quotes: "One should not derive any benefit from the wood and stones of the *Beis HaMikdash* and if he does, he must bring an offering" (*Hilchos Me'ilah* 6:7). That is the simple meaning of saying that the *Beis HaMikdash* is a place of sanctity. With his answer to Plato, Yirmiyahu was saying, "It is from the holiness and unique sanctity of the *Beis HaMikdash* that I have derived all my knowledge."

Of course, a philosopher cannot understand this idea, which is not something that can be perceived by the human intellect. Plato, like the other philosophers, did not believe in *hashgachah pratis*, individual Divine Providence, but only in what he saw with his own eyes. Sanctity meant nothing to him, and he therefore could not understand the meaning of a "holy nation." Yirmiyahu's response to Plato told him, "There is something in our nation that we call sanctity and it raises the individual to a level above human logic."

We see this concept of sanctity and specialness pointed out in a famous author's remarks about the Jewish people:

> The Jews constitute but one percent of the human race. It suggests a nebulous dim puff of star-dust lost in the blaze of the Milky Way … his commercial importance is extravagantly out of proportion to the smallness of his bulk. His contributions to the world's list of great names … are also away out of proportion to the weakness of his numbers. He has made a marvelous fight in this world, in all the ages; and has done it with his hands tied behind him … The Egyptian, the Babylonian and the Persian rose, filled the planet with sound and splendor, then … passed away; the Greek and the Roman followed,

and made a vast noise, and they are gone; other peoples have sprung up and held their torch high for a time, but it burned out, and they sit in twilight now, or have vanished. The Jew saw them all, beat them all, and is now what he always was … All other forces pass, but he remains. What is the secret of his immortality?

The writer could not understand the greatness of the Jew who, despite being only a small proportion of the world's population, is always outstanding in every field. And yet there is so much anti-Semitism because of jealousy against this small nation that excels. The secret of our greatness and success is simple, even though others will never understand it. It lies in the fact that we have a holy Torah, a living Torah that gives us everlasting life and binds us to Hashem. We are His children and are therefore like Him and remain forever.

Our Sages tell us that there was no other prophet like Moshe among the Jews, but there was one among the nations of the world and that was Bilaam (*Yalkut Shimoni, Devarim* 967). Our Sages say that Bilaam's stature was somewhat equal to the greatness of Moshe Rabbeinu.

Some of our commentators are surprised by this comparison and think it slightly obscure. With a beautiful parable, Rav Chaim of Volozhin explains what is meant (*Torah Temimah, Devarim* 34, footnote 26). He says that the two prophets are compared to the eagle and the bat. Both have a certain sense of when it is sunrise and sunset, but there is a vast difference between them. The eagle loves the sunrise but at night its vision is dulled. It only enjoys life when the sun is present. The bat, on the other hand, starts off in the darkness of night. It fears daylight and hides itself when day arrives. Consequently, the two differ greatly. The eagle senses when the sun is coming out and will rise to enjoy life. The bat also feels the sunrise, but to the bat daylight is the taste of death and thus it hides from it. When sunset arrives, the eagle knows that it is time to rest; the bat, however, dashes around freely in the darkness.

Both Moshe Rabbeinu and Bilaam knew Hashem's thinking — but from two totally divergent points of view. There are two opposite times in the world: the time when Hashem uses the attribute of *chesed* and *rachamim*, mercy, and the time when the strictness of *din*, judgment, is employed. We rely on *chesed* and *rachamim*, for who can win in a time of *din* when one's deeds are so closely examined?

Both Moshe Rabbeinu and Bilaam knew these two different times but, as our Sages tell us, Moshe used his prophecy to improve *Klal Yisrael*'s situation. When Moshe Rabbeinu appeared, it was a wonderful time of joy and happiness, like the sunrise. He was always seeking *chesed* and *rachamim* for *Klal Yisrael* at times of judgment. He never used his prophecy to seek punishment for *Klal Yisrael*.

Bilaam did the exact opposite. He leapt to the fore whenever he saw the attribute of *din*. He rushed to complain and curse *Klal Yisrael*, and when it was a time of *rachamim* and *chesed*, he hid himself.

Both prophets, then, possessed the greatness to know *daas Elyon*, Divine intent, but each used this ability for opposite ends. The evil Bilaam was a vicious, cruel individual. The Midrash explains that Hashem chose Bilaam because he was the most highly respected leader of the nations of the world (*Tanchuma, Balak* 4). Hashem gave Bilaam prophecy so that the nations would not be able to use their lack of having a Moshe Rabbeinu as an excuse for not becoming a great nation like the Jews. Hashem chose this leader of the nations of the world, yet we see what Bilaam accomplished in comparison to Moshe Rabbeinu. Bilaam brought only destruction to the world; he only wanted to use his knowledge to curse and punish the Jewish people.

We might ask, "What caused such a vast difference between these two great leaders of these two peoples?" What made Moshe Rabbeinu the great individual he was and Bilaam, *lehavdil*, the mean and vicious one? Both possessed so much greatness and knowledge!

It was their character that made the difference. The good-natured Moshe Rabbeinu is likened to the eagle, which loves the sunrise and loves to do *chesed*. His nature is to rise and enjoy light. Bilaam's nature, however, was vicious. The basic difference is that without Torah, a person can be the greatest philosopher — and yet the meanest creature in the world. Lions and tigers would not do as much damage as this evil Bilaam, for although he had intellect, it was worthless without Torah. Hitler, may his name be blotted out, used his knowledge to curse and bring destruction to the world. This difference is why Yirmiyahu wept and Plato could not understand why. Only that which possesses sanctity and holiness can refine and refashion a person to bring him to an elevated spiritual level of greatness.

When one possesses this purity and sanctity, such questions as Plato's are non-existent. Our greatness does not lie in the fact that we have knowledge but rather that we are a nation of holiness. We possess all the knowledge in the world because we are part of Hashem. The Ramban says in his preface to the Torah that the Torah includes all branches of science. Whenever you look in the Torah, you will find everything else as well. But that is not the greatness of the Torah. It is the holiness of the Torah that lets us use our knowledge in a way to benefit humanity. It is the holy Torah that elevates an individual to that sublimity of refinement, to a character filled with lovingkindness, graciousness, and goodness — all of which exemplify Torah.

Yirmiyahu wept over the stones and wood because he knew that the Jewish people, through the Torah, possessed this greatness. A non-Jew, of course, did not understand this. We are immortal because we have the soul, the eternal living Torah within us. All that is material eventually dies, but that which is spiritual never degenerates or disintegrates. The unique quality of spirituality is that it is everlasting. The Torah gives life to the soul and makes the Jewish people immortal. All the nations of the world will fade but we will be everlasting.

Yirmiyahu wept not only over what we had lost, but because the Jewish people had not understood the Torah's lesson. Every morning we say the blessing over the Torah, "Who has chosen us." The Jewish people of that time did not utter this blessing, as the Ran says in the name of Rabbeinu Yonah (*Nedarim* 81a), because the Torah held no special significance for them. They regarded Torah as another branch of knowledge, not realizing its uniqueness in comparison with other branches of knowledge. True, Torah contains vast knowledge, but there is more to it.

It is remarkable that although the Jewish people studied the Torah so diligently, no one understood the reason for the destruction of the *Beis HaMikdash*. Finally, Hashem told them that it was due to this lack of understanding of Torah's importance, without which all the diligence means nothing. A student of mathematics, for instance, can study his field diligently and become an expert in it. Torah, too, is a magnificent piece of knowledge, but the real task for us is to understand its beautiful importance and uniqueness. Since the Jewish people lacked this understanding and appreciation of the Torah's holiness, it became for them no more than another branch of knowledge, and this is why the *Beis HaMikdash* was destroyed. Adding the virtue of sanctity to Torah puts it in a totally different category. Learning Torah then refashions the individual's character to make him holy, like the Chofetz Chaim, and not just an ordinary human being. This is the very essence of Torah: to elevate human nature to the highest level of holiness and lovingkindness in its truest form.

I often think to myself: How can we, in our era, correct this lack of the realization of the Torah's importance? Today we find many students studying Torah. There are even professors who lecture on the Talmud, and non-Jews who know *Mishnayos* and the Talmud as well. But what is lacking in all this is an understanding of the Torah's unique importance.

When a rav passes by, very few children stand up for him. This shows a lack of appreciation for Torah. Why shouldn't they stand up and show respect for one who is studying Torah? The Gemara says that *kavod HaTorah*, honor for Torah, stands higher than studying Torah (*Megillah* 3b), and yet there are so many students who study the Torah but do not stand up for a Torah scholar. It hurts me to see Torah treated like ordinary knowledge, without any recognition of its greatness. This was the cause of the destruction of the *Beis HaMikdash*, and as the Chofetz Chaim used to say, if it has not yet been rebuilt, it is because the reasons for its destruction are still prevalent. If these causes were removed, the *Beis HaMikdash* would already have been rebuilt (see *Yerushalmi, Yoma* 1:1).

A child should be taught the importance of honoring his parents. He should be told that when Papa or Mama come into the room, he should stand up and show respect. A child raised like that will listen to his parents in later years. Children who are not taught when they are young to respect their parents, will not do it when they get older. So, too, if you do not teach a child this respect for Torah, even if he studies Torah when he grows up, the *kavod haTorah* will still be lacking, and that is devastating.

Torah without *kavod* is destruction. Without Torah's importance, knowledge only brings destruction, as we see with nuclear weapons, which are used only to bring devastation to the world.

The very basis of Torah is not only the study of it but the respect for it. This is the message to all mothers. You must teach your children that the cause of the destruction of the *Beis HaMikdash* was a lack of realization of what the Torah means to the Jewish people. When we realize that Torah is our life, our sanctity, that it refines a person's character to fashion him into a whole and sanctified individual, we can be instrumental in rebuilding what was destroyed.

QUESTIONS & ANSWERS

Q If a rav is getting on a bus, is it considered modest for me to give him my seat? Should I give him my seat even if there are other empty seats behind me? Should I give up my time to let him go ahead of me in line?

A The answer is definitely yes. There is no question of modesty here if you are young and he is an old man. On the contrary, you would be criticized for not getting up.

Likewise, you should get up even if there are other empty seats. You can move to another seat. You should let an elderly person go ahead of you in line. Your time is precious, but you are required to honor the elderly. Even if your husband is waiting for you so that he can go to learn Torah, you would be required to do the same thing, as would he. Wouldn't you do this for your father and mother?

Q I have a 9-year-old daughter who, if she sits next to me, will *daven* and follow *krias haTorah*. Toward the middle of *davening* there are not enough seats. Should she get up for a woman?

A Definitely. She is not obligated to hear *krias haTorah*. She is also younger than the woman, so why can't she stand? She should get up out of respect.

Q If one sees a *Rosh Yeshivah* outside and is already standing, is it enough to stand silently as he passes by or should a woman say hello? What about a man or boy who sees a *Rosh Yeshivah* walking to shul — should he say hello or should he remain quiet?

A A woman does not have to greet him. A man or boy should greet him properly. A man should address one whom he considers a dignitary.

Q If I am sitting on the bus and an elderly *talmid chacham* is getting off the bus, is it right to stand up for him?

A Definitely. One should always show respect for *chachamim* and respect for age.

Q When should you get up if the *gadol* is not within *daled amos*, in the immediate vicinity?

A It is always better to get up, even if you have to go out of your way.

Q How can we correct the lack of honor for Torah we see today?

A We are very much responsible for the lack of honor and love for Torah today. We are responsible also for the lack of honoring parents, which, the Gemara says, is the most stringent of commandments. Parents should instill respect in their children. They should make their children stand up for them. A child should stand up for his parents. They brought him into this world and the child owes them a lot, so let him give his parents the proper respect.

Children should be taught to stand up for a *talmid chacham* and they should see their parents standing up for a *talmid chacham*. You stand up for a *talmid chacham*, not for a professor. This is giving honor to Torah. In this way, respect for elders, respect for *chachamim*, is inculcated into the child. When the child sees that the attitude to Torah is different from the attitude to all other forms of intellectual learning, he will have respect for Torah. Torah is not just merely another branch of learning. But these attitudes must be inculcated in the child in his early years, from the age of 5 when he becomes old enough to understand. When he sees a dignified Torah scholar he should be made to stand up. This makes an impression that will last for life.

Q **Is it proper for men and women to stand up for a woman over the age of 70?**

A You don't have to — only if she's an *eishes chaver*, the wife of an esteemed Torah scholar. But on the bus, of course you have to give her your seat — that's *derech eretz*!

Q **What is the proper way to do *teshuvah* after the passing of a *gadol*?**

A We should try to fill the gap by learning more Torah and supporting more Torah study.

Q **If you take a chartered bus to a wedding and there are not enough seats, what is the proper mode of *derech eretz*? Should a young man get up for a man or a women or a single girl? Should people get up midway and switch places with those standing? Should a strong, healthy girl get up for a tired young man?**

A The best answer would be to get a bigger bus!

These are complicated questions. The Torah always comes first. For instance, one always gets up for an elderly woman. I personally would get up for a woman. She should defer in *kavod haTorah* but it would be my duty to show her this kindness. It is incumbent upon the individual not to be self-centered. This all depends on the circumstances, so it is hard to give a *psak*. I would probably just go all the way to the back of the bus.

Q **Should a young person get up for an elderly woman?**

A By all means! She should get up out of respect for the elderly woman. Today's youth have not been taught to ask their elders. They have their own opinions, their own mind, and act on their own. This is a tragedy — and it all stems from the fact that we don't train our children in their youthful years to respect their elders.

Q **May I change diapers in front of *sefarim*?**
A Yes, but if possible, avoid it.

Q **Are you allowed to carry a soiled diaper past a *mezuzah*?**
A If it is covered, yes.

Q **Can you say *divrei Torah* in the street where sewage water runs? What if you do not smell an odor?**

A If you do not smell or see it and you are also *daled amos* away, then it is permissible.

Q **Are you allowed to write, in Hebrew, names that have the *yud* and *hei* that spell Hashem's Name next to each other, like the name Yirmiyahu, for instance?**

A It is customary to write a dash before or after the letter.

Q What should a person do with the *baruch Hashem* and the *bs"d* that are on letters? Are they *sheimos*?

A Some are strict about this and some are lenient. If you can, rip off the letters, put them all in a *sheimos* bag, and give them to your local shul, which probably has some arrangement for burying them. Do the same with verses on wedding invitations. I don't write it on my mail, I just write 'בע. Many people take mail into the bathroom so it's best not to use anything that signifies Hashem's Name like the 'ה. But some are lenient.

25 TORAH THROUGH HARDSHIPS

The question is often raised: Why did Yaakov Avinu and Rachel and Leah have such hard lives? The other Patriarchs, as we know, did not have it so hard. Our Sages have observed that even the way in which they found their *zivugim*, mates, was quite different. Yitzchak had the *zechus* that his *zivug* came to him without his having to go into *galus*. Yaakov Avinu, though, had to go to look for his *zivug*, and we know what kind of *galus* he had with Lavan the Arami.

But why should Yaakov Avinu, who symbolizes Torah, which is so important and precious to us, have to go through life in such a hard way? We would think the opposite should be true. Yaakov Avinu, as the *shakdan* and *masmid* in Torah study, the diligent learner to whom every minute is so precious, should be spending his time at the Gemara and his *zivug* should come to him instead of him having to go into *galus*. Yet we know that from beginning to end, Yaakov Avinu's life was a hard, bitter struggle, full of trials and tribulations.

Our other *Avos*, Avraham and Yitzchak, didn't have it so hard. Avraham, as a great philosopher, was crowned as king by the nations of his time. He had honor, prestige, and wealth, as did Yitzchak. But Yaakov, known as the most important of the *Avos*, did not have such an easy life.

Rashi, in answer to this puzzling question, brings down the Midrash on the verse, "Yaakov settled, *vayeshev*, in the land of his father's sojourning" (*Bereishis* 37:2), and says this means Yaakov wanted to settle down in tranquility. We must remember that back then, this didn't mean having free time to relax, but total immersion in the study of Torah. Yaakov Avinu desired a life that would be free of trials and tribulations. He yearned for a tranquil life that would leave him free to sit and study Torah. But Hashem answered him, "Isn't what lies in store for the righteous in the next world enough for them? Do they still want to live in peace here?" It is impossible to have this world at ease. And therefore, "The tragedy of Yosef came upon him." Yaakov Avinu said, "My troubles came one right after the other without letup" (*Bereshis Rabbah* 84:3).

When Yaakov Avinu asked for tranquility and peace of mind to sit and learn Torah, the answer was that his reward would await him in the World to Come, for this world is not a world of ease, but one of nonstop toil.

Yaakov Avinu's life represents Torah life in its fullest sense. Such is the way of Torah. The development of a *ben Torah* is with just a piece of bread, salt, and a measured cup of water.

Why do we have to suffer so much? Logic would dictate to us that a beautiful mansion, with no troubles, with peace of mind, would make Yaakov Avinu into a better individual. It seems to us that troubles and distress distract from growth in Torah.

But it is not so. Our Sages have beautifully stated: "One who labors on the eve of Shabbos will eat on

Shabbos. And one who doesn't labor on the eve of Shabbos, what will he eat?" (*Avodah Zarah* 3a). This is emphatically stating that it is not the preparation for Shabbos but what goes into the preparation! He who toils will get his reward on Shabbos. I always picture in my mind what the rebbetzin goes through when she toils on erev Shabbos. It's the extra effort you make that counts most. A store-bought cake, even with all the same ingredients and spices, does not taste the same as the one you made yourself. It might be delicious but it doesn't have the same *geshmack*. Our Sages tell us that "a man prefers one measure of his own more than nine of the same measures from his friend" (*Bava Metzia* 38a). It isn't "what you have," it's "how you came to have it."

In the same line of thought, there are mothers who have children with no *tzaar gidul banim*, and then there are mothers who have a great deal. Who enjoys the child more, later in life — the one who went through the hardships or the one who had it easy? Going through the hardships of raising a child brings with it this same type of gratification. "Those who sow in tears, will reap in joy" (*Tehillim* 126:5) is a true fact of life: In order to enjoy the accomplishments, you have to go through difficulties. That satisfaction doesn't just result from the accomplishment — it comes from the work put in.

This definitely applies to Torah. Something you toil over gives you a sweet sense of satisfaction. As a matter of fact, the harder one works the more the pleasure one has afterward. It isn't only sowing with hardship but with *tears*. Those are the people who will reap with joy.

Therefore, this was the only way for Yaakov Avinu, who embodies Torah, to accomplish and attain the high levels of the sanctity of Torah. He had to grow and live the hard way in order for Torah to mean what it did to him.

We see this in yeshivos today. A *bachur* who is a sharp,

outstanding student often does not produce as much as the student whose mind is of lesser caliber. The smarter student may be more talented but he will often not delve deeply enough into the learning to see the truth. To get the most out of your Torah learning you have to work harder.

Rachel is another example of how overcoming difficulty in life builds a person. Rachel was the mainstay of Yaakov's home. We may think that, logically, Leah should have been the mainstay for it was she who gave birth to most of the *gedolei Yisrael* who were the tribes of Israel. Yehudah, who symbolizes monarchy and from whom will come Mashiach ben David; Levi, the priestly tribe; and Yissachar, the symbol of idealism in Torah — all came from Leah. Rachel, however, only had two sons. Spiritually, wasn't Leah the mainstay of the home?

But we are told that this isn't so. In *Megillas Ruth* it says, "May Hashem make the woman who is coming into your house like Rachel and like Leah, both of whom built up the House of Israel" (*Ruth* 4:11). Rashi comments: Rachel is mentioned first! Even though all those present at this event were of the tribe of Yehudah and thus descendants of Leah, they admitted that Rachel was the true mainstay of Yaakov's home and therefore mentioned her first. But why was she chosen? We must remember that it wasn't because of love or beauty but because of her spiritual virtues. This answer lies in the Midrash describing the destruction of the *Beis HaMikdash,* when all the *Avos* and *Imahos* pleaded for *Klal Yisrael.* Leah and Rachel also came pleading to Hashem, with Rachel coming last.

We are all aware of what Rachel went through when Lavan fooled Yaakov Avinu and gave him Leah instead of Rachel. Now she said, "Master of the World! It is revealed and known to You that Yaakov loved me with a greater love and worked seven years for me and that when he finished them and the time came for my marriage to my husband, my father wanted to give my husband to my sister instead of me and it was very difficult for me." Yaakov and Rachel had arranged secret signs between them to prevent just such an eventuality — but Rachel told Leah the signs, and we all know what Rachel went through because of Yaakov's marriage to Leah. Rachel goes on to say to Hashem, "If I, who am only flesh and blood, dust and ashes, was not jealous of my rival and did not let her suffer shame and disgrace, then why should You, Living Eternal G-d and King, Who is merciful, be jealous of idolatry, which is meaningless, and exile my sons to let them be slain by the sword?" Immediately Hashem's mercy was evoked. "For you, Rachel, I shall return Israel to their place," as is written in *Yirmiyahu*, "A voice is heard on high ... Rachel is weeping for her children" (Introduction to *Eichah Rabbah* 24).

Why did Hashem hearken to Rachel and not to Leah? For the very reason that the Midrash states: Rachel went through many hardships! It was only through her efforts that Leah merited becoming Yaakov's wife; therefore, all the great sons that Leah bore were because of Rachel. The very hardships and tribulations that Rachel went through are the foundation of *Klal Yisrael*. True, Leah produced great tribes but it was all due to the hardships and sufferings of Rachel. And that is what counts the most. Therefore, Hashem listened to the voice of Rachel and not to Leah.

Suffering is rewarded. The purpose of hardship is only to help us find enjoyment and delight in Torah study, so that Torah becomes an integral part of us, part and parcel of our nature. A yeshivah student is called a *ben Torah*, a son of the Torah. He is not just a student but a son, because Torah becomes part of him. A *ben Torah* is one whose personality is refashioned by his Torah learning. And this is achieved through toil, struggle and travail.

These lessons apply to the wife of a *ben Torah*, too. She has an equal share in his accomplishments. And as he must endure hardship, so must she. But in the wake of these hardships is untold satisfaction, untold joy. *Ashrecha* — fortunate are you not only in the World to Come, but also in this world (*Pirkei Avos* 6:4).

I recall the suffering I endured over 60 years ago. There were times when we didn't have the money even to purchase food for Shabbos. Some of my students, who also endured hardship, are today *gedolei Torah* and *roshei yeshivos*. The Torah's way is not one of ease and it is only through hardship that one can achieve greatness in Torah. But in the end, honor will come (*Nedarim* 62a) and one will look back and say, "How happy we are. What a beautiful life we have."

QUESTIONS & ANSWERS

Q Weren't there some "Rabbi Doctors" who were acceptable?

A Yes, there were some rabbis who had secular knowledge. Polish Jewry didn't accept some of their ways, such as congregational singing, but they saved German Jewry and only for that purpose did they receive the title of Doctor. It is similar to the Rambam's bemoaning the fact that he had to study foreign wisdoms to save *Klal Yisrael*. Yet this was a *horaas shaah,* and he saved many thousands of people with his *Guide to the Perplexed*. Today, though, people do things just to compete with others and to show that they too know philosophy as well as teach Torah. The Rambam condemned the Greek philosophy of his time, yet he had to refute all of their methods by forcing himself to subjugate himself to the *horaas shaah*. Not just anyone can decide to become a professional, only someone who has experience with *chochmas haTorah*. Also, a person can never be a halachic authority for himself because he is so caught up in his own emotions that he doesn't see the truth.

Q

How can a wealthy person fulfill the Mishnah that says a person should learn Torah by living a hard life?

A

Even if a person is rich it doesn't mean he has no problems. One could have trouble from his learning partner, his child, or other problems at home. A life of Torah is a hard life full of struggle. One is rewarded for all of his mitzvos together, and Torah study outweighs them all. We must remember that *lefum tzaara agra*, the reward is according to the effort. Two people may do the same mitzvah, but the one who had more *tzaar* receives more reward.

Q

I heard that the *Rosh Yeshivah* doesn't believe in vacation breaks. Why?

A

I tell my *talmidim*, if your health or your wife's requires it, then of course you can take a rest. Otherwise, time is too precious to waste. The same is also true of unnecessary breaks. The Maharsha, who lived 400 years ago, criticized people who vacationed unnecessarily.

Q

What is the purpose of *yissurim*, suffering?

A

Yissurim have a twofold purpose: as a *kaparah*, atonement, and as a signal to us to scrutinize our deeds. Everyone suffers, but suffering atones for our sins and we view it in that way.

There are some transgressions for which *teshuvah* alone cannot atone unless they are accompanied by *yissurim*. Poverty, *Chazal* say, atones for one who was destined to die. A poor person is considered as dead, so Hashem has mercy on him and makes him poor.

Q

How should a person respond when a child must go into the hospital?

A You must understand that this was the greatest *chesed*; something worse could have happened. Remember: There is always something predestined for the individual but Hashem, the source of all mercy, turns it into the easiest form of suffering and for that you should be happy.

Undergoing an operation, experiencing poverty, or being stricken with blindness — all are literally a matter of atoning for something worse that could have happened. If you could buy off death with money, you would. So if you don't get the check sometimes and the poverty causes you some suffering, be happy about it.

We know that the Egyptian exile was originally supposed to last 400 years but Hashem reduced it to 210 years because the Jewish people had suffered so much. He cut it short but He also made it a little harder. All *yissurim* are *chesed v'rachamim* in every phase of life, even though we do not understand it completely. The Rambam says that Hashem does not judge transgressions by quantity but by quality. For example, two people did not perform a certain mitzvah but the one who didn't do it because he didn't feel well is not punished the same as the other one. In the same way, if two people fulfill a mitzvah but one has it hard while the other has it easy, the one who worked harder receives more reward.

We come to this world for a few years and think we can understand *hashgachah pratis*. Everything is *min haShamayim*, and all the trials we go through in life should be taken as *chesed v'rachamim*. The Vilna Gaon used to say that if not for *yissurim* there would be no *tekumah*; we would have no World to Come. You should be thankful for *yissurim.* The Ramban says that all of the *yissurim* of Iyov are not even one-sixtieth of the fire of *Gehinnom*, so what we pay here is minimal compared with those *yissurim.* Looking at it that way, we cannot even imagine the *chesed* that is being done for us.

If a child is run over and hurt, people might ask, where is the *chesed?* But we must realize that something worse could have happened.

How do we understand that Yaakov complained to Pharaoh that his days were full of *tzaar* and consequently he was punished?

The commentators say that Pharaoh was surprised because Yaakov Avinu looked like a very old man. Yaakov Avinu then explained that it was due to *tzaros*, but he was still punished for this. We are not allowed to complain, and it's only when we do complain that we feel the hardships.

Which is the best way to look at *yissurim*?

It is not a good idea to be depressed. There are two spiritual reckonings: one of the *yetzer tov* and one of the *yetzer hara.* What's the difference? In the *yetzer tov*, a person says to himself in a constructive way: "I've erred, I've faltered in some way and my task now is to improve myself." This is the exact opposite of the advice given by the *yetzer hara,* who tells you to brood, that you are no good. Of course you will become depressed — and that is what the *yetzer hara* wants. We must work in a constructive way, saying, "Hashem! I erred somewhere and now I'll try to improve myself." The case is then closed. Remember: no dwelling or brooding, just a short *cheshbon hanefesh* which will *be'ezras Hashem* prod you further.

Q How do we understand the reason for the *yissurim*?

A Today we can't understand this because we do not have any prophets to explain the meaning to us; we just have to take it as *min haShamayim*. Remember: The first step is not to bicker or complain to Hashem. If a child is sick, take it as *min haShamayim*. I wouldn't say to take it with a grain of salt. The proper attitude is to take things with a grain of sugar. You should look at the *yissurim* as sugar-coated, where you don't know the contents but somehow it is sweet.

Q Why do we say *lo liy'dei nisayon*, not through trials, if undergoing trials and tribulations successfully is what makes us great?

A We are asking that we should become great from tests we are already going through. But we should never ask to be put into such situations. After the 10th *nisayon*, Avraham Avinu wasn't tested any more because he had already reached the highest level.

Q About cause-and-effect actions, should we try to figure it out on our own? Should we say, this particular suffering was the result of such and such an action? How do we know if we are right?

A We are told to examine our deeds but to say that we can pinpoint the cause is beyond us. Only the *gedolim* can see this.

Q Do our Sages say that there is such a thing as *mazal*?

A Yes, but Jews are above *mazal* and their merits can overpower and negate *mazal*.

This volume is part of
THE ARTSCROLL SERIES®
an ongoing project of
translations, commentaries and expositions
on Scripture, Mishnah, Talmud, Halachah,
liturgy, history, the classic Rabbinic writings,
biographies and thought.

For a brochure of current publications
visit your local Hebrew bookseller
or contact the publisher:

Mesorah Publications, ltd

4401 Second Avenue
Brooklyn, New York 11232
(718) 921-9000
www.artscroll.com